Supervising the Successful

School Music Program

MALCOLM E. BESSOM

Parker Publishing Company, Inc., West Nyack, N. Y.

PRINTED IN THE UNITED STATES OF AMERICA

B & P

Dedication

*To my parents Harold and Mina Bessom
for the musical life.*

THE PURPOSE OF THIS BOOK

While the literature of music education is abundant in the areas of elementary and secondary school teaching methods, and in the techniques of vocal and instrumental instruction, a surprisingly small amount of material has been offered which relates specifically to the duties of the music supervisor or director of music.

School music supervisors generally work into their positions through classroom teaching. Although such experience is an important aspect of a supervisor's preparation, many take over their jobs with little or no formal training in the specialized practice of supervision, and they are in need of useful suggestions, rather than philosophical statements, on how to set up and operate a functional program. This book has been written to serve such a need. The author has experienced the typical and not-so-typical problems faced by most supervisors, and he is confident that the techniques and solutions he discusses in this book will work effectively for directors of both large- and small-scale programs in systems of various sizes.

The book is primarily for the in-service music director—whether he is new to his job or an experienced department head looking for more practical techniques. It will also be of use to administrators who wish to gain further insight into the requirements of a successful music program and to members of the music staff who are involved in supervisory work (such as elementary music consultants and specialists working with classroom teachers). Furthermore, the book should serve a sizable need in college and university music departments, where a practical text is required for courses in the administration and supervision of music education.

Fundamentally, the book is organized as a guide to the supervisor's relations with the administration, the teaching staff, and the community as a whole; to the understanding and execution of his special responsibilities; and to the processes of organizing and developing a curriculum in music education. Its practical approach offers the reader workable suggestions in such areas as justifying the music program; determining curriculum content and organizing the curriculum for sequential growth; working out scheduling problems; making out the music budget; developing an in-service program to aid teachers through observations, demonstrations, conferences, and workshops; writing curriculum guides and instructional bulletins; selecting textbooks and music; interviewing and selecting personnel for the music faculty; using the mass media effectively to build community support for the school program; providing necessary materials, equipment, and physical facilities; handling business transactions; evaluating the program; and many other problems with which the music director is concerned daily.

Among the special features of the book are the presentation of important factors in human relations, a primary concern of the successful music supervisor; an in-depth study of techniques of public relations, a subject largely overlooked in other literature; and detailed material on the basic content of the general music curriculum and of special high school courses such as music history, theory, and comparative arts.

The author has dealt with his subject in as comprehensive a manner as possible. He has had experience in teaching many phases of elementary, junior-high, and senior-high school music, and is familiar with the needs and problems encountered at each level. He has set up new courses, restyled old ones, and worked with teachers in developing new materials. This experience, together with research, observation, and common-sense thinking, has yielded a body of practical ideas and techniques which should prove useful both to those now in the field and to those about to enter the music education profession.

MALCOLM E. BESSOM

ACKNOWLEDGEMENTS

Acknowledgement is gratefully made to *The Music Journal, Inc.,* New York, for permission to use material I wrote for them in an article entitled "Music Education: What Are We Trying To Do?" published in the January 1966 issue.

I also wish to thank Harold E. Bessom for his assistance in compiling the appendices; Dr. Robert A. Choate, Dr. Lee Chrisman, Dr. Jack O. Lemons, and Dr. L. Eileen McMillan for contributing to my thinking on supervision and curriculum development; and the following organizations and publishers for permission to quote from copyright works:

American Association of School Administrators, Washington, D.C.
Music Educators National Conference, Washington, D.C.
Oxford University Press, Inc., New York
Prentice-Hall, Inc., Englewood Cliffs, New Jersey.

CONTENTS

1. THE SUCCESSFUL MUSIC SUPERVISOR   1

Agencies of Supervision (2)
Types of Supervision (7)
Responsibilities and Duties of the Supervisor (8)

2. VALUE AND PURPOSE OF THE SCHOOL MUSIC PROGRAM . . . 15

The Aesthetic Value of Music (16)
Building a Program on Aesthetic Value (20)

3. ORGANIZING THE ELEMENTARY MUSIC CURRICULUM 23

Elementary School Music Experiences (25)
The General Music Program (26)
Basic Content in General Music (31)
Providing for General Music (37)
The Non-General Music Program (41)

4. ORGANIZING THE SECONDARY MUSIC CURRICULUM 47

General Music Classes (47)
General-Special Music Classes (54)
The Vocal Program (65)
The Instrumental Program (68)
Content in Performance Classes (71)
Balance and Credit in Music Classes (73)
Special Activities (76)

5. RELATIONS WITH THE ADMINISTRATION 81

Principles of Human Relations (82)
Problems and Procedures (83)
Scheduling (85)
Planning Music Facilities (96)

6. RELATIONS WITH THE TEACHING STAFF 103

Full-Time Personnel (103)
Part-Time Personnel (109)

7. RELATIONS WITH THE COMMUNITY 113

Person-to-Person and Group-to-Group (114)
The Mass Media (122)
Programs of Community Involvement (127)

8. THE EFFECTIVE IN-SERVICE PROGRAM 131

Visitation (132)
Conferences (136)
Observations and Demonstrations (137)
Bulletins (138)
Professional Library for Classroom Teachers (139)
Teacher's Meetings (139)
Workshops (141)

9. IMPLEMENTATION AND DEVELOPMENT OF THE CURRICULUM 143

Curriculum Guides (143)
Supplementary Bulletins (145)
Selecting Textbooks (146)
Selecting Music (149)
Enriching Instruction (150)
The Testing Program (154)
Self-Growth (156)

10. ADMINISTRATIVE DUTIES OF THE MUSIC SUPERVISOR 157

Supplying the Schools (157)
The Desk Job (163)

APPENDICES

A. General Educational and Cultural Organizations (169)
B. National Music Organizations (171)
C. Musical Instrument, Equipment, and Supply Companies (175)
D. Music Publishers (185)
E. Recommended Organization for Filing Music Materials (189)
F. Selected Music Periodicals (195)
G. Basic Music Book Series for the General Music Program (201)
H. Selected Literature on Music Education (203)

1

The Successful Music Supervisor

In the early years of the eighteenth century, an institution known as the singing school was established in towns throughout the Colonies, developing with particular concentration in New England where it was a flourishing activity by the 1720's. Here, in meeting halls, churches, and homes, itinerant singing masters would meet with the people of a community for a short period of four or five weeks, mainly to instruct them in their singing as members of church congregations. These singing masters eventually became the first music teachers in American public schools.

Today's music teachers, of course, have changed considerably since the days of the itinerant songster. Seldom is a single person still looked to for the total musical instruction of a community. Teachers now have become more and more specialized, just like professionals in many other fields. It is quite common to find those who work solely within the area of a vocal music program and others who work strictly in the instrumental field. In fact, it is not uncommon to find teachers handling even more specific assignments. An elementary school, for example, may have one teacher to handle the general music program in the primary grades, another for general music in the intermediate grades, and still another for private and class instruction on instruments. In a sizable junior high school, individual music teachers may handle the general music classes, the instrumental groups, and the vocal groups, and large high schools may be specialized to the point of having one or more persons for band, one for orchestra, one for vocal activities, and one for music appreciation and theory classes.

Clearly, the field of music education has grown over the years—and it continues to grow. But, with today's specialization, with music programs staffed by a number of teachers in a school system, and frequently, with music instruction being given at the elementary level by classroom teachers who may or may not have had any musical training, little chance of quality exists throughout, unless one other factor is present; that factor is the music supervisor, the person who organizes the music program.

Supervision is required to ensure the most efficient operation possible of a music curriculum, for the music supervisor is the one person who is

1

in a position to coordinate *all* music activities—to provide continuity throughout a system from one level to another, to analyze difficult situations and move for improvement, to advise and stimulate teachers, and to expedite the acquisition of essential teaching materials. He, too, is a specialist—in the *total* music program.

The processes of administering and supervising a successful program of music education frequently overlap in their realms of operation. Generally, however, administration is concerned with providing the conditions under which a program may be carried out, whereas supervision deals with the actual working of what is called the "teaching-learning" situation. It is through supervision that one is able to establish the means for realizing an educational policy that has been formulated with the administration, by providing leadership in as many ways as are necessary to promote pupil growth.

Consequently, developing a proper setting for the learning experience involves many things: the recognition of objectives to be met, the cooperative planning of the means of achievement, the creation of a good environment, the provision of opportunities for teacher growth, the improvement of methods and materials of instruction through cooperative effort, and a continual evaluation not only of the product, but also of the aims and processes themselves.

AGENCIES OF SUPERVISION

The scope of supervision in music education is not limited to the local school system. It begins at the national level and extends downward through state and county to the individual community. Since education, by virtue of the United States Constitution, is a function of the separate states (and, in turn, the direct responsibility of each city and town), the federal government does not administer, nor supervise, a program of public education, except in federally-operated schools. Nevertheless, the government and many other national organizations provide guidance in the organization of educational programs. The Office of Education, in the Department of Health, Education, and Welfare, serves this purpose in music education through a music and art specialist, whereas the National Education Association (NEA), a non-governmental agency, speaks principally through its member organization, the Music Educators National Conference (MENC).

It is of considerable importance for the local music supervisor to be aware of such agencies, and of their activities and offerings. Through them, he can enlarge his vision of the entire educational field, advance himself professionally through the circulation and exchange of ideas, and define his perspective in regard to his own position. It is not only through music organizations that the supervisor can grow. The MENC, for example, is only one of a number of departments under the National Education Association. These departments include, among others, the National Association of Secondary School Principals, which has published a report on the place of music in the secondary school curriculum; the National Elementary Principals Association; the Association for Supervision and Curriculum Development; the Department of Classroom Teachers; and the American Association of School Administrators, which has published the proceedings of its conference devoted to the creative arts. (See Appendix A for a listing of educational organizations.) Since the supervisor must deal with his subject in terms of the total curriculum, an awareness of what is happening in other branches of the educational profession is vital.

Among the music associations, the most important to the supervisor is the Music Educators National Conference, which has, as an auxiliary organization, the Music Industry Council. The MENC exists, not as an organization in the nation's capital, but in the activities of each of its 55,000 members throughout the country. The actual work of the MENC office is directed by the National Executive Board, consisting of the national president, vice-president, and president-elect, the presidents of the six divisions, and the president of the Music Industry Council who is a non-voting member. The National Assembly, which meets at biennial conventions and constitutes a forum, is composed of the presidents of the federated state associations and the presidents of the MENC's auxiliary and associate organizations.

The various publications of the MENC, including those of the now-defunct National Interscholastic Music Activities Commission (formerly an auxiliary organization), are the results of professional research by individuals and by commissions especially formed to study certain problems. These publications include monthly and quarterly journals, books, resource guides, and specialized studies which offer considerable guidance to the supervisor in formulating and directing his program. They should be available in a school system's professional library for use by the entire music staff.

A number of other agencies, devoted exclusively to music, are also of interest. One of these is the Music Teachers National Association (formed in 1876) which is of particular importance at the college level. Through the state association, however, it can also aid the local supervisor in coordinating the school curriculum with the instruction of private teachers in the community. Other groups include the National Catholic Music Educators Association, the American String Teachers Association, the American School Band Directors Association, the National School Orchestra Association, the National Association of Teachers of Singing, and the National Music Council. (A more complete listing is given in Appendix B.)

State and County Supervisory Programs. Some 35 states now employ a total of over 50 music supervisors or consultants in state departments of education, and many others carry out some program of music supervision without an actual department head. While the direct line of responsibility generally extends from the state department to the local boards of education, and then down to the director of music, the local school music department may also be guided by two indirect lines of supervision. These stem from the office of state supervisor of music, which derives its responsibility from the state superintendent of public instruction, and from the office of county supervisor of music, coming under the direction of the county superintendent of schools.

Frequently, a music consultant is available from the state department to schools which seek advice in developing their programs, organizing courses, working out schedules, providing building facilities, and evaluating instruction. This is of particular importance in rural areas, where music teachers may not be employed on a wide basis and where state and county offices are looked to for providing a minimum program in music. There are many services which the state supervisor may provide. He may:

1. Issue bulletins on instruction, program events, etc.
2. Assist in the selection of books, recordings, and other materials, particularly in states which require a state-wide adoption of texts.
3. Serve as a liaison between national organizations and state groups.
4. Serve as a liaison between lay and professional groups, including state education officials and teachers.
5. Promote state, regional, and local conferences.
6. Promote university research.
7. Coordinate research and distribute instructional information.
8. Organize festivals.
9. Advise on workshops and in-service programs.
10. Develop extension programs and summer clinics.
11. Advise community and civic groups.
12. Promote state arts councils.
13. Advise on legislative bills.
14. Offer leadership in curriculum development.

At the state level, guidance may also come from associations of local teachers and supervisors. A state meeting of music supervisors, for example, may result in many projects that will benefit all the schools. Special booklets of supplementary materials may be published; research studies may be organized; resource units may be developed for use in general music classes; a state-wide curriculum guide may be produced; resource projects for correlating music with other subjects may be initiated; teaching materials may be evaluated; and a traveling workshop may be provided.

Between meetings of the state organization, regional meetings can be held to carry on the work. One of the most valuable activities of the state association can be in extending the local curriculum through special district and state-wide performing groups made up of the most capable students throughout an area. Such organizations can provide the student with musical experiences of a calibre not possible in most individual schools.

The county music supervisor is able to provide many of the same services as the state supervisor, but with the added advantage of focusing upon the needs of a smaller region. At this level, inter-school activities may be promoted and festival-type programs, involving several school systems, may be organized. In addition to promoting a general program of music education in schools throughout the area, the county office may:

1. Promote local and regional conferences, demonstrations, and workshops.
2. Provide speakers.
3. Promote public relations with newspapers, radio, and television.
4. Help determine the music needs of individual school systems.
5. Advise school systems in curriculum development and evaluation.
6. Aid schools with scheduling problems, financial considerations, building plans, etc.
7. Help organize in-service programs.
8. Issue bulletins.
9. Provide a central library service for distributing special instructional materials and equipment.
10. Promote research studies.

Supervisory Organizations Within School Systems. When it comes to local school systems, the authority of the music supervisor's position is apt to fluctuate from town to town. It is important that the music supervisor always be certain of knowing to whom he is responsible in any given situation. Although this may seem obvious, it is worth emphasizing that his relations with others on the supervisory and administrative staffs are of utmost importance to the smooth functioning of the music program.

Depending on the school system involved, the line and staff organization of supervision will vary. Line officers include the superintendent, assistant superintendents, division directors, principals, assistant principals, and department heads, as well as any special positions that may come between these, such as coordinator of secondary subjects. There are two types of staff officers. Those in charge of service divisions would include librarians, psychologists, guidance officers, statisticians, and others. The second type, including the music supervisor, would be those in charge of major departments in the curriculum.

If the supervisory organization is a vertical structure, the supervisor is responsible for instruction throughout the system, at all levels. If the organization is horizontal, the supervisor is usually responsible for just certain levels or certain schools. A third type of organization is the coordinate system, in which a building principal and the supervisor function at the same level of authority. In the case of music supervision, there is usually a combination of all three types. Thus, the director of music education is in charge of the program throughout the system (vertical), but functions at the same authoritative level as a principal (coordinate). Then, below the director are several other supervisors who are in charge of a particular area, such as the elementary program in schools A and B, or the instrumental instruction at the secondary level (horizontal).

The title which a supervisor holds depends upon the staff organization of the system, but frequently, a single title is used differently from one community to another. The most common positions are as follows:

1. *Director of Music.* This person bears the full responsibility for the music program, and all other music supervisors are responsible to him. He, in turn, is directly responsible to the superintendent, on whose authority he operates. *Throughout this book, the terms "director" and "supervisor" will be used interchangeably in reference to this position, unless they are otherwise qualified.*

2. *Supervisor of Music.* The supervisor, in this case, is one who deals primarily with teachers. He is in charge of the curriculum and has the responsibility of seeing that it is carried out. He is responsible both to the principals of the schools in which he works and to the director of music. In smaller systems, the director and supervisor may be one. A supervisor who works under a main director will be referred to in this book with a qualifying term, such as "elementary supervisor" or "instrumental supervisor."

3. *Music Consultant.* The consultant is an "on-call" supervisor — primarily a resource person who enters the classroom only at the invitation of the teacher or principal.

4. *Music Coordinator.* Although the duties of the coordinator generally fall within the scope of the director's position, a separate person may be employed. He maintains balance as far as the totality of the school system is concerned, sees that the music program is essentially the same throughout the schools, and coordinates music with other areas of the curriculum.

5. *Music Specialist.* The specialist is not a supervisor, except over his own work. He is a teacher who deals directly with the children in classes or schools to which he is assigned. He is responsible to the principal of a school, and through him, to the director of music.

There is a trend in some areas — particularly in county supervision — toward the employment of a general supervisor over all subjects. This is usually a person who has come up through the classroom structure and, possibly, has taught several subjects. Although the coordinating function of such a position is admirable, it has a major drawback: No one person can know all there is about a single subject, let alone a number of subjects. Consequently, when one person is in charge of all supervision, certain areas of the curriculum are likely to suffer. It is precisely for this reason that many classroom teachers have difficulty with music in the elementary grades. It is preferable, therefore, to have a supervisor with special training for each of the major divisions of the curriculum. A coordinated system may still be maintained through a director of instruction or an assistant superintendent.

TYPES OF SUPERVISION

The supervisory duties that are performed depend upon the philosophy with which the office of supervisor is organized. Several types of supervision are, or have been, common. Under the type known as *autocratic supervision,* the supervisor is essentially a dictator. The only way in which something may be done, and the only way in which music can be taught, is the way the supervisor sets forth. It is true, of course, that certain elements of business must be decided by the supervisor without consulting the teachers. However, authoritarianism generally stifles the learning situation, limits the opportunities for teacher and pupil growth, and results in poor relations between members of the teaching staff.

In some systems, *representative supervision* has been practiced, since it is believed that a democratic climate is promoted by allowing teachers to elect their own leader. Thus, a teacher is elected for one year to act as supervisor within a given area. Since the position is a temporary one, however, no authority is behind the office. A policy that is put into operation may not be carried through to completion before a new supervisor takes office, and in some cases, a teacher will not try very well, knowing that his work is not permanent. Furthermore, a teacher may not wish to give directions, since the situation will be reversed within a year, and awkward situations may arise.

Invitational supervision, in which teachers ask consultants for help, is quite prevalent. Although it is theoretically fine, a consultancy is not practical, for most teachers who are in need of aid are afraid to seek counsel, whereas those who do solicit visitation are generally the ones who are doing well in music and would like to exhibit their success. In cases where relations with principals are solid, the consultant may be able to ask for an opportunity to visit; however, this is usually not possible on a regular basis.

A rather outmoded form is *scientific supervision,* which consists of simply visiting schools for testing purposes. Obviously, this overlooks the many supervisory processes that must occur before techniques of evaluation are employed. In addition, it does not even account for a valid form of evaluation, which must be based on much more than just objective tests.

The preferable type of supervision is one with a democratic form of leadership provided for all areas of the music curriculum. *Democratic supervision* recognizes the values which other people can contribute to the teaching process, as well as their needs; and it builds upon them, deriving supervisory action from the situation at hand, rather than imposing a set formula upon it. This allows for a flexible, functional program through cooperative group effort and through a certain degree of experimentation. It is this type of supervision with which this book is concerned.

RESPONSIBILITIES AND DUTIES OF THE SUPERVISOR

The people to whom the music supervisor is responsible fall into five main groups, each of which expects a different type of relationship. Before outlining some of the actual duties of the supervisor, it might be well to look at each of these relationships briefly.

1. *Teachers.* The classroom teacher looks to the supervisor as a source of help. Depending on the teacher's musical abilities, the supervisor may be welcomed or feared, but generally his value is recognized. Therefore, the teacher expects sympathetic understanding from him, and a willingness to help by providing specific suggestions and materials. Regular music teachers will also look to the supervisor for guidance in planning their work, suggestions for certain activities, and materials with which to work.

2. *Principals.* The principal, as administrative head of a building, expects cooperation from the supervisor. He does not want to feel that the supervisor has authority over him. Consequently, he expects coordination and integration of musical activities in his school, help for his teachers, justification for the music program, consultation and reports on activities, and, most important, respect for the authority of his position and for his own personal integrity and judgment.

3. *Superintendent.* Since the superintendent is responsible for the educational policies throughout all the schools, he expects the supervisor to provide a music program that is in accordance with the general objectives and philosophy of the system. The superintendent should be consulted for his own ideas on the program, and he should be furnished with regular reports on what is taking place. Ultimately, he expects justification for and interpretation of the program that he takes before the board of education.

4. *Board of Education.* The board looks to the music supervisor as a leader and an adviser — one who can interpret a sound program, support the budget that is required, and advise them on purchases. He is expected to build cultural relations between the school and the community, and is

expected to work with the superintendent in providing a balanced and up-to-date program.

5. *The Community*. The community wants the supervisor to interpret the school program, to cooperate with professionals in the area, and to provide cultural leadership, not only in the school, but also in civic and social activities.

Together, these groups expect of the supervisor human values, guidance, musicianship, knowledge, teaching skill, educational understanding, and community leadership.

The day to day duties of the supervisor, in meeting these responsibilities, are so numerous that compact categorization seems impossible. However, allowing for duties that defy a single classification, five main areas of activity may be outlined: (1) curriculum organization and development; (2) provision of materials, equipment, and space for implementation; (3) direction and improvement of the teaching-learning situation; (4) professional growth; and (5) evaluation and interpretation. To provide an overall view of the demands on the music supervisor, some of the duties encompassed by each area are given below. The provision of leadership, of course, transcends each category. It is also assumed, without explicit statement in the list, that these duties are performed with the cooperation of teachers and administrative officials.

CURRICULUM ORGANIZATION AND DEVELOPMENT

1. Formulation of objectives and policies.
   a. Surveying and evaluating the present program to determine its strengths and weaknesses.
   b. Determining for whom the program is to be planned.
   c. Outlining the aims of the program.
   d. Determining the objectives of separate phases of the program.
   e. Coordinating the objectives with the educational philosophy of the entire system.
2. Planning activities and the course of study.
   a. Determining what is needed in view of stated aims.
   b. Determining what is presently available.
   c. Establishing a long-range program of activity.
   d. Planning emergency steps for immediate action.
   e. Keeping teachers and the staff informed of new ideas in curriculum development.
   f. Working with teachers in setting up experimental phases of instruction.
   g. Holding regular meetings with teachers and the administration to advise of recommended changes and formulate new proposals.
3. Coordination and articulation of instruction.
   a. Meeting with teachers to help coordinate activities within individual classes.

b. Holding grade-level meetings to determine the specific needs at each level.
c. Ensuring articulation of instruction between levels by providing for the sequential development of experiences throughout the schools.
d. Coordinating the music program with other departments of the curriculum.

PROVISION OF MATERIALS, EQUIPMENT, AND SPACE

1. Materials.
   a. Selecting, with the staff, texts, music, and recordings for regular course needs.
   b. Selecting, with the personnel involved, materials for special programs and activities.
   c. Selecting materials for the student library, and providing the librarian with recommended bibliographies.
   d. Providing a list of available instructional materials.
   e. Providing supplementary materials in the form of bulletins and guides.
   f. Determining the best means of distribution of materials.
   g. Preparing directions for the use of materials.
   h. Appraising materials in use.
   i. Planning a budget to allow for long-range and emergency purchases.
2. Equipment.
   a. Appraising equipment presently owned by the school.
   b. Determining what is needed.
   c. Devising a long-range plan for purchases and replacement.
   d. Providing for immediate equipment needs.
   e. Preparing specifications for equipment.
   f. Advising the school board on purchases.
   g. Providing for the repair of instruments and other equipment.
   h. Working with the audio-visual department in the distribution of equipment.
3. Buildings.
   a. Determining the spatial requirements of the music program.
   b. Providing storage facilities for materials and equipment.
   c. Advising the board of education on plans for new buildings.

DIRECTION AND IMPROVEMENT OF THE LEARNING SITUATION

1. Employment of personnel.
   a. Determining personnel requirements.
   b. Soliciting applicants for positions.
   c. Participating in the selection of personnel.

    d. Placing employees according to curriculum needs and personal qualifications.

    e. Advising personnel of policies and procedures.

    f. Assisting in problems of adjustment.

2. Improving staff relations and working conditions.

    a. Cooperating with the administration and the teaching staff in meeting personal needs and instructional needs.

    b. Advising and helping in distributing the teacher load fairly.

    c. Working with the administration and the board of education in providing a favorable teaching environment.

3. In-service program.

    a. Consulting with teachers as to their needs.

    b. Cooperating with teachers in planning a program for professional growth.

    c. Providing for workshops, teacher meetings, conferences, and demonstrations.

    d. Arranging for observations.

    e. Providing professional literature and specially prepared bulletins on instruction.

    f. Arranging for special programs, concerts, and exhibits.

    g. Promoting professional organizations.

    h. Encouraging enrollment in extension courses, summer clinics, etc.

PROFESSIONAL GROWTH

1. Professional affiliations.

    a. Attending and participating in meetings of local, regional, state, and national professional organizations.

    b. Serving on educational committees.

2. Research and study.

    a. Participating in surveys and research studies.

    b. Keeping informed on research projects.

    c. Enrolling in courses for advanced study.

    d. Conducting experiments on instructional problems.

    e. Keeping in touch with new publications in music and education.

EVALUATION AND INTERPRETATION OF THE PROGRAM

1. Maintaining records.

    a. Keeping temporary and permanent records of student enrollment in music activities.

    b. Keeping records of students in special programs.

    c. Maintaining an inventory of libraries of music, books, and other materials.

    d. Maintaining an inventory of instruments and other equipment, and keeping a record of repair information.

    e. Keeping accounts of proposed music programs and of present activities.

2. Evaluation.
   a. Working with teachers and administrators in determining the means of appraisal.
   b. Evaluating the results of the program (pupil growth) in light of the objectives.
   c. Evaluating the activities and instruction used.
   d. Evaluating the teaching personnel.
   e. Re-evaluating the original objectives and program of instruction.
   f. Evaluating the program of supervision.
3. Interpretation.
   a. Interpreting the purposes and nature of the program to the teaching staff, the administration, and the board of education.
   b. Keeping principals informed of plans and activities within their respective buildings.
   c. Keeping the superintendent up to date on plans and activities throughout the school system.
   d. Filing an annual report with the administration describing the year's work and evaluation.
   e. Filing other reports as needed or requested.
   f. Keeping the community informed of the school music program, and music in general, through school concerts, community performances, mass media, and adult education programs.

The duties outlined above are by no means inclusive of the entire responsibilities of the music supervisor. The list offers only the main divisions, under which many more specialized activities may take place. Some of these will be noted in greater detail in the following pages.

Having these duties arranged before the eye in this way makes it obvious that the successful music supervisor must possess a number of different qualities. The most important are: (1) skill in human relations; (2) musical sensitivity and skill; (3) knowledge of teaching techniques and the ability to use them; (4) educational understanding; (5) extensive professional training; (6) imagination and determination; (7) the ability to perceive and direct musical growth; (8) knowledge of his own field and an active interest in others; (9) confidence in his own abilities and those of his associates; (10) respect for the contributions of others; (11) enthusiasm for his work and his profession as a whole; (12) a sense of purpose and responsibility; and (13) friendliness and happiness.

Some of these qualities are inherent personality traits; others are rather objective qualities which can be acquired in a variety of ways. Knowledge and understanding can be advanced through graduate study in music and education, including courses in curriculum development, supervision and administration, and other specialized areas. However, while such training is basic, a great deal of supervisory insight can also be acquired from actual teaching experience, observation, reading and personal research, and from plain reasoning. No one type of background will provide the qualifications necessary for the supervisor. More important than the fact that an individual has taken certain courses or has had certain teaching experiences is the fact that he himself recognizes the demands of a supervisory position and identifies his own strengths and weaknesses. Then, the individual can take whatever steps seem necessary for him to develop his abilities. The in-service supervisor (as well as the prospective head of a music department) would do well to begin his self-evaluation by comparing his status to the following checklist.

The successful music supervisor:

1. Has a definite philosophy of the role of music in American life and the role of music in the schools.
2. Is informed of current trends in music, education, and music education.
3. Is informed of the school system's over-all curriculum.
4. Has a clear definition of his responsibilities and duties.
5. Keeps ahead of the program through sound planning.
6. Plans with both long-range and immediate goals in mind.
7. Enlists the cooperation of administrators, teachers, parents, and students in the advancement of the program.
8. Provides leadership in curriculum development, and paves the way for changes.
9. Involves himself and his staff in experimentation and research.
10. Facilitates instruction through supervision of materials and equipment.
11. Makes judicious use of funds.
12. Utilizes a variety of resources.
13. Is informed of teachers' achievements, problems, needs, and activities.
14. Shows a genuine interest in teachers and students, and contributes to teacher morale.
15. Has the mutual respect of his associates.
16. Is open to suggestions and seeks the opinions of his staff members.
17. Works with the administrators rather than against them.
18. Works with the teachers rather than above them.
19. Provides a variety of methods for in-service training.
20. Handles supervisory problems democratically.
21. Stimulates groups and individuals to positive action.
22. Is professionally active in local and state organizations.
23. Is efficiently organized.
24. Keeps records and handles reports simply, but completely.
25. Maintains effective public relations.
26. Promotes music in community life as well as in the school.
27. Interprets the music program soundly and intelligently.

2

Value and Purpose of the School Music Program

"Why do we bother to teach such an impractical, unnecessary, fringe-benefit subject like music in our schools?" The implications of an expanding space age have undoubtedly caused a question such as this to be raised in the minds of many educational administrators. The increasing demands of scientific knowledge, pressing on an already-crowded school day, have led many school systems to take a second look at subjects that are sometimes referred to as the "frills" of education. As a result, some music programs have suffered for lack of clear justification, and others have just managed to hold their own. Nonetheless, some have prospered, in spite of the pressures, because their value has been recognized. Obviously, the music supervisor must be well prepared when he has to justify his music program to a school committee, superintendent, principal, or group of parents.

A great deal has been written on the purpose of music in the schools. The subject, in fact, has become somewhat traditional in literature in the field and at conventions. Certainly it is an important consideration, one on which a school's entire program rests. But all too often, the stated aims of the music education profession seem to be afterthoughts — contrived theories to justify an existing program or its desultory expansion. As a result, music is sanctioned by everything from developing a youngster's lungs through singing, to developing his muscular coordination through rhythmic activities. These may possibly be by-products of the music program, but they can hardly be justified as the program's *raison d'être*. (They are, instead, worthy aims for the school's department of physical education.) Similarly, it is often reported that a purpose of the music program is to promote the student's ability to work cooperatively with others, or to foster democratic ideals. Cannot these aims, however, be met equally well by other areas of the curriculum?

The problem here is that there has been too much of a backdoor ap-

15

proach to justifying music in the schools. This approach looks first at the desired outcomes of education in general, and then attempts to fit music into the pattern. Good citizenship and self-discipline, for example, are worthy aims of the educational process; therefore, music should be taught because it contributes to these outcomes. If this is the only defense for the existence of a music program, there appears to be every reason why music should be tossed aside entirely in favor of other subjects that can do the job much better.

THE AESTHETIC VALUE OF MUSIC

The major objection that should be raised to such thinking is that too many teachers are overlooking the unique contributions which music can make to an individual's education. Although it may support and broaden a student's development in many other areas, music (and for that matter, the arts in general) provides an experience that is not offered in other subject areas, such as math, the social and natural sciences, and the language arts. Its contribution is in that rather nebulous area of human experience which is best described by the term "aesthetic." Indefinite as it may seem, the aesthetic quality is the strongpoint of the music education profession; and the supervisor is off on the wrong course if he neglects it in favor of other supposedly "concrete," but truthfully irrelevant values. Educators are not even at the root of the subject when they speak of developing the voice or increasing musical skills, for these are only the means by which the true objectives can be reached.

If the value of music lies in the area of aesthetic experience (more will be said about this), the question remains why such experiences deserve a place in the curriculum. Here is the proper place for the supervisor to consider the purposes of general education. Although there may be contradiction among educators as to what these purposes are, it is perhaps safe to say that general education is concerned with learnings that are essential to everyone in community living, learnings that provide tools for personal and social adjustments, and learnings which would generally not be acquired informally.

Now, there is no doubting the fact that we have informal contact with music of all types. In fact, it would be almost impossible to avoid it in some form in daily living. Whether we hear music on radio or television, on records or at a concert, as part of a worship service, as an adjunct to a sports event, as an accompaniment to a dentist's drill, or piped into the local supermarket, office, or bank, it is undeniably all around us. This does not mean, however, that we necessarily hear music as an aesthetic experience, whether it is in informal or formal surroundings. For there is more to music than what is heard on the surface; and it is the in-depth involvement in music that results in the truly aesthetic. The average person usually lacks the understanding necessary for such involvement, which explains why "popular music" is popular. It is music that is obvious; most of the meaning and interest lies on top in the melody, and there is little need to look any further. Although there is a large amount of good popular music, a vast amount of good classical music and jazz also exists now primarily for a minority public — since the average listener cannot hear below the surface. Indeed, a great many people have trouble discriminating between the good and the poor in the field of popular music alone! To acquire the ability to probe beneath the surface and discover real meaning in musical sound *is* a process that requires some degree of formal guidance, then, and this places music within the domain of the school.

Fortunately, the music supervisor rarely has to justify his program from the standpoint of whether it develops musical understanding. This much is usually granted him. However, he does often have to face the problem, sometimes evident as an administrative attitude rather than a spoken thought, of why this is so important. Part of the resistance to a strong music program may be that while those in authority see the emotional, therapeutic, and social values of music, they fail to see its value in terms of the intellect. Of course, it does have intellectual value; music is a powerful force that reaches individuals emotionally, spiritually, physically, *and* intellectually. But its intellectual value is not the real importance of music. It is its aesthetic value that is misunderstood, and this is the value with which the supervisor should deal whenever he has to justify his program.

In terms of the purposes of general education, we may ask whether music is an essential learning. The answer is decidedly "yes." If we look back into history, we find that throughout the ages, the arts have embodied each culture's conceptions about itself, and it is the arts of a nation that have survived for centuries after its battles and conquests have been forgotten. The average, intelligent adult could probably tell you little or nothing about Russian history of the nineteenth century without running to an encyclopedia, but he is likely to be familiar with at least the existence and general work of a Tchaikovsky or a Dostoyevsky. Similarly, one who is familiar with the names of Michelangelo, Tintoretto, and Palestrina, could probably relate little offhand of what was happening in Italy in the 1500's when these men were sculpting, painting, and composing. Great art works have survived because man has always recognized a need to symbolize experience, and music through the ages has been a prime means of symbolizing the most important feelings of a culture. This fact was recognized by the President's Commission on National Goals when, in 1960, it stated: "In the eyes of posterity, the success of the

United States as a civilized society will be largely judged by the creative activities of its citizens in art, architecture, literature, music. . . ." [1]

In this sense, the study of music serves the purpose of passing on the cultural heritage of mankind. But a deeper concept is involved in music education. Psychologists like Jules Masserman tell us that man has a basic need for aesthetic expression — that man has an aesthetic function that contributes to his entirety. It is a function that involves feeling as well as thinking. In other words, to know intellectually is to know only partially. Knowledge without feeling and appreciation develops an unbalanced personality and can lead the individual into anti-social behavior.

The great value of music lies in its symbolic insight into the depths of reality. To be sensitive to art and music is to be sensitive to life. This is especially true of music more than the other arts because of its quality of abstraction and, at the same time, its greater precision in defining feeling. "Sound," says psychologist Max Schoen, "is the natural utterance of feeling, since the very and only meaning of sound is the feeling it evokes. The media of the other arts *have* feeling; but tone *is* feeling." [2] More precisely, music reaches the spirit of man because it can relate those feelings for which there can be no verbal description. It is possible to be moved by music in an almost imperceptible way — to respond without being aroused to sorrow, or joy, or outrage, or love, or any other emotion that we can identify by name — and yet still be moved. Obviously, then, there are kinds of human feeling that can be expressed in music but not in language, and to be lacking in the aesthetic experience is to be lacking an awareness of, fulfillment in, and self-satisfaction through the totality of human emotion and feeling.

Even those emotions which are identifiable can take on new meaning in music by being raised to the level of universal feeling. The composer Richard Wagner stressed this when he said that music expresses feeling in an infinite, ideal sense. The tragedy, or love, or passion that we hear in a musical masterwork is not an expression of how the composer personally felt on a certain occasion, but it is the composer's interpretation of the emotion itself on an absolute plane. This, said Wagner, is a timeless expression of a quality foreign to any other language.

Music, then, is the symbolic thought of life. It makes evident, intensifies, and interprets life's subtleties of feeling which practical experience can keep from our observation. There is the story of a concert pianist who, having just concluded the performance of a masterpiece by Beethoven, was asked what it meant. He answered by playing it again. How else could

---

[1] President's Commission on National Goals, *Goals For Americans.* (Englewood Cliffs, N.J.: Prentice-Hall, Inc., 1960), p. 9.

[2] Max Schoen, "Psychological Problems in Musical Art," *Journal of Research in Music Education,* III, 1 (Spring 1955), pp. 29-30.

it be explained? True, within a single work a hundred different listeners may interpret a hundred different shades of meaning, but in its infinite variety of expression and impression, music can communicate a myriad of emotional nuances that the reality of one's life can never exhaust. The music program thus offers a completely different type of experience for the student—an experience that is essential to his emotional development and well-being, and one which cannot be gained in any other area of the curriculum.

The importance of such experience was recognized by the administrative branch of the profession as early as 1927 when the Department of Superintendence resolved in Dallas that ". . .we are rightly coming to regard music, art, and other similar subjects as fundamental in the education of American children. We recommend that they be given everywhere equal consideration and support with other *basic* subjects."[3]

Further support was lent to the music curriculum in 1959 at the national convention of the American Association of School Administrators. Meeting at Atlantic City, the AASA devoted their entire convention to the creative arts and adopted this resolution:

> We believe in a well-balanced school curriculum in which music, drama, painting, poetry, sculpture, architecture, and the like are included side by side with other important subjects such as mathematics, history, and science. It is important that pupils, as a part of general education, learn to appreciate, to understand, to create, and to criticize with discrimination those products of the mind, the voice, the hand, and the body which give dignity to the person and exalt the spirit of man.[4]

Now, how is such aesthetic sensitivity gained? It can come only through extensive exposure to the arts — through an analysis of art works, performance of art works, and the development of factual knowledge and ideas about art. In fulfilling the role of music in the schools, it is important that students be guided in their ability to analyze music of all types so that their experiences become conscious, precise, and disciplined, thus making possible critical discrimination. It is also important to provide performance skills — not to develop performers, but because music cannot be fully experienced without some degree of performance. Certainly, if music has any impact on the casual listener, it must have greater impact on the person who can sing or play with a certain proficiency. It is important, too, that the student develop concepts of music that will carry

---

[3] Resolution of the Department of Superintendence, Dallas, 1927. Used by permission.

[4] Resolution of the American Association of School Administrators, Atlantic City, 1959. Used by permission.

over into his out-of-school life, thus making it a rewarding experience for him.

BUILDING A PROGRAM ON AESTHETIC VALUE

Based on these concepts of man's aesthetic function and the real value of music, we can now get down to the more precise job of outlining the basic aims of a public school music program. (These are aims that legitimately apply to any school; it is the job of the supervisor to determine the specific "objectives" encompassed by these aims that apply to his particular situation.) The five aims presented below, although general in nature, appear to cover all the specialized arguments that might be raised. They are derived from the important needs of students to which music education can contribute vastly. A program that is based on these needs is likely not to wander aimlessly. Furthermore, specific long-range goals, immediate objectives, desirable outcomes, and the expected outcomes of these activities are all suggested by each basic premise. If the "why" is known, the "how" is much less of a problem, for certain types of experiences present themselves as necessities if these five basic needs are to be met.

First, the music program should develop the aesthetic responsiveness of the individual.

Aesthetic responsiveness can be attained only if we provide experiences in making and listening to music that increase the pupil's sense of beauty, his concept of discrimination, and his receptivity to a wide range of human emotions.

Secondly, the music program should develop a sensitivity to the cultural heritage of the world through an understanding and appreciation of music in its many forms.

Such a broad sensitivity will be developed only if we provide participative experiences with music of many lands and peoples, of many composers of different eras, and of many types and styles — both vocal and instrumental music in the classical, folk, and popular fields.

Third, the music program should develop the creative potential of the individual through making and responding to music.

To develop this potential, it is necessary that the school provide many, varied experiences in singing, playing, and listening to music that enable a pupil to increase skills in music reading, in vocal and instrumental techniques, and in the ability to interpret music, both as a performer and a consumer.

Fourth, the music program should develop the student's interest in, and respect for, music as a form of lasting enjoyment, a means of relaxation, and a profitable occupation, whether as a profession or a leisure activity.

This aim will be met if we provide a sufficient variety of musical activities to interest all pupils and create a desire in each to participate in music for personal satisfaction.

Finally, the music program should promote the personal and emotional adjustment of the pupil as an individual and as a member of society.

This adjustment, which recognizes the importance of music to man's psychological well-being, can be furthered by providing musical experiences that offer opportunities for self-expression, opportunities to unite with other men through shared emotions, and opportunities to meet and adapt to a variety of social situations as a result of mental, emotional, and spiritual development through music.

The educational profession today is coming to realize more and more the important purpose that music fills in our lives. Undoubtedly, the results of the Tanglewood Symposium, convened in 1967 to study the role of music in American society and in the schools, will influence the shape of music education in the coming years. The symposium emphasized the aesthetic basis of music education, recognized the importance of music of all periods, styles, forms, and cultures, and called for music to be placed in the core of the curriculum.

In today's crowded curriculum, where music is frequently pushed aside, it is the program based on a clear understanding of purpose and need which will survive. The program which is sound and the one that develops along with the whole of education can evolve only when false objectives are recognized as such and cast aside.

3

Organizing
the Elementary Music Curriculum

A curriculum, according to the modern educational concept, is not just a fixed body of subject matter nor a course of study. Rather, it consists of all those experiences which a student has under the guidance (and mis-guidance) of the school. Classroom activities certainly account for a large portion of these, but not all of them; many important experiences come to the student through club and social activities, guidance services, after-school programs, and community trips. The so-called "extracurricular" activity, then, is not outside the curriculm at all. A better term for it might be "extra-class."

The development of a comprehensive music curriculum requires a consideration of all the possible experiences in music both in and out of class which the school can provide, and it begins with an analysis and evaluation of the existing program to determine its strengths and weaknesses. Then, with the strengths known and ready to be drawn upon, the supervisor can start afresh in building the type of curriculum that is best for his particular system. It is not wise to try to fit a school system to a pre-conceived, standardized curriculum plan, for what works in one community may not be suitable for students elsewhere. Although certain basic experiences may seem desirable for every child, the specific nature of these experiences, the actual materials to be used, and the methods of presentation — all elements of curriculum development — must vary from one school to another to meet the needs of the pupils. Neither should a new program, even a specially-tailored one, be imposed upon a teaching staff; it should be worked out with the administration and teachers themselves, generally by a committee organized especially for this purpose.

There are three main steps to follow in organizing a curriculum:

1. The committee must first decide why music deserves a place in the schools and set forth aims and objectives that are in accordance with the general philosophy of the total school curriculum. This statement of belief should be available on paper, in simple terminology, to teachers, parents, and anyone else who is interested in the work of the school. From this

point, it can be determined what musical experiences are desirable and necessary for every student in order to realize the stated objectives.

2. The second main step is to identify what is needed to bring these experiences about. This includes the environment that is necessary; the materials, equipment, and space that must be provided; the knowledge and abilities required of teachers; the number of teachers needed; and the amount of time required each week. When these factors are known, the step is completed by determining how to provide these things, and then by actually obtaining them.

3. The final step is in drawing up a syllabus, a course of study, or a curriculum guide that combines everything in the first two steps. That is, the desirable experiences are re-stated as specific objectives; possible teaching procedures are outlined; a projection of sequence is made with outcomes; and materials are coordinated as resources for the teacher.

None of these steps is ever actually completed. Objectives and experiences must be constantly re-appraised, better materials and teaching conditions must be worked on to replace the old, the teaching-learning situation must be re-evaluated, and the curriculum must be re-designed in various ways to meet new needs.

As with many important projects, the most difficult step in organizing a curriculum is often the first. The formulation of objectives cannot be handled lightly, nor in hurried fashion. It is, to be sure, a kind of philosophic stage which is not much good by itself; but it is also *the stage from which all practical, successful maneuvers and techniques are developed*. To begin, general aims should be worked out with a cross-section of the music staff. These aims need to stress the importance of the art, the purpose for its inclusion in the curriculum, and the principle methods of understanding its structure and content which will further the aesthetic communication of music. (See pages 20–21 for examples of such aims.)

Prior to the initial meeting of the aims committee, the music director might ask his staff members to organize their thoughts separately on the place of music in present-day society and in the life of the individual. Then, in group meetings, these thoughts can be brought together, analyzed, and related to the school in terms of what the school should do to support, advance, and encourage the role of music. The music education program that will ultimately evolve must serve the present and look to the future; therefore, during these meetings, the changes taking place in society and in education as a whole must be kept in mind. It is important, too, to consider the needs of the wide variety of students for whom the school is responsible and to keep in mind the focus of the total curriculum. In covering each of these points, it is valuable for the director to provide resources in books and pamphlets for consideration by the committee.

The basic *aims* which are drafted should apply to every phase of the program. These are then translated into *objectives* for each level. For this purpose, additional staff members — specialists in the various levels and departments of the program — may be consulted. Objectives, like general aims, need to relate to the current society of which the school is a part. They must also be concrete statements, written in behavioral terms. That is, objectives for a given level will describe a change in, or action of, the learner when he has achieved the stated goal; it should not attempt to summarize the content of the learning experiences. When a clear concept of sequential behavioral patterns has been formulated by levels, then objectives can be refined and detailed more for specific courses. This leads, naturally, to the second major stage of curriculum development as stated above — the identification of materials and other needs required to realize the objectives. (For specific suggestions on how to lead organizational and other staff meetings, see Chapter 8.)

ELEMENTARY SCHOOL MUSIC EXPERIENCES

The elementary music program should be mainly investigative. This is a time for the child to explore music in every aspect that will have meaning for him—to listen to it; to respond to it physically through free and controlled, bodily movement; to sing and discover the nature of his own voice; to play it on instruments; to manipulate the possibilities of musical sound through his own creative impulses; to relate it meaningfully with other phases of his life, both in and out of school; to explore the various ways in which music is made and performed; and to experience the expressive power of music. At this level, children learn best by doing, so the development of their aesthetic sensitivity should be promoted principally through the area of performance, an extensive involvement in the making of music.

Each type of musical learning needs to develop progressively from the general to the specific, from the concrete to the abstract. (Learning notation, for example, is abstract and needs to be preceded by aural experiences with tonal concepts.) Since music in its most concrete form is still rather abstract, specific learnings need to be reinforced continuously throughout the grades — with numerous and different experiences being offered for the illumination of one idea, and with a single experience being examined from many, different angles. (This is the basis of the "spiral curriculum.") Gradually, throughout the elementary years, the knowledge of musical facts and more abstract concepts can be increasingly stressed until this becomes a strong approach at the secondary level.

In essence, then, the elementary curriculum should provide:

—Experiences derived from specific objectives.
—Experiences based on the needs and interests of the students.

—Experiences that involve all the students actively and meet the special needs of individuals.

—Experiences allowing for investigation and exploration.

—Experiences that provide real meaning for students.

—Experiences offering a variety of approaches to musical understanding.

—Experiences that build interest, appreciation, and good attitudes.

—Experiences that allow for sequential musical development.

—Experiences that build a child's musical skills and self-respect for his skills.

—Experiences that allow for and develop creativity.

—Experiences with music of real worth and aesthetic value.

To provide such a program, a director of music obviously needs to know a great deal about children. The child's changing interests from grade to grade will dictate a certain type of song text that is appropriate. His emotional development and relationships with his family, peers, school, and community will call forth specific needs that can be met through the proper selection of curricular experiences. Also, his physical growth will suggest the appropriate time to introduce a particular type of activity. For example, the maturation of a child's muscles will determine his ability to move rhythmically to music and to coordinate in the playing of instruments. Although the characteristics of child growth and development are beyond the scope of this book, they must be considered by the supervisor in terms of their implications for the music program.

THE GENERAL MUSIC PROGRAM

The general music curriculum in the elementary school is often based on a "five-fold program," which varies to some degree but usually includes activities designated as "singing," "playing," "listening," "reading," and "rhythms." Sometimes "creativity" is added as a sixth area or substituted for either "rhythms" or "reading." In essence, the classroom program is really *three-fold*: singing, playing, and listening. While the other subjects have a definite place in the curriculum, there is a fallacy in labeling them as separate areas since this suggests a teaching approach that isolates these other subjects as individual entities from a meaningful musical context.

Creativity, for example, is too often thought of only as the making of instruments or the setting of a poem to music — thus, the separate category. But creative experience is much more; it can and *should* be inherent in those activities that constitute singing, playing, and listening. Creativity is essentially perceiving and responding to things in a new or different way. It grows out of a child's curiosity about his environment and is manifested in his ability to integrate all his experiences so that when he concentrates on one area, something new occurs in his response. This is not something that necessarily requires a certain level of intelligence. In fact, psychologists have found that some of the less bright students are much more creative than those with high intelligence quotients. Nor does it matter whether the child is dealing with something new in itself. He may react in an entirely novel way to something already familiar, for creativity is basically a re-ordering of existing ideas and experiences.

The field of music — one of the "creative arts" — would seem to be a natural medium for developing a child's creative instinct, but it is frequently taught with the idea that the creative experience is ouside the realm of general musical activity. Such an approach to teaching is not unique to music. It seems that one of the greatest faults of our educational system, in all parts of the curriculum, is the stifling of creativity. A student is told what to do, what to think, what *the* answer to a problem or question is; and at the upper levels of his schooling, he is still being told what subjects he should take regardless of his interests. He is disciplined, rather than helped toward self-discipline. He is piloted away from personal feeling and original thinking toward seeking what he believes his teachers want him to think. His curiosity is dulled to cautiousness as he discovers that the unconventional and the unexpected do not lend themselves to high test grades. He is taught, perhaps, to have insight, but not invention — insight into the past without inspiration for the present. And he is taught to conform to the point of rebellion, rather than allowed to become a creative individual who will contribute to the betterment of society.

The implication here for music is that more attention needs to be given to processes, not just to results. In performance and listening activities, the child must be given a wide variety of experiences, a sufficient number of tools of expression to work with, numerous opportunities to experiment with music and to apply his own ideas in performance, opportunities to discover recognizable feeling in musical sound, and time to form his own ideas and concepts about music and to identify himself with it.

Singing and playing *can* be creative; it does not matter that someone else has already written the tune. If this were not so, orchestras would only *re-create* the works of the masters, and one recording of Beethoven's *Fifth* would probably be as good as another. That listening can be a creative experience, too, is demonstrated by the fact that no two people will react in an identical way on hearing a single work, nor will an individual usually respond the same way twice to the same composition. And if this were not so, music could easily become time-worn and boring. Clearly, the most common approach to creativity in music that is practiced is a limited one, and as long as it is thought of as a separate type of activity it will remain limited.

Reading and rhythm activities should also be integrated in the classroom program. They can have real meaning only when they are related to the three basic areas. To teach reading without relating the symbols of notation to sound is useless, for symbols have no meaning except in terms of sound. A child learns to read a language, not by seeing black letters on the printed page but, by hearing words spoken and then relating their sound and meaning to a visual impression. Before he learns to read for himself, others read to him; he speaks and is spoken to long before he attempts the visual approach. The same is true in regard to the language of music. One learns to read music through singing and playing it. Thus, the reading program is really part of the performance program.

It is the same with rhythms. Rhythmic response in bodily movement takes place while the child listens to music. There can be no response to accent or beat unless there is an accent or beat to hear. Consequently, an abstract, verbal presentation of rhythmic elements is senseless. It is possible, of course, for a person to respond to music that exists in his mind alone, but he is still hearing something, even if he is alone in his experience. The isolation of the rhythm program is obviously not the same as the situation in music reading. Rhythmic experiences are normally a part of some other activity, as in the playing of instruments or the creation of a rhythmic accompaniment. So the problem here is not one of teaching rhythm without relationship to sound (although that is done as an aspect of instruction in music reading). Rather, the fault lies in the common practice of concentrating solely on the rhythmic activity and letting all else become background music. The student should be helped to recognize rhythm as one of several things that are occurring simultaneously and to feel its movement in terms of the total sound effect. When this is done, he has a greater awareness of rhythm in all musical activities, whether in singing a melody, playing a harmony part, or listening to an orchestra weave its parts together.

The five-fold program, then, ought to be reduced to the three-fold program if every experience is to be presented meaningfully. It might be even more precise to say that there are only two basic types of experience: *making music* (singing, playing, composing) and *responding to music* (listening, dancing, free bodily movement). To clarify the program as much as possible, however, it will be more useful here to speak in terms of the three areas of singing, playing, and listening.

Singing.   Singing has traditionally been the core of the elementary music program, and for good reason. Every child can sing. Some can sing better than others, to be sure, but all children can find satisfaction in singing because it is a means of personal expression and emotional release. We all know of certain adults who love to sing even though their voices may be hoarse and out of tune. Seldom is such a person deluded about the quality of his voice; he simply cannot resist the joy of song. With children this love is even greater, and they can be taught to find increased satisfaction through guided development of their voices. The discovery of aesthetic and emotional pleasure in free, natural singing is not limited to a few. Even the uncertain singer (once referred to erroneously as a "monotone" because his vocal attempts had not progressed beyond the stage of "speaking" a song) can be taught to carry a tune. Although not everyone can be a fine singer with a beautiful voice, anyone who is capable of learning can be taught to sing better and can develop standards of taste in regard to tone quality and interpretation. In addition to the joy of vocal performance, a wide range of musical learnings can be gained through singing. And unlike playing an instrument, which requires a good deal of time and practice to attain some degree of sensitivity and control, singing can be a successful, even artistic experience from the start.

The singing program needs to be developed in three stages throughout the elementary grades: (1) a period of free imitation, wherein the students can come to understand their voices and the pleasure of singing; (2) a period that develops an "eye-plus-ear" approach to music reading; and (3) a period that leads to the independence of eye and ear so that the student is able to hear what he sees and see what he hears without a mutual dependence on the written note and the aural sound.

Many aspects of notation, form, style, and so on can be taught through singing, but the song literature must be chosen as well in terms of the child's voice, his vocal development, and his other needs. This means that songs must have suitable vocal ranges and phrase-lengths within his normal breathing capacity. There should be unison songs throughout the grades and opportunities for part-singing at the middle and upper levels. Songs need to be included that will lend themselves to the reading program, as well as others that are appropriate for action and rhythm activities. As the child grows, his repertoire should expand with his interests through a broadly balanced offering of folk, art, and popular songs, including spiritual, patriotic, and seasonal material.

By the time the child reaches the upper elementary grades, there needs to be a more careful appraisal than is generally made of the material selected to meet his interests. In grades five and six, students are listening more and more to popular music on radio, television, and records. Many of them become attracted to the rhythmic vitality of the poorer types of this music simply because they have never been exposed to good popular songs. Folk tunes, calypso songs, and occasional melodies extracted from larger works by the masters are not the whole of song literature, and the students know this. It is no wonder they look for music with a little more excitement than that which they are fed in the elementary program. Surely, the inclusion of good popular songs, *appropriate to their level,* would save many students from marooning themselves in rock 'n roll, folk-rock, and pop-rock. It has been my experience that those students who are familiar with good popular music are the same ones who have a healthy interest in classical music, while those who have been forced to seek their own popular outlet in poorer idioms are the ones who have no interest whatsoever in the classics. It would seem that the loss of students to limited forms of musical expression is due in part to the blindness of music educators themselves. The singing program must use literature that will develop standards of taste for a number of styles.

Playing. The use of instruments in the general music classroom is intended to give children a fuller musical experience. Since not all music is sung, playing rhythmic, melodic, and harmonic instruments places music in its more natural setting. Such instruments as rhythm sticks, drums, triangles, bells, and Autoharps can be used for accompaniment, for dramatizing songs, for exploring tonal and rhythmic concepts, and for composing music. Many types of musical learning can be introduced or reinforced through the use of classroom instruments: pitch, tempo, beat, accent, melodic contour, harmony, style, mood, form, notation, etc. Although in the primary grades rhythmic and simple melodic instruments are used most, the piano can be effectively employed by children for exploring tonal relationships, and the Autoharp can add a great deal of interest by enhancing a song both rhythmically and harmonically. Toward the end of the third grade, but more normally in the fourth, pre-band instruments like the Tonette and Flutophone are also used.

One of the important principles to keep in mind is that these instruments should be used to bring about rhythmic, melodic, and harmonic growth—not performance growth. Becoming an accomplished performer is something that takes place in the instrumental class rather than in the general music class. The students do, of course, need to attain some proficiency in the manipulation of classroom instruments, but they should be led, beyond this stage, to make their instruments sound good in context and to discriminate in the selection of instruments for accompaniments.

As in the area of singing, instrumental activities should begin with aural experiences, before symbols are introduced. Once again, there are three main stages of use: (1) imitation, free self-expression, and the development of basic aural concepts; (2) relating rhythmic and melodic experiences to notational symbols; and (3) developing the ability to look at symbols and imagine the rhythm or melody represented.

Listening. Listening is an integral part of each phase of the music program, for it is involved in rhythmic activities, in playing instruments, in creating original tunes, and, of course, in singing, whether it be in learning a song by rote or producing good tone quality and accurate pitch in a song that is already known. The successful program, however, must also include listening activities for their own sake and enjoyment, principally through the use of a wide variety of recorded material (although live performance should not be neglected).

The listening program is a prime means of enlarging the student's knowledge and appreciation of music literature since it can extend the experiences of the child beyond his own musical abilities. This widening of cultural awareness comes through a portion of the music curriculum in which all students can take part with a fair assurance of success. For through listening activities, the child who has not yet found his "singing voice," nor perhaps been able to coordinate rhythmically, may at last discover the path to musical success, which is so important in making music a meaningful part of his life. Through the listening program the child can increase his knowledge, appreciation, and enjoyment of different musical styles, structural and dance forms, instruments and voice types, the works of great composers, the descriptive qualities of program music and the intrinsic values of absolute music, and the wide range of moods and human emotions that can be expressed through music. In addition, the listening program can increase the child's knowledge and understanding of other people, races, nationalities, customs, and art-forms. It can also stimulate intellectual, physical, and emotional responses, and foster creative expression. At the same time, listening activities can increase the child's appreciation of musical skills and develop his sensitivity to elements such as melody, harmony, rhythm, instrumentation, meter, etc., and basic concepts of tone quality, volume, pitch, and tempo.

Through all of this, if the listening program offers a balanced diet of styles, types, and media, it should develop discrimination and taste in music on the part of the individual student and should contribute to the betterment of his life through enjoyable musical experiences.

BASIC CONTENT IN GENERAL MUSIC

It has been said that although specific experiences will vary from school to school, certain basic learning might be expected in any successful and comprehensive general music program. Such experiences are outlined in this section by grades. The idea of assigning particular learnings to grade levels should not be taken too exactly, however. This list has been arranged in a logical, sequential order, but it is quite possible that something listed under grade three might be learned earlier in one school, or even later in another school. The important thing is *developmental readiness*, which does not necessarily follow grade-level lines.

However, since most teaching is conducted within the structure of the graded school, it is of value to see where certain learning might be expected to come. It should also be kept in mind that a specific learning is not confined to one grade. Although AB form can be recognized in the first grade, it may not be clearly understood until later, and should still be experienced through other examples in the sixth grade. Only by reinforcement will the learning be firmly grasped.

FIRST GRADE

Singing

>   Symbol-free experiences; learning songs by rote.
>   Matching tones.
>   Comparing the singing and speaking voices.
>   Short, simple songs, both active and quiet.
>   Singing games, action songs, dramatizations.
>   Building a repertoire: songs about self, home, seasons, animals.
>   Clapping to the beat and free rhythmic response.

Playing

>   Playing rhythm instruments to feel the beat and to
>   create accompaniments.
>   Playing melody bells, resonator bells, tone bars, etc.
>   Discriminating among instruments to use for accompaniment.
>   Keyboard exploration to contrast high-low, up-down.
>   Making simple instruments.

Listening

>   Identification of high and low, fast and slow, loud and soft, smooth and
>   short, in both singing activities and listening to recordings.
>   Feeling accents in the music.
>   Responding to phrases and cadences.
>   Listening to moods.
>   Walking, running, skipping, hopping to rhythmic changes.
>   Responding to AB and ABA forms.
>   Identifying the trumpet, violin, piano, snare drum, and cymbals.

SECOND GRADE

Singing

>   Learning songs by rote.
>   Matching tones.
>   Singing games and dances; action songs.

Free rhythmic activity to songs.

Building a repertoire: songs about self, community, friends, the out-of-doors.

Rounds in two parts.

First use of books to identify familiar songs.

Recognition of the scale and melodic patterns in the notation of familiar songs.

Connecting lines and verses in reading the score.

Introduction to the treble staff and to sol-fa syllables.

Identifying basic note values by play names: whole note (sleeping note), half note (slow note), quarter note (walking note), and eighth note (running note).

Identifying like and unlike phrases in note reading.

Identifying scale degrees by numbers.

Association of physical response to notation.

Playing

Making and/or playing accompaniments on rhythmic and melodic instruments.

Playing simple accompaniments on the Autoharp.

Selecting instruments for accompaniment.

Playing simple beat patterns.

Playing melodies by numbers and letters.

Keyboard exploration and experimentation with steps, skips, and repeated rhythmic patterns on one or two notes.

Experimenting with sound relations by playing strings, bars, bottles of liquid, etc.

Listening

Identifying simple themes, changes in mood, dynamics, and tempo.

Aural recognition of stepwise and skipping motion.

Feeling the phrase, recognizing contrasting sections, and recognizing like and unlike phrases.

Feeling accents.

Response through marching, skipping, dancing, etc.

Identifying AB and ABA forms.

Identifying the tuba, string bass, flute, bass drum, and glockenspiel.

THIRD GRADE

Singing

Learning songs by rote.

Learning simple songs by note: identifying like and unlike phrases, rhythmic patterns, and tonal patterns.

Singing games and dances.

Rounds and descants.

Building a repertoire: songs about group activities, time, events, patriotism, the community, and school.

Use of letter names and the "movable do" system.

Familiarity with lines and spaces of treble staff.

Use of real names for identifying the whole note, half note, quarter note, and eighth note.

Recognizing rhythmic duration by understanding and feeling the number of beats in various note values.

Recognizing simple dotted rhythms.

Understanding the hold, tie, slur, repeat signs, and dynamic marks.

Understanding the sharp and flat.

Understanding meter signatures: 2-4, 3-4, and 4-4.

Understanding the major scale pattern.

Understanding key signatures and identifying the keys of C, F, and G.

Playing

Accompanying with rhythm and melody instruments, and with the Autoharp.

Exploring the keyboard.

Writing simple accompaniments, introductions, and codas.

Playing descants to singing.

Playing melodies by notation.

Clapping and playing simple rhythmic notation.

Selecting I, IV, and V chords for song accompaniment.

Use of classroom instruments such as the Song-flute to aid in learning musical notation.

Listening

Listening for themes, for like and unlike sections, and for rhythmic and tonal patterns.

Begin study of composers. (Mozart, Schumann, and Debussy are well-received at this level.)

Identifying meters by listening for the movement of music in "two's" and "three's."

Distinguishing the sounds of the I, IV, and V chords on the piano and Autoharp.

Recognition of ABA and rondo forms.

Recognition of the clarinet, trombone, harp, timpani, and tambourine.

FOURTH GRADE

Singing

Learning songs by rote.

Learning songs by notation that include skips of thirds and fifths as well as steps.

Three-part rounds, descants, chants, dialogue songs.

Singing in parallel thirds; with a stationary part against a moving line; and with a scalar part against a skipping melody.

Building a repertoire with longer songs: songs of reality, patriotism, heroes, science, transportation, and songs with foreign texts.

Setting poems to music.

Singing to folk dances.

Discriminating in style of phrasing in singing.

Understanding meter signatures: 2-8, 2-2.

Understanding chromatic signs.

Understanding basic dynamic markings.

Songs with more dotted rhythms.

Awareness of sixteenth-note values.

Review of music-reading symbols, and use of real note names.

Locating keynotes in songs.

Understanding and identifying key signatures of C, F, G, B-flat, and D.

Use of letter names and syllables.

Use of musical terms such as legato and staccato.

Emphasis on sound of major scale, tonic major triad, and tonic minor triad.

Playing

Accompanying with harmonic, as well as rhythmic and melodic, instruments.

Playing primary chords on the piano and Autoharp.

Playing original melodies on the piano.

Building scales on the piano.

Writing original accompaniments.

Playing pre-band instruments such as the Song-flute and recorder.

Listening

Listening to both program and absolute music.

Identification of the soprano, alto, tenor, and bass voices.

Identification of common rhythms and meters.

Recognition of moods, themes, tempos, and dynamics.

Study of composers representing various periods and types of music. (Bach, Schubert, Grieg, Foster, and Tchaikovsky are well-received at this level.)

Recognition of ABA, rondo, suite, and march forms.

Identification of dance forms such as the minuet and waltz.

Recognition of the French horn, bassoon, cello, and xylophone.

FIFTH GRADE

Singing

Learning songs by rote.

Learning songs by notation that include skips of fourths and fifths.

Three-part and four-part rounds, two-part songs, descants.

Dialogue songs and boy-girl songs.

Building a repertoire: songs of America, of exploration, of work and occupations; folk songs, spirituals, and patriotic songs.

Writing songs.

Organized dance movement to songs.

Developing sense of balance and blend in part-singing.

Reviewing and developing an understanding of music-reading symbols.

Use of letter and syllable names.

More use of dotted rhythms and syncopation.

Understanding meter signatures: 3-8, 4-8, 3-2.

Understanding construction of minor scale.

Understanding and identifying key signatures: C, F, G, B-flat, D, E-flat, A, A-flat, E; and A minor, D minor, and E minor.

Playing

Writing original accompaniments.

Playing accompaniments from a score on the Autoharp, percussion instruments, and melodic instruments.

Keyboard experience.

Experimenting in chording familiar songs and original melodies.

Listening

Recognizing by ear themes that have been presented in notation.

Listening to both program and absolute music, with increased awareness of non-programmatic elements.

Identifying the soprano, alto, tenor, baritone, and bass voices.

Study of composers representing various periods and types of music. (Gershwin, Foster, Sousa, MacDowell, Anderson, Copland, Grofe, and Rodgers are appropriate in connection with the study of America, but a balance should be maintained with European composers.)

Identifying meters in listening.

Recognizing syncopation in listening.

Understanding and recognizing forms such as the fugue, theme and variations, suite, overture, ABA, march, and rondo.

Recognizing dance forms such as the polka, tango, and waltz.

Recognizing the saxophone, guitar, and organ.

SIXTH GRADE

Singing

Learning more difficult songs by rote.

Learning songs by notation; experiences in reading stepwise patterns, jumps in major and minor chords, and other simple jumps.

Two-part and three-part songs; four-part rounds.

Building a repertoire: traditional songs of America, songs of and about foreign countries.

Making up original songs.

Discriminating in vocal interpretation.

Understanding 6-8 as a meter signature.

Understanding and recognizing triplets.

Understanding unusual meters.

More use of dotted rhythms and syncopation.

More use of chromatics.

Use of both letter names and syllables.

Understanding and recognizing the minor scale.

Identifying all major and minor key signatures, and constructing all major scales.

Playing

Playing rhythmic, melodic, and harmonic instruments.

Using basic chords to accompany singing.

Accompaniment with other instruments by students taking class and private instruction.

Notating rhythmic and melodic lines that have been made up.

Introduction of bass clef in playing instruments.

Listening

Listening to folk music of various countries.

Listening to both program and absolute music.

Study of composers representing various periods and types of music. (Brahms, Grieg, Tchaikovsky, Beethoven, Verdi, Chopin, and Sibelius are well-received at this level, but American composers should not be neglected.)

Recognition of principal themes and their development.

Understanding and recognizing forms such as the symphony, tone poem, fugue, theme and variations, suite, overture, march, opera, and art song.

Recognition of dance forms and styles such as country dances, ballet, the waltz, and Spanish dances.

Recognition of the viola, oboe, and five basic types of voices.

PROVIDING FOR GENERAL MUSIC

Personnel. Originally, music was taught in the elementary schools by specialists, but today it is handled extensively by the classroom teacher. There are advantages and disadvantages in both practices.

Some schools have a specially-equipped music room where students are taken for instruction by a music specialist. With such a system, it is expected that the trained specialist can provide better instruction than the classroom teacher, who generally lacks the specialized skills in music. Such an independent type of program, however, isolates music from the rest of the curriculum, and rarely is music introduced into the other daily activities of the classroom. An additional disadvantage is that children are apt to feel that music is not so important if the teacher, whom they have for almost every other subject, is not involved in the music activities.

When music is taught by the teacher of the self-contained classroom, it can be used at any time of the school day when it best meets the needs of the students. Music holds added meaning in this arrangement, since the classroom teacher is able to know, understand, and help each child much more personally than the specialist. On the other hand, when music is taught solely by the classroom teacher, there is likely to be a narrower range of experience, as well as limited continuity of the music program from grade to grade. Although the classroom teacher may be deserving of considerable admiration for her ability to teach a number of subjects and meet a variety of student needs, few have sufficient skills, training, and insight into music education to do the total job.

To provide a strong elementary music program, then, it is clear that *both* the specialist and the classroom teacher are needed to combine their talents in a cooperative teaching endeavor. The specialist, coming into the classroom on a regular schedule, can provide a balanced offering of activities, supply the necessary special skills, see what experiences are needed in terms of the total music curriculum throughout the grades, provide proper resources and materials, and make suggestions for activities to be carried on while she is absent. This does not leave the classroom teacher out of the program. She can provide music daily at the appropriate times by reviewing familiar material, adding new verses to old songs, teaching new songs from recordings (if she lacks music reading ability), using simple instruments, giving listening lessons, establishing a music corner (where children can explore at will instruments, musical charts and pictures, books on music, and so on), and offering other experiences of enrichment. The teacher is also of considerable value in preparing a class for a lesson to be given by the specialist.

It would be ideal, of course, for each elementary building to have a resident music specialist who would be able to give sufficient time to each room. Although this is done in some communities, most school systems do not feel able to handle the added expense of this practice. Consequently, the specialist is apt to serve two, three, or even more school buildings. She may schedule classroom visits only once every one or two weeks and act as a consultant to the teachers on the activities that they provide from day to day. In some cases, the specialist serves only as a consultant, and her visits are limited to observations and conferences with the teachers. (There are instances where a specialist serves 200 or more teachers; obviously, she can be little more than an occasional consultant.) It is preferable, though, for the specialist to do the actual teaching on a regular basis, with time set aside for consultation. How often a specialist will teach each class naturally depends on the number of rooms she has to visit, but meeting a class once a week would seem to be the minimum if there is to be any continuity. And it is assumed that all the classroom teachers will be able to carry on a good program during the interim, for one regular music lesson per week is not sufficient to develop musical growth. If it is at all possible, the specialist should see each class at least three times a week.

Most elementary teachers are willing and anxious to cooperate in providing continuity and enrichment when they are given ideas to follow and materials to use. For this reason, the specialist should leave with the teacher an outline of her own lesson, including suggestions for follow-up activities. Or, preview material may be provided for the teacher to use in preparing the class for a coming lesson. It is only when the classroom teacher is left without resources and useful ideas that she is inclined to avoid musical activities between the specialist's visits. Even the teacher who feels musically limited can and *will* do a great deal if she is offered assistance.

Perhaps the following first-hand experience will point up the type of cooperation that is possible and the kind which the supervisor should promote: Once when I was producing a musical play for high school students, an elementary music supervisor suggested that it would be of interest to pupils in the fifth and sixth grades. I agreed and prepared a short television program that could be presented to all the intermediate classes in the school system at the same time. The twenty-minute program featured students from the high school cast and offered background material on the play, its author and composer, and how a show is put together. Since this was a one-program lesson in music appreciation, it might have had little meaning by itself. However, I prepared a bulletin that was circulated to all the elementary teachers the week before the viewing. This included an outline of the program and information on the play, its writers, the types of voices that would be heard, the style of the music, how it differed from other types of music theatre productions, and so on. With this in hand, the teachers eagerly prepared their classes for the program to come, so that the televised lesson was the culmination of an activity, rather than the total experience. Significantly, the teachers were most thankful afterward for having been given material they could use, on a personal basis, with the children and for being able to participate in the music program. Such an attitude among these "non-music" teachers is usually present if they are given tools to work with, and if they are not left to carry on the music program by themselves.

Thus, the elementary music curriculum requires a team approach. Neither the classroom teacher nor the music specialist can do the job alone. But working together, they can create an excellent climate for musical experience.

Time.   The MENC recommends a minimum of twenty minutes of music daily (100 minutes weekly) in grades 1-3, and a minimum of twenty-five to thirty minutes daily (125-150 minutes weekly) in grades 4-6. In 1963, the Research Division of the NEA published a study including a national survey of elementary school practices. Based on 657 replies to 790 queries sent to a random selection of schools, the report stated that the median time allotment for music in the elementary grades was about eighty minutes per week. The average elementary school, therefore, needs to provide more time for music in order to attain reasonable standards of growth.

Practices will still vary, of course, from room to room within a single school. Some teachers devote an equal amount of time to music daily, while others prefer to have longer sessions two or three times a week. Although the weekly minimum can be realized by either method, it is recommended that some musical activity take place each day whether in equal time periods or not. Generally, students will learn and retain more in shorter sessions daily than in longer sessions that are spread apart. However, where fewer but longer periods are desired, it still would be of value to use music incidentally as a short, change-of-pace activity in the course of each day. Class singing after a period of individual study, an activity song following a long period of sitting, or a musical interlude to establish a desirable class mood can all be used effectively outside of the scheduled music lesson to serve both non-musical purposes and musical growth.

It is important, though, that fully-organized music lessons with clear objectives are not sacrificed to the use of incidental musical activity solely for the purpose of meeting minimum recommendations for time allotment.

Equipment. In order to execute a music program, certain basic equipment is needed. Each elementary classroom should be permanently stocked with a set of music textbooks for its level, a phonograph, a set of basic recordings for the grade, a pitch pipe, a music-staff chalk liner, a set of resonator bells, at least two drums (one high-pitched, one low-pitched), several pairs of rhythm sticks, a triangle, a tambourine, and a few sand blocks.

In addition, each elementary school should have the following equipment available for rotational use among its classrooms; pianos, 12-bar Autoharps, a tape recorder, filmstrip and motion picture projectors, pictures of composers and instruments, supplementary recordings for all grades, books on music for children, and additional rhythmic and melodic instruments.

Among the instruments that may be supplied are:

tom-toms	bell sticks
bongo drums	castanets
barrel drums	cymbals
hand snare drums	finger cymbals
rhythm sticks	tambourines
wood blocks	cow bells
clave tone blocks	gongs
temple blocks	Swiss bells
claves	song bells
sandblocks	wooden tone bars
coconut shells	Tonettes
maracas	Flutophones
shakers	recorders
guiros	ukuleles
triangles	guitars
sleigh bells	portable electric organ

THE NON-GENERAL MUSIC PROGRAM

Choruses. Although there should be ample opportunity for all children to sing as part of the classroom program, there is still a place for a special chorus at the intermediate level. Especially-talented students in the upper elementary grades deserve and can profit from part-singing in a selective chorus. Such a chorus can take them beyond the level of classroom performance, reinforce classroom experience in part-singing, and provide a good introduction to choral performance that may encourage them to participate in choral activities at the secondary level. To serve these purposes, it is advisable that the elementary ensemble perform music that, for the most part, is not found in their basic classroom texts. This identifies the chorus as a special group, encourages student interest, and extends the children's experiences as well as abilities.

Although there may be a primary-grade unison chorus, it is not necessary. The chorus serves its purpose best in the fifth and sixth grades, where harmonic singing is being developed. Since fifth-graders usually sing in two parts, whereas sixth-graders are capable of handling three parts, it may be desirable to form two groups. The sixth-grade chorus could then work on three-part arrangements, and a combined fourth-grade and fifth-grade chorus could sing in two parts. The division, of course, would depend on the number of interested and capable students available.

The students may be selected easily by the music specialists during regular class lessons. Unlike instrumental groups, in which a certain basic instrumentation is required, an elementary chorus can function and perform well as either a large or small ensemble. Fifteen to twenty students, or several times that number, can form a good chorus. The students are usually assigned to "high" and "low" parts (or high, middle, and low). However, if the music is chosen carefully, ranges of the different parts will usually be close enough to permit a transferral of parts, so that the same section will not always be singing melody or harmony.

Rehearsals for the chorus should be held at least once or twice a week, and preferably three times a week, for periods of twenty-five or thirty minutes. These may be set up at a regularly-scheduled time or on a rotational basis (see Chapter 5 for scheduling practices). To make the goals of the group more realistic for the children, public performance is desirable — at a school assembly, a PTA meeting, or a special public concert involving organizations from each of the elementary buildings.

Instrumental Instruction. The use of pre-band instruments (recorders, Tonettes, Flutophones, etc.) in general music classes helps in the teaching of music reading, introduces children to instruments, stimulates their interest in instrumental study, and is worthwhile in determining a student's potential ability in playing an instrument of the band or orchestra. This leads naturally to specialized instrumental study at the intermediate level, available to students having the interest, talent, and aptitude for it.

The beginning program. Instruction normally begins in the fourth or fifth grades, but provisions should be made for students through the seventh grade to be able to begin lessons. A student should not be denied the opportunity to learn an instrument simply because his interest is kindled a year, or two, or three after beginning classes are available to him. As for how early a child may start, there is no definite answer. Musical aptitude tests and achievement in other school subjects may indicate something about a student's readiness, but these are not accurate gauges by any means. In fact, a child who does not do well on an aptitude test could very well turn out to be an excellent performer, if he has the interest and perseverance. A much more important consideration is the child's physical development, particularly his coordination of small muscles and his proportions in relation to the instrument he is going to play.

Muscular control is necessary for beginners on any instrument, but physical size is relative. Stringed instruments, for example, are available in junior, intermediate, and standard sizes to fit the performer; but in other cases, a child may need fingers big enough to cover clarinet holes or arms long enough to manipulate the trombone slide.

Some educators prefer that pupils wait until the fifth grade or even later to begin the study of a musical instrument. This is a moot question, and much depends on how often the student will have his lessons. If lessons are far apart (once a week), skills are developed less rapidly, and younger students are less likely to maintain interest. Others feel that most instrumental instruction should begin in the fifth grade, but that string players should start in the fourth grade since it takes longer to develop basic coordination and skills on stringed instruments. Generally, it may be said that if a student is physically capable and has the interest, it makes little difference how old he is or what grade he is in.

The choice of an instrument, aside from the matter of physical restrictions, rests primarily on what appeals to the child, and to a lesser degree on maintaining a balanced instrumentation. Since the choice of instruments in elementary school will determine the fullness of instrumentation later in secondary school organizations, it is naturally desirable if all the beginning students do not select the snare drum and trumpet. However, this is generally not a major problem since there is likely to be a reasonably good distribution of instruments, and some students can easily transfer to instruments which are needed. Educator Dr. Lee Chrisman suggests that a basic guideline in projecting instrumentation of future groups is to see that for every student who starts percussion lessons, about four start on brasses, six on woodwinds, and eight on strings.

Certain schools start pupils only on basic instruments — violin, trumpet, clarinet, snare drum — and transfer them to other instruments later, when they join the band or orchestra. However, students need ensemble experience with mixed instruments right from the beginning; and if the child is physically mature, he should be able to start on any instrument.

Since we are dealing here with music in free (tax-supported) public schools, it would seem logical that the schools own every instrument necessary for instruction. In practice, however, there are relatively few schools that do this. Most schools own only those instruments which parents probably would not buy because they are too large, too expensive, too limited in terms of available solo literature, or simply not popular. A medium-sized elementary school, then, might be expected to own a minimum of two or three violas, three or four cellos, one or two string basses, one or two oboes, two to four French horns, one or two baritones, two tubas, two or three snare drums, one bass drum, a pair of cymbals, and a piano. These instruments should be made available free of charge to students, although some schools rent them for $2 to $5 per semester.

Arrangements can be made with instrument companies, distributors, or local music stores to rent other instruments to students for a trial-period of three months. If the parents and child decide to continue instruction, the rental fee is then applied toward the purchase price. This plan allows parents to postpone buying an expensive instrument until they are sure that their child has the interest and talent to benefit from it.

Recruiting. A performance by existing elementary-school organizations, or by junior-high and senior-high bands and orchestras, can do much to interest students in beginning instrumental study. But still there is needed a more direct effort toward arousing their interest. Usually, a demonstration of instruments will be given by members of the staff, or by a local dealer-distributor servicing the school. Such a demonstration may be given at each of the elementary schools, or during an evening at the high school auditorium, so that interested parents can participate. The presentation should make evident the tone quality, features, and capabilities of each instrument through visual, mechanical display and through the performance of short, representative, melodic selections. Time should be allowed afterward to answer questions. A display of basic instruments, or pictures of them, may also be set up in each school.

Before this demonstration is given, a letter should be sent home to all parents of eligible students: setting forth the purposes and advantages of the program; providing information on lessons, securing instruments, and cost; and calling attention to the demonstration that will be presented. This letter might take a form similar to the following:

RIDGELAND PUBLIC SCHOOLS

Dear Parent:

Because music is an important part of every child's education and is a rewarding experience that will enrich your child's life for years to come, the Ridgeland Public Schools offer beginning and advanced instruction in playing instruments of the band and orchestra.

This program is offered during school time to students in grade four and beyond who are physically mature enough to handle their chosen instruments. Since it is difficult to determine which children may develop rich musical talent and will benefit most from instruction, trial class lessons are the only sure way to discover potential. Wouldn't you like to give your son or daughter this opportunity?

Instruments may be rented for a reasonable fee of $10 for a three-month trial period. If you and your child wish to continue instruction, this fee is later applied toward the purchase price of the instrument. Some school-owned instruments are also available on loan.

You may ensure your child's place in our program now by filling out and returning the slip below. If you would like to learn more about the instruction, have assistance in selecting the right instrument, or arrange for an instrument rental, please come to our demonstration at the high school auditorium, Wednesday evening, September 17th, at 7:30 p.m. We'll be happy to answer your questions, and if you wish, you may enroll your child at that time. We hope to see you there.

Sincerely,
David Cutter
Music Director

To the Principal:

I would like my child, _____, age _____,
                              (name)

to have instruction in playing the _____ .
                                          (instrument)

☐ I will come to the demonstration to arrange for rental of an instrument.

☐ I already have an instrument for him (her).

☐ I am undecided, but will attend the demonstration.

Parent's name _____
Address _____

Child's school _____ Tel. _____

Class organization. There are several ways of organizing instrumental instruction. Private lessons are ordinarily too expensive from the standpoint of the number of teachers required and the time involved in teaching, unless the school is very small. Although there is an advantage in personalized instruction, there is also a lack of ensemble experience, which is very important. At the other extreme is the mixed class of all instruments; this arrangement is objectionable because it is unwieldly, techniques are unrelated, and progress is slow.

It is preferable to teach the children in classes of five to fifteen, grouped by like instruments (all clarinets, all trumpets, etc.) or by families of instruments (all woodwinds, all brass, etc.). In either case, the groups may be organized by like ability or varying ability. Classes of like instruments and like ability are best. Usually these can be set up without much difficulty in the large school. In medium-sized schools, where grouping by ability is apt to draw students from more than one grade, it is not so easy. In this case, grouping by family, but still with like ability, will usually draw together enough students in the same grade to make a class. Classes of like instruments, but varying ability, are the next best combination and usually work in the smaller school. Less desirable is the family class of varying ability.

There should be beginning and advanced classes for each instrument or group. Intermediate classes may be added in a well-developed program. The average school, then, grouping by families, should have:

> Beginning string class
> Advanced string class
> Beginning woodwind class
> Advanced woodwind class
> Beginning brass class
> Advanced brass class
> Beginning percussion class
> Advanced percussion class
> Beginning piano class
> Advanced piano class

Ideally, each group should meet daily, but at least two or three times a week for thirty minutes. In a large group that meets less often, and where the student is not playing constantly, a longer period of forty-five minutes might be possible. Since elementary students and beginning instrumentalists tire easily, shorter, more frequent periods are desirable.

The brass, woodwind, and percussion classes at each level should combine in at least one meeting a week to form:

1. Beginning wind and percussion ensemble
2. Advanced wind and percussion ensemble

The wind and percussion ensemble and the string ensemble (string class) are recommended in place of an elementary band or orchestra because of the usual lack of instrumentation required by the latter groups, and because of the limited literature that is available for this level. This is simply a matter of terminology relating to full instrumentation. The elementary school should be concerned with providing beginning stages of instruction and ensemble experience, but not necessarily the experience of a full "band" or "orchestra"; this experience can be realized in the junior high school. Although there is a growing list of educational material written specifically for an elementary band or orchestra, for the most part four-part ensemble music will offer music of higher calibre and will provide a better balance of sound. In this sense, the terms "wind and percussion ensemble" and "string ensemble" are more appropriate.

4

Organizing
the Secondary Music Curriculum

It has been stated that the program in the elementary school ought to be designed to lead the child through an investigation and exploration of music. If that program is well-structured, there should be no need for any new *type* of activity in the junior high school. If the student at the elementary level has had good experiences in singing, playing, and listening, has developed an understanding of the basic mechanics of musical notation and begun to acquire skills in music reading, then he should be offered a secondary curriculum built for musical *refinement,* with experiences that will broaden his understanding, knowledge, enjoyment, and skill.

These experiences will be new only in the sense that they are different and more advanced. To develop refinement, two basic directions are taken. First, there is the general music program, intended to meet the needs of all students throughout the secondary grades. Then, with this as the core, other offerings are made to meet the needs of special groups.

GENERAL MUSIC CLASSES

The term "general music" lacks precise definition in the schools today, but it is fundamentally a class for every student and is centered around singing, playing, and listening activities, as well as a more formalized study of musical subjects. It is a mistake to think that the class is intended mainly for those students who are not members of performing groups, because every member of a secondary school band, orchestra, or chorus needs the type of exposure to music that a good general class can provide. Many students in performing organizations tend to experience only the part they are singing or playing; they seldom are aware of total musical content. Even if they possessed such an awareness constantly, they would still be experiencing a very small portion of musical literature — and at that, a portion that is limited to their own performance abilities. The truly great works of symphonic literature, chamber music, choral music, jazz, and the musical theatre would never reach their ears in school if the performing group were their only formal contact with music. Thus, the general music class is for the performer as well as the non-performer.

Perhaps it is more precise to say that the lack of definition is not of the term "general music," but of the content of the course that term labels. More than any other area of music education, the general music class has suffered from instability. No two schools seem to teach this course quite the same. Although it is a required course in the seventh and eighth grades throughout many states, it is usually taught with little sense of continuity or basic content. Depending on the particular group of students in a class, the teacher often volleys back and forth between listening to records, re-teaching the recognition of instruments (which students should be expected to know by this stage), assigning research projects which often result in oral reports about popular musical groups, and relating class activities to whatever is being studied in the social studies class. Sometimes, worth-while centers of attention are presented and serious musical literature is examined, but the time between these points is so great that there is no cumulative learning of any real value; and what is learned in one class meeting may not be followed up in the next because the course jumps almost at random from one topic to another. This practice appears to be the rule rather than the exception in school systems around the country.

Certainly, if the general music class is such an important concept — and its need *is* recognized — there ought to be substance to its content. More-over, this substance should provide successive groups of students with cer-tain common experiences from year to year. Yet, there is probably no other course in the school curriculum which changes its direction so much; students taking general music one year cover units that are completely different from those to be given the following year.

Since this is the last period of formal musical study for a vast percentage of students, it would seem that a more settled approach is needed — an approach that is organized with the musical *consumer* in mind, because most students, after graduation, will be consumers rather than performers. What are the most important needs of the prospective consumer? Essen-tially, he needs to be aware of the many forms and styles of music, and he needs to have an understanding that will permit him to select the best in musical activity and to find enjoyment in the wide range of musical experiences he meets in everyday life. In other words, he needs a back-ground that will give personal meaning to the music he hears, whether it is music he seeks out or music that comes to him without formal invitation.

Although elective courses in general music may be offered in the ninth grade and beyond, let's consider the content of the course in the seventh and eighth grades. Unless meaningful activities are offered there, few students will choose to elect the continuing course later. To serve the purposes described above, the class in the seventh grade should be organized differently than in the eighth, with the two forming a unified whole that moves in a single direction.

In the seventh grade, the course should bring together all the experiences of the elementary grades into a single, meaningful concept. Hopefully, the seventh-grade student has had rewarding singing activities, has known the delight of singing in parts, has used instruments to experience music in a wider context, and has listened to many types of music. But what does it all mean to him? How do these activities fit together? The seventh-grade general music class can bring these things together through an examination of *the significance of music, its function in our lives, and its existence as a medium for expression of the thoughts and actions of man* (man in both the individual and collective sense). It can examine more closely the materials of which music is made and the forms it takes. Handled correctly, with the aim of giving music meaning for the individual, this can provide the background for developing in the eighth grade an enlarged appreciation of our musical heritage through an understanding of styles and literature of various types.

The diversified unit approach would still have its place in the seventh-grade class, but only to the extent that each unit — whatever its topic and organization — draws the student closer to the personal meaning of music. A unit on the music of Africa, then, would be valid if it were organized to illustrate how music expresses African life and how it has served daily, functional purposes. But it would not be valid if it were presented as a look at Africa, simply because that continent is being studied in the social studies classes. It would perhaps be best for the excessive regional or national orientation of units to be played down here, drawing instead on the music of a number of countries in a single unit concerned with a basic concept. That concept, of course, still might be the creation of music to express national feeling (any national feeling). An exception would be a study of American music, since this would relate music more directly to the students' lives.

Some of the possible units that would satisfy this concept of organization are the following:

American music
The architecture of music
The art song
Chamber music
The concerto: the individual and the group
Dance forms in music
Eastern music: a different dialect in musical language
Elements of music: how they work together
Emotion in sound
Folk music of America

Great choral music
How music began
How we respond to music
Indian music
The language of music
Latin-American music
Marches and human spirit
Musical words become sounds
Music and legend
Music for festive occasions
Music for worship
Music in your life
Music of Africa: expression of a continent
Music of American wars
Music of early America: the voice of an emerging people
Music of Russia
Music of the rivers and seas
Nationalistic music
Percussion music and our response
Performance media
Program music vs. absolute music
The role of instruments
The science of musical sound
Selecting recordings
The suite
The symphony
Theme and variations
The tone poem
The voice
Work songs

The eighth-grade class, according to this type of organization, would be more specific in terms of unit topics. Amount and selection of content would still be necessary variables due to the differences in individual groups of students, but the general approach for all classes in this grade would be similar if an appreciation of our musical heritage is to be taught. Styles and important examples of the literature in the areas of classical music, folk music, jazz, popular music, and music theatre can be presented to create an awareness of the many types of music with which the student will be in contact. However, an historical approach is not the most appropriate means of developing understanding at this level. It is more important for students to understand the differences between these styles, to know what to listen for, how to judge music, and how to find meaning in these styles. It does not really matter whether the student knows how a particular form developed or how many symphonies a certain composer wrote. It does matter that he can follow those elements which characterize different styles, can hear relationships in music, and can distinguish between good and not-so-good examples. If he is to be a fully-aware consumer, the student needs to have some concept of discrimination. This means that he needs to be able to recognize elements which may be appropriate to musical meaning in one style but not in another. Thus, the characteristic rather than the historical approach would seem most logical. What characteristics can be recognized for deeper enjoyment in classical music, or folk music, or jazz? This is the critical question to keep in mind in planning experiences.

Some of the possible units that would lend themselves to this aim are the following:

> Baroque music: the grand and noble sound
> Classical music: an art of balance and refinement
> Folk music: the combined voice of a people
> The joys of jazz: the performer as composer
> Modern music: expressions of the present
> Music in the theatre: an integrated art
> Popular music in America: its changing styles
> Romantic music: its divergent emotional forms

In organizing and teaching these units, it is important to think of them as "centers of activity" rather than as isolated topics. Each one, though different in content, should contribute to a common objective — the development of aesthetic sensitivity to all music.

If an elective class is offered for ninth-grade students, it may be organized to allow for a considerable number of individual projects — directed research and examination of areas of special interest to each student. Full class activities would be centered primarily in performance experiences and in the sharing of results of individual study.

Singing. Singing is still the central activity of the general music program in the junior high school, because it is the most natural way to involve everyone in direct and personal musical expression. There is probably no better way to sense an emotion in music than to be involved in the actual making of that emotion vocally. Vocal activities lend themselves to every concept about the meaning and significance of music which the teacher wants to present.

Teachers often think that boys at this age do not want to sing and should not be forced to; consequently, we frequently find an emphasis on listening activities. Actually, boys *do* want to sing and there is no need for any coercion if the situation is analyzed. Naturally, a junior-high student, and particularly the male student, will resist singing any kind of material that seems childish. If the teacher were to put himself in the place of a seventh or eighth grader, recalling the interests and feelings of students at that age, and then were to read the words and titles of many songs in general music books, he would easily recognize how degrading they are to the students' maturing egos. Music with interesting melodies and harmonic parts, varied rhythms, and words to which the student can relate are a necessity if the student is to be interested in classroom singing. This does not limit the topics of songs as much as one might think. All sorts of material, including even love songs, will appeal to the junior-high pupil if they are carefully selected.

The second obstacle that causes students to feign disinterest in singing is their physical growth. They are constantly forced to do things which their changing voices will not accommodate. Although girls' voices will mature and extend in range during this period, boys' voices will change completely, dropping an octave below their former child voices. During the period of mutation, the voice narrows in range, ultimately expanding again as it settles into either a high or low register. This, most assuredly, is not the time for boys to stop singing; rather, it is a time for careful guidance so that their voices will develop healthily toward a mature adult quality. On the other hand, the teacher should not try to force adult vocal quality in an attempt to get a full sound. Such a quality does not come normally in the junior high school.

Because of the changing voice, or "cambiata" as it is called, part music is a necessity. Unison songs are still good, but there is difficulty in selecting worthwhile songs that have a small enough range to permit unison singing by both changing and non-changing voices. During these years, four-part music should be comfortably attainable — not SATB music having adult ranges, but part-music including provisions for sopranos (and unchanged boys' voices), altos (though not the mature alto), cambiatas, and baritones. Allowing for parts with cambiata ranges will preserve voices that will ultimately settle into tenor or baritone-bass parts. Using only baritone parts will force prospective tenors into a lower range and harm the quality of the voice. In selecting music, care should be taken not only to choose proper ranges but also to maintain the proper tessitura for each part. There needs to be a constant re-classification of students throughout the seventh and eighth grades so that voices will function freely and settle naturally.

The music reading program also needs to be continued here through singing activities. Sight-reading skills can be developed in learning new songs through the use of syllables, letters, rhythmic chanting, and so on. Music-reading drills, on the other hand, are dull and should be avoided.

Playing. There are numerous opportunities for instruments to be used in accompaniment of singing activities in the general music class. The piano, guitar, Autoharp, percussion instruments, and others, all have their place here for the purpose of involving all the students in instrumental activity.

However, there is another aspect that should not be overlooked. Many students will have attained some proficiency on band and orchestral instruments by the time they are in junior high school, and they can give solo or small ensemble performances for the class. This can be rewarding not only for the performers but also for the rest of the class. Instrumental timbre, performance skills, blend, phrasing, interpretation, melody, harmony, and form are just a few of the possible topics that might be examined by the group in connection with a student's playing for his peers.

Listening. Listening is a very important part of the course. Although singing is perhaps the most direct way to make music a personal experience, the students need to become familiar with an abundance of great music. Listening is the only way in which this can be accomplished — through recordings, broadcasts, and occasional field trips to concerts. A large record collection should be available for instant use. With good materials and carefully-planned, directed listening, a great deal can be absorbed in a short time to make students more intelligent, discriminating, and involved consumers.

Providing for General Music. Establishing a good course of this sort requires the same three essential elements that are needed throughout the music program: sufficient time, proper materials, and qualified personnel.

Teachers employed to work in the general music class require special sensitivity to the needs of early adolescence and particular knowledge of how to deal with the changing voice. The ability to think abstractly in drawing significance from musical works and to communicate concretely in developing awareness is of paramount importance; so, too, is an interest in and knowledge of music of many forms and idioms.

The teacher with keen sight into the physical, emotional, and social changes taking place in this age group can do much with very little equipment and a lot of ingenuity. Success comes easier, of course, when there are materials to work with. Every room used for general music activities should be supplied with a quality phonograph, record collection, books on music, song books, charts and pictures, a piano, a guitar or Autoharp, percussion instruments, a chalkboard, and ample display space. A phonograph with headphone equipment would be valuable for students pursuing individual projects.

In the seventh and eighth grades, these classes should be scheduled at least twice a week, and preferably three times a week, for periods of forty-five minutes, during both semesters. The most carefully-planned sequence of lessons can yield much less than is hoped for when classes meet only once a week, for then it is difficult to maintain a feeling of continuity. In a schedule based on a seven-period or eight-period day, classes can also be established for ninth-grade students.

GENERAL-SPECIAL MUSIC CLASSES

It is often suggested, and rightly so, that the general music type of course should be offered as an elective subject in grades nine through twelve. The term "general music," however, is perhaps not the best title for advanced courses in this area. In keeping with the purpose of refinement in the secondary grades, later courses should aim toward the organization of instruction in music appreciation, music history, and comparative arts. The music theory class would also be in this category.

Such courses are usually considered "special" offerings, and this is true in the sense that they are not required and that they ordinarily draw those students who have a special interest in music. These courses, though, should not serve only special students. Even the theory class, which would be highly valuable for future musicians, composers, and music teachers, can be an exciting venture and a musically broadening experience for one who will be involved in music solely as a consumer.

To be sure, these courses are organized differently than the general music classes of the junior high school, but that is no reason to consider them exclusively for the specialist, any more than one thinks of the chemistry course (rather than general science) as being only for future scientists. If scheduling is well organized and the right courses are offered, the average musically-interested student should be able to schedule both singing activity (in a chorus open to everyone) and a music appreciation or literature course — all in the same block if necessary. The only difference, then, is that the content of the general music class is broken up at the senior-high level into two separate "part-time" classes for more concentrated study within a given period.

There are two important points involved here from the standpoint of administrative opposition. Administrators sometimes feel that (1) these courses cannot be justified because they are of value to only a select group of the student body; and (2) because of scheduling and staffing difficulties, the study of theory and literature should be introduced into other courses, such as band and chorus. The music director may present several strong arguments to these objections. First, the general student *can* find value in "specialist" courses if they are properly organized. Secondly, even if these were intended only for special students, the school should recognize an obligation to meet the needs of exceptional pupils. Third, at least one of these appreciation courses could be scheduled in a six-period day (perhaps alternating from one year to the next with a second course), and several such courses could be programmed in curriculums operating on a seven-period or eight-period day. Fourth, although the teaching of theory and appreciation in performing groups is good, the teacher cannot spare enough time from actual rehearsal to go into any topic in depth. Even if he could, it would, in this case, definitely be to the advantage of special students only — performers being specialists in comparison to the general student body.

To meet the needs of all students, including future listeners, amateur performers, and professionals, several courses may be offered. These would include a major-subject course in music history and appreciation, a part-time course in music literature for students unable to schedule a full-credit subject, and major-subject offerings in music theory (including harmony and composition) and comparative arts (or humanities).

Music History. There have been two broad views regarding the teaching of courses in music history and appreciation. Both consider history a science and appreciation an art, but while one separates the two, the other endeavors to join them. Some authors, educators, and musicologists believe that although the appreciation of an art lives by interpretation and criticism, these factors have no place in a history course. Consequently, there should be two different courses, each with a different emphasis. Others (including the author) believe that science and art are complements, and at this level at least, the two should be brought together in a single course to develop greater insight into the art of listening through historical perspective. However, the full-credit, music history and appreciation class might be supplemented, whenever possible, by a part-time course in music literature (the non-historical, listening approach), simply to accommodate students with tight schedules.

The approach to teaching a history-appreciation class varies widely. A chronological approach is commonly used, although reverse chronology is also found, beginning with the twentieth century and working backward. The class might also begin at a point of high interest, such as music of the nineteenth century, and then progress to earlier and later musical idioms. None of these systems is perfect. The straight chronological plan leads the student through a great deal of unfamiliar music (and difficult music from the standpoint of the contemporary listener) before he reaches music that is recognizable and easier to enjoy. On the other hand, each of the other methods makes it more difficult for a student to understand how certain forms and styles have developed over a long period of time, or why certain composers and works are considered important points of culmination rather than innovation. Another possibility is the unit approach, organized around forms, types, media, and selected composers. This is appropriate for the literature class, but for the history course it presents the same problem as the reverse-chronology and high-interest plans: historical understanding is limited without considerable repetition of factual data.

Deciding upon the proper organization requires the consideration of one other matter. As in the general music class, it is important that study is not limited to the classical field. To the often-heard cry that there is little time to study anything else, I can only say — time should be, and can be, made. There is no valid basis for neglecting the important things that have taken place in other areas of music, for neglecting the great amount of non-classical music that can be enjoyed (and is worthy of enjoyment) by the musically literate, or for neglecting the fact that other styles are unavoidable in everyday life and demand from music educators an obligation to prepare students as *total* consumers.

The most practical organization of a history-appreciation course at the high-school level is perhaps a combined chronological-unit approach. The plan outlined in the following pages has been proven successful over a period of several years of development with high school classes. This course is organized into seven basic units of different lengths, each unit, with the exception of the first, being taught chronologically. The first unit, on the elements of music, is introductory and draws upon examples from many styles to illustrate elements which can be recognized in each type of music throughout the course. The other six units deal with the development of classical music from the Baroque period to the present, the development of jazz, folk music in America, early music through the Renaissance, the music theatre, and popular music in America. The breaking-up of traditional composed music into two units, pre-Baroque and Baroque to the present, avoids a long stretch of music that is relatively unfamiliar to the student and yet retains a large enough time period in each portion to offer historical perspective.

It is important that each of these areas be given attention for its unique values. The old practice of using jazz or popular music as an "ear-catcher" and an "introduction" to Bach or Mozart should have no place in music education. When this is done, it suggests that the teacher is not really convinced of the musical value of these forms; consequently, he is doing his class an injustice in using material he feels is not of quality. The indiscriminate use of inferior music, whether it is in the jazz field or any other area, is a negative approach to teaching. If a teacher needs this type of stepping-stone to interest his group in a classical work, there is something lacking in either the work selected or in the teacher, and in many cases it is the latter. Good works in any of these fields speak for themselves, if the student knows what to listen for (and even that is not always necessary). Therefore, the use of any type of music should be for its own merits. Upholding the value of individual styles does not mean, of course, that each unit should be isolated from the others, nor isolated as an end in itself. As in the general music class, it is important to think of these units as vehicles for providing aesthetic experiences that are integrated in the student's understanding and resultant sensitivity.

The over-all plan of this course, which can be adapted in many ways to fit the individual school, is as follows:

I. The Elements of Music
  A. Main elements
  B. Structural elements
  C. Elements that vary by interpretation
II. The Development of Classical Music
  A. Baroque era
  B. Rococo and pre-Classical periods
  C. Classical period
  D. Romantic era
  E. Post-Romanticism
  F. Twentieth century
III. The Development of Jazz
  A. Backgrounds and beginnings
  B. Traditional jazz era
  C. Mainstream jazz era
  D. Revival period
  E. Modern jazz era
IV. Folk Music of America
  A. Defining folk music: its characteristics
  B. British and African traditions in America
  C. Folk styles around the country
V. Early Music
  A. How music began
    1. Origins and functional uses of early music
    2. Music of ancient civilizations
  B. Music of the Middle Ages and the Renaissance
    1. Music of the early Christian Church
    2. Early polyphonic music
    3. Music of the Renaissance
VI. Music Theatre (Opera is covered under the classical unit.)
  A. Backgrounds of American musical theatre
  B. Operetta
  C. Vaudeville and musical revues
  D. Musical comedies
  E. Musical plays
VII. Popular Music in America
  A. Development and trends
  B. Popular song forms
  C. Dance-band and vocal styles

The range of topics may appear to allow only superficial coverage of the more important areas. However, each part should not be of equal length, and a great deal depends on the careful organization of the units.

In addition to information on composers and performers, their contributions, and the significance of their music, each unit should focus attention on the melodic, rhythmic, and harmonic properties of the music; the treatment of thematic material; principal characteristics of style; instrumentation and orchestration; form and design; interpretation; and so on. There also should be relationships, though not comparisons, drawn between the major unit topics and individual works that are examined. (Relating types of music is a completely different technique than using one type to "introduce" another.)

Meeting daily as a full-credit subject and requiring outside preparation just as other major courses do, this class can offer a thorough, detailed introduction to the major developments of music history. *It is not an easy course to teach.* Nor are most teachers equipped by their college training to handle such a class with authority. This course requires a teacher with a deep knowledge of many styles of music, an understanding of the major items of importance to listeners, a wide background in music literature, an ability to organize the course without the use of a textbook, and an ability to make all kinds of music important to the students.

To increase the effectiveness of the class, sources of music other than recordings should be used. These may include radio, television, motion pictures, live performances by students in class, and outside concerts. It is necessary, too, that there be an ample assortment of materials, equipment, and facilities to use—including the usual boards, charts, pictures, recordings, and phonograph, as well as a piano, tape recorder, scores, and books and periodicals on music and musicians. Furthermore, there should be some arrangement by which students can listen to the music being studied outside of class, either in special listening rooms or in the regular classroom. A headphone-listening center in the main school library may serve this purpose.

Music Theory. The high school music theory course is perhaps the most specialized of the non-performing classes. Yet, there is cultural as well as professional interest in the study of theory. The cultural values of the course are in helping students to hear more detail in music, thus increasing response in listening, and in developing an understanding of how a composer uses his musical resources. The theory course is, in fact, as much a study and appreciation of the techniques and practices employed by composers as it is a study of harmonic "rules." The fact that these values exist opens the theory class to general students.

For the student with professional interests, the course will sharpen the ear, develop ability in reading scores, develop skills in composition, and increase knowledge of the functions of tones so that the student may improve as a performer. For both the general student and the specialist, the class can develop musicianship and musical taste through an understanding of the elements of music and an understanding of form, design, and style. Although different students will find different values in studying theory, the basic purpose of the course is actually the same for all: to give insight into the nature of music through an examination of its materials.

The theory course is offered under a variety of titles. Some of the most common are "Theory of Music," "Harmony," "Fundamentals of Music," "Structure of Music," and "Essentials of Music." Although the title is chosen often for its psychological effect on the student, it may also reflect the approach taken within the class in regard to its content. Usually, the content will include a few, or all, of the following topics: pitch, rhythmic duration, notation, intervals, chords, inversions, harmonization of melodies and basses, sight-singing, melodic dictation, and keyboard experience. Courses in theory "fundamentals" or "essentials" often cover little more than notation and scale formation. Such a format serves little purpose, unless a student is expected to find emotional release in writing scales. In fact, most high school courses in this area underestimate the capabilities of students. The course outlined below is equal to as much as a year and one-half of many college courses, but it has been successfully taught at the high-school level in the period of one year.

As in the case of any subject, much more can be learned, retained, and used by students when the sequence of topics is organized logically. It is also important that the study of theory be immediately functional; that is, it should be applied by the student in a practical way at the time he learns it, and not stored for future use. One way of making the course functional is to include work in composition. No matter how limited the student's harmonic knowledge is, he should be encouraged to compose. This may begin with exercises in transposition, extend to arrangements of short piano selections for small ensembles, and then move into the actual composition of original material in simple forms.

To encourage creativity, harmonic rules should be taught with room for variation. It is not enough that an exercise is correct because no rules have been broken; it is better to break a few in order to make the music sound good. Many theory instructors insist on teaching by means of the figured bass, with the result that students have no choice of chords to be used, and the melodies that ensue are generally unmusical. To study melodic writing at an early point in the course and to approach harmonic exercises at times from the melodic voice will give the student greater freedom of harmonic choice and much more opportunity to make the music "sound," melodically, harmonically, and formally. There should be considerable opportunity for experimentation in composing for vocal and instrumental combinations, and for *hearing* the results. There is also a need to extend harmonic usage beyond the seventeenth century. This does not require knowledge of more complicated chords so much as a different method of using traditional harmonies.

To increase the aesthetic functions of the theory class, there should be opportunity to hear fine music literature of all types, either on recordings or in student performances. This practice will increase not only the student's knowledge of music literature, but also his understanding of harmonic usage in different styles, form in composition, and the treatment of the various elements of music.

Finally, if the course is to cultivate aesthetic sensitivity as well as technical facility, there must be provisions for developing the ear. Here there is a need for keyboard experience, sight-singing, melodic and rhythmic dictation, aural identification of written examples, and analysis of melodies and harmonies that are played.

The following course outline was developed over a period of four years in classes with high-school juniors and seniors. It was used successfully with both future music majors and general students with limited musical backgrounds. The course is organized for cumulative experience in working with musical materials. To avoid redundancy, ear work (keyboard and sight-singing activities) has not been indicated in more than a couple of units, although this should take place throughout the course.

Unit 1: Clefs, staves, pitches, rhythmic duration, meter signatures
          Simple rhythmic dictation
Unit 2: Scale construction in major keys; key signatures
          Relationship of keys
          Relative minor scales (three forms)
          Analysis of diatonic melodies
          Singing of major and minor melodies
          Melodic transposition
Unit 3: Intervals
          Analysis of two-part music
          Aural identification of intervals
Unit 4: Triadic harmony; types of chords
          Aural identification of major, minor, augmented, and diminished triads
          Primary chords; connecting primary chords in root position
Unit 5: Inversions of primary chords
Unit 6: Harmonization of bass lines and melodies
          Cadences
          Use of passing tones and auxiliary tones
          Keyboard experience in harmonization with primary chords
          Harmonic transposition
Unit 7: Principles of melodic writing
          Melodic dictation

Unit 8: Secondary triads
The leading-tone chord
Unit 9: Chordal progressions
Aural identification of chords in progression
Unit 10: Harmonization of original melodies
Unit 11: Dominant seventh chords
Transcription of a chorale for wind instruments
Unit 12: Dominant ninth chords
Unit 13: Composition of theme and variations (melody with harmonic analysis)
Unit 14: Diminished seventh chords
Unit 15: Song composition in ternary form (melody with harmonic analysis)
Unit 16: Non-dominant seventh chords
Unit 17: Modal interchange
Secondary dominants
Unit 18: Other non-harmonic tones
Unit 19: Arrangements and transcriptions for small instrumental ensembles
Unit 20: Composition in march form (melody with harmonic analysis)
Unit 21: Higher dominants
Unit 22: Other secondary relationships
Unit 23: Modulation
Unit 24: Piano accompaniments and piano reductions
Unit 25: Modern chord symbols

The music theory course should be offered as a full-credit subject, meeting daily and requiring outside preparation. In some high schools it is a one-year course; in others, it is taught in a two-year sequence. The above plan is adaptable to either time period. However, while it has been used effectively in a one-year course, in most situations a two-year plan would be more appropriate, allowing more time for composition, individual projects, analysis of significant works, and the gradual training of the ear. Materials required for the class include a music chalk board, manuscript paper, recordings, a phonograph, a piano, and scores.

Humanities and Comparative Arts. In recent years, a most welcome and valuable experiment has been taking place with considerable success in high schools throughout the country. It is the significant trend toward the unification of the secondary curriculum through courses that involve a team of teachers for the purpose of relating ideas and experiences in different subject areas. Whereas in the past pupils have studied secondary subjects in isolation, gaining little or no over-all perspective on how one subject relates to another or to themselves, today there are courses that teach history and English together, music and art together, or combinations of several subjects. Of interest to the music education field are those courses, often labeled "Humanities," which draw parallels and comparisons among the various arts—music, painting, sculpture, architecture, literature, poetry, drama, and dance—and other disciplines. Usually, these are taught by a team of teachers—specialists in the fields of music, art, literature (or English), and history. Their combined efforts can unify the curriculum, including the creative arts, in a way that makes the several subjects more meaningful and useful in the students' lives.

The value of such a course can be recognized instantly when one listens to a random selection of high-school seniors discuss their secondary education. I have heard student after student—intelligent, honors students—say that high school has meant almost nothing to them. The reason, upon questioning and analyzing, is that their classes have no direct relation to anything else in their lives. There is seldom an attempt made to pull together into a "whole" everything they have learned. The humanities course can help do this.

Amid the widespread enthusiasm for this movement, however, the music educator should be alert to one danger. In no case should a humanities course be a replacement for the offering of any other basic course. Rather, it should be a complement. In schools where the course is heavily slanted toward the integration of the arts, there is the possibility that during its development it might become a substitute for other arts courses. While furthering the humanities program, the music director must still uphold the position of music as an independent discipline, requiring its own curriculum offerings.

One of the main problems in establishing either a humanities or integrated arts course is the availability of the necessary teachers at the same time. No one teacher can be expected to have the complete background necessary in music, art, and literature, as well as other related fields. For this reason, two different types of courses are described below: one is essentially a music course (taught by an individual), the other a comparative arts course (taught by a team). Both courses are of primary interest to the music department (in contrast to the multi-department involvement in the humanities course), although the ideas presented here can be applied by the music director in contributing to the humanities program.

Music and humanities. Since it is difficult to organize a team-teaching program without long-range planning, an immediate step may be taken by setting up a "Music and Humanities" course. This can be taught by a music teacher alone if he is well trained, has a wide range of other interests, and is a capable researcher. The purpose of the course is to relate music to other areas of the curriculum, including science, history, literature, sociology, and the fine arts. This is still a *music* subject, but it promotes a wider understanding of music through relating it to other areas of our knowledge and culture. In essence, this might be thought of as an application of the "core" principle, in which everything is brought to bear on one main topic. It serves the dual purpose of being a worthy end in itself (as a second-year course directed toward the development of musical breadth after enrollment in a music history-appreciation class), and a preliminary step toward a comprehensive arts course.

In this class, the last third of the year should be devoted to a comparison of music and other arts (a condensed version of the second course, discussed below), whereas the first two-thirds should be concerned with music as it reflects other subjects. "Music and Science," for example, could consider the nature of acoustics in music, the acoustical basis of performance, and the application of acoustics to composition. It could also examine activities in electronic music and *musique concrète*. A section on "Music and Literature" might have two main points of departure: the use of music to accompany drama (opera, operetta, musical comedy, musical play, incidental music), and the use of literary themes as the basis of musical works. The latter would offer many possibilities for seeing how one idea can find infinite varieties of expression in different musical styles (the Berlioz, Tchaikovsky, Prokofiev, and Bernstein treatments of the Romeo-Juliet theme; or Liszt's, Berlioz', and Wagner's interpretations of *Faust*); or it might involve a study of music based on poetry (Delius-Whitman; Thompson-Frost; Debussy-Mallarmé) and on ancient and medieval tales.

The reflection of history through music can be approached through the effects of social movements on the composer's status and style, through musical descriptions of historic events (in folk music or composed works like the *1812 Overture*), through musical portraits of famous figures (Copland's *Billy the Kid* or Roy Harris' *Sixth Symphony,* on Lincoln), and through industrial ballads and topical songs.

"Music and Sociology" opens a wide field to exploration, viewing music as an expression of a social group or social system. The unit can be organized around nationality (musical styles of selected countries; various national styles in the United States); race (concentrating on primitive, Oriental, and folk music); worship; government (governmental influence on music, governmental support of music); geography (the effect of geography as seen in regional work songs, sea songs, or urban vs. rural music); work (industrial folk music, functional music); and music as an industry (the roles of composer, performer, distributor, and listener).

Such a course requires a great deal of research on the part of the teacher, but it can be a stimulating experience for high-school students. Frequent use of discussion sessions and theoretical excursions involving the interplay of students' ideas have proved valuable in making this a music course of unusual depth for upper-class students.

Comparative arts. The comparative arts course involves extensive planning with personnel from outside the music program. Since this ordinarily requires a team of teachers, just any representatives of the participating departments will not do. It must involve teachers who have interests in each area of the course, and who are willing to learn along with the students. It is most important to avoid the pattern of alternating teachers from one day to the next. Each of the teachers should be present at every class meeting, prepared to take over whenever the topic leans toward his particular field of authority. A study of rhythm, for example, might involve the music, art, and English teachers all on the same day—not necessarily in a pre-determined order, but whenever each has something to offer because of the direction a lesson has taken at a given moment.

This is a class that reaches its height when ideas are tossed back and forth by teachers and students alike—the teachers, of course, always being in the guiding positions. Having all teachers present at each class provides for the proper unification and balance of materials. For the purpose of remaining on the right track, however, a lead teacher is recommended to guide each unit. The position of "leader" may alternate back and forth from unit to unit.

The comparative arts course can be organized in a number of effective ways. The class might begin with an open-discussion unit in which a definition of "art" is formulated through an examination and creation of art works, and in which basic groundwork is laid for the development of concepts and criteria for judging art. Then, the first semester might be devoted to an analysis of style and form, relating all the arts through an investigation of elements found in each. The second semester could tie these together more through an historical survey of the arts. A basic outline of suggested content follows.

Semester I: A. The nature of art
               B. Style and form
                  1. Themes
                  2. Symbolism
                  3. Line
                  4. Rhythm
                  5. Color
                  6. Planes
                  7. Texture
                  8. Size and density
                  9. Closed and open structures
               10. Form
               11. Cyclical development
Semester II: C. Historical survey
                  1. Pre-historic art
                  2. Ancient art

    3. Middle ages
    4. Renaissance
    5. Modern (or post-Renaissance)
    6. Primitive art
    7. Art in America

With a significant number of high schools carrying on programs in this area, colleges have begun to offer not only single courses in the related arts, but also major fields of concentration in the subject. Hopefully, the trend will continue to grow, with an increased number of teachers being properly prepared to give instruction in this field and with a large number of students choosing enrollment in this type of course at the secondary level.

THE VOCAL PROGRAM

A design for a vocal program in the secondary schools must account for two large student groups: those with average voices who want to participate in choral activities, and those with special talent who need experiences of a higher calibre. To accommodate everyone requires a combination elective-selective program, consisting of some, or all, of the following:

Junior High School
    Mixed Chorus A (elective; all grades combined; 2-5 times a week)
    Mixed Chorus B (elective-selective; all grades combined; 3-5 times a week)
    Boys' Glee Club (elective; seventh and eighth grades; 2 or 3 times a week)
    Boys' Glee Club (elective; ninth grade; 2 or 3 times a week)
    Girls' Glee Club (elective; all grades combined; 2 or 3 times a week)
    Vocal Ensembles (variable)
Senior High School
    Mixed Chorus (elective; all grades combined, usually freshmen and sophomores; 3-5 times a week)
    Concert Choir (elective-selective advanced chorus; all grades combined, usually juniors and seniors; daily)
    Boys' Glee Club (elective; all grades combined; 2 or 3 times a week)
    Girls' Glee Club (elective; all grades combined; 2 or 3 times a week)
    Mixed Glee Club (elective; all grades combined; may consist of boys' and girls' glee clubs together; 1-3 times a week)
    Chamber Singers (elective-selective advanced ensemble; daily)
    Voice Class I (3 times a week)
    Voice Class II (3 times a week)
    Vocal Ensembles (variable)

Mixed Choruses. At the junior-high level, there is some question as to whether a mixed chorus should be selective or open to everyone. Some educators argue that it definitely should be selective because there is still provision for everyone to sing in the general music class. Others believe that because of changing voices, it is difficult to organize a balanced group that is really select; thus, every student should be allowed to join. The answer does not necessarily lie on either side.

Even though the average student should be having vocal experience in his general music class, an elective chorus will offer him a different choral sound, different literature, and a different musical purpose and spirit. Everyone should have the chance to join such a group. At the same time, although there is, perhaps, not the need for such selective grouping as is practiced in the senior high, talented students still deserve the opportunity to perform with a special organization. Thus, two separate mixed choruses are needed. Each should be comprised of students from seventh, eighth, and ninth grades; and each, ideally, should meet daily. If two choruses cannot be scheduled five times a week, both might be scheduled for the same period, meeting on alternate days. In junior high schools that have only seventh and eighth grades, it will be more difficult to select a boys' section to balance the girls'. Nevertheless, if the school is large enough to support both groups, the dual system should probably be maintained, even when the selective chorus has to be reduced in size to retain balance.

At the senior high school, there is a definite need for both groups. It is desirable that both the beginning group (open without audition) and the advanced group (open only to those who meet special qualifications) meet daily. If this is not possible, an alternating schedule might again be the solution. However, every attempt should be made here to rehearse the advanced chorus five times a week in order to reach appropriate goals. The beginning chorus, if reduced in class time, still ought to have a minimum of three meetings a week. For those students whose schedules permit, a music-literature class meeting on the other two days would fill out their continuing education in general music.

Once the selective group is established, its purpose should not be defeated by allowing the distribution of parts to become unbalanced for lack of boys. If necessary, the size of the group should be cut down to retain the proper ratio between sections.

Glee Clubs. Glee clubs have a special attraction—especially to boys—at both secondary levels. Although neither the repertoire nor the range of tone colors is as varied as in the mixed chorus, full, artistic, and enjoyable sounds can be produced by these groups. Both boys' and girls' glee clubs should meet for a minimum of two rehearsals a week.

In the junior high school, these groups are desirable for two important reasons: first, many students at this age prefer to participate in groups exclusively of their own sex; secondly, their interests are particularly met by the type of literature that is available for these organizations. Therefore, if two mixed choruses cannot be scheduled, it may be best to offer boys' and girls' glee clubs that are open to all, maintaining only one mixed chorus as a selective group. The glee clubs can still be brought together once a week for mixed choral singing.

The junior-high girls' organization should consist of seventh-grade, eighth-grade, and ninth-grade students. If school enrollment permits, the boys' glee club would function best in two units—one made up of seventh-graders and eighth-graders, the other of ninth-grade students. Although boys' voices naturally do not change at the same time, nor suddenly, there is generally a large enough difference in the ninth-grade voices to warrant a separate glee club.

In the high school, both the boys' and girls' groups should be a cross-section of all grades. These groups might also be complemented by a mixed glee club, formed by bringing together the two individual units in a combined rehearsal once a week. This would allow them to work on their parts, or on separate literature, in their individual meetings.

Small Ensembles. Boys', girls', and mixed ensembles—including trios, quartets, quintets, sextets, and others—offer valuable experiences in developing balance, blend, tone quality, ear training, and sight reading. Many of these can be organized either during school time or after school by allowing the students to rehearse by themselves, with occasional guidance from the music teacher. Ordinarily, the teacher will not have the time to direct each one personally.

However, a select group of chamber singers should also be organized under the teacher's direction. This should be a regularly-scheduled, daily class, preferably comprised of the top vocalists in the advanced chorus or concert choir. Consisting of between twelve and fifteen students (more than this number would destroy the special quality of the small ensemble), such groups are often formed under the name "Madrigal Singers." The chamber group, however, should not be restricted to singing madrigals alone, delightful as they are. Rather, it should cover the full gamut of choral literature, concentrating on the more challenging numbers in each field.

A select group of this sort is likely to learn quickly. Therefore, less than daily rehearsals would not be as limiting as in the larger choruses. Much depends on the length of the individual rehearsal, but as a general rule, three meetings a week should be a minimum.

Voice Classes. Every chorus, glee club, and ensemble is actually a course in singing. But for students who want more direct instruction in the development of the voice, special classes should be offered. A desirable plan would be a two-year course ("beginning voice" and "advanced voice"), meeting three times a week.

Some educators maintain that the purpose of the voice class is to study and appreciate solo literature. More correctly, it is to study, appreciate, and develop one's own voice. (An appreciation of the medium can be acquired in general music or music appreciation classes. One would hope, of course, that the student would also gain deeper appreciation of songs while learning how to sing.) Very few high school students realize that there is a correct way to sing. The voice class, then, should concentrate on developing correct breathing, tone quality, resonance, placement, diction, and interpretation through fine solo literature.

THE INSTRUMENTAL PROGRAM

In building an instrumental program, some or all of the following courses may be established, depending upon the size of the school, community support, and the development of the elementary program, which will serve as a "feeder" system:

Junior High School
    Orchestra A (beginning group; elective; all grades; 3 times a week)
    Orchestra B (advanced group; elective-selective; all grades; daily)
    Band A (beginning group; elective; all grades; 3 times a week)
    Band B (advanced group; elective-selective; all grades; daily)
    String Class I and II (each twice a week)
    Brass Class I and II (each twice a week)
    Woodwind Class I and II (each twice a week)
    Percussion Class I and II (each twice a week)
    Piano Class I and II (each twice a week)
    Instrumental Ensembles (variable)
Senior High School
    Intermediate Orchestra (elective; all grades; 2 or 3 times a week)
    Orchestra (advanced group; elective-selective; all grades; daily)
    Wind and Percussion Ensemble (elective; all grades; 2 or 3 times a week)
    Concert Band (advanced group; elective-selective; all grades; daily)
    Marching Band (elective-selective; all grades; twice a week)
    String Class (2 or 3 times a week)
    Brass Class (2 or 3 times a week)
    Woodwind Class (2 or 3 times a week)
    Percussion Class (2 or 3 times a week)
    Piano Class (2 or 3 times a week)
    Stage Band (elective-selective; all grades; twice a week)
    Instrumental Ensembles (variable)

Instrument Classes. Students who have not had previous training in playing a band or orchestral instrument should find provisions for beginning instruction in the junior high school. Such provisions will also accommodate students who wish to transfer to another instrument or those who are needed on another instrument in the band or orchestra.

Two classes (beginning and intermediate) may be offered for each family group: strings, brass, woodwinds, and percussion. Beginning and advanced piano classes are also desirable. Each of these should meet at least twice a week. If a beginning band and beginning orchestra can be organized, each rehearsing three times a week, then two weekly meetings for the instrument classes would be sufficient. By combining the two types of courses, students could then have both ensemble experience and specialized instruction in a program that gives them five periods of instrumental music weekly. This is especially suitable for a student who is in the intermediate instrument class but has not yet advanced enough to join the regular band or orchestra.

In the senior high school, instrument classes might be organized in single sections, two or three times a week—not for beginners, but for students with previous experience. These would provide for further development of individual skills, would assist some in learning a second instrument, and would introduce students to ensemble literature for strings alone, woodwinds alone, brass alone, and even percussion alone. An intermediate orchestra and a wind-and-percussion ensemble could meet on alternating days to fill out the time block for students in these classes, to offer mixed ensemble activities, and to serve as a preparatory course from which qualified performers could move into the selective senior-high band or orchestra. Piano classes at this level are especially attractive to students, many of whom have a sudden, awakening interest in the keyboard.

Orchestra. Although the orchestra is the most prominent medium of performance in the field of professional music, it is still a relatively undeveloped organization in American schools. (Interestingly, the band has become *the* instrumental institution in our schools, though few professional concert bands are in existence.) In the junior high school, there should be an elective-selective orchestra in addition to the beginning group mentioned above. This should meet daily. Its members ought to be encouraged to study in one of the instrumental classes, or to have equivalent experience in private instruction.

The senior-high orchestra should also be a selective group, meeting five times a week. Less advanced students, unable to join this organization, would still be able to participate in the intermediate orchestra and in string class or one of the other instrumental classes. The orchestra is quite adaptable in size, and its number, if selective, should be determined by principles of balance. Usually, there will be no problem in finding an adequate number of qualified non-string players; rather, there may be too many who are qualified but cannot be accepted for the sake of balance. These can still find a place in the concert band.

Band. The junior-high band, like the orchestra, should be organized as an elective-selective group with daily rehearsals. (Again, this is to complement an elective band-and-instrument class program for students who are at early stages of instruction.) It is at the junior-high level that something resembling band instrumentation starts to appear; this may even involve the transferral of some students from their original instrument to a related instrument in order to fill out the group. Here, the organization should be thought of only as a concert band, as there is no real need for a junior marching band. Any marching band literature of value can still be studied within the format of the concert band.

At the senior high school, both a concert band and a marching band may be organized. It would be best to keep these groups separate in membership (though many students will be in both), since the concert group would be a more selective band that rehearses daily. There has been much controversy over the value of the marching band—first, because of its literature, and secondly, because a group cannot play at its best while marching. Actually, there is a great deal of marching band music that is good literature. It should not, however, be the only literature that a student learns during football season or during any other marching season. Adequate time to participate concurrently in the performance of concert band music must be provided. This may be done by holding marching activities after school, or by scheduling the concert band three times a week and the marching band twice a week (expanding the former to a daily rehearsal schedule during "concert season").

Although it is true that a musician cannot perform at his best while marching, it is also true that a marching band *can* play well. This can be accomplished without extra rehearsals if marching and playing are kept in their proper places. It would seem best that marching drills themselves and the learning of formations should be practiced outside of regular band rehearsal time since they are non-musical entities. This should not be interpreted as a denial of the organization's deserved position. The marching band is an art in itself, combining several disciplines, and it deserves respect for its own values in the same way that other part-musical artforms (including ballet and opera) are respected. (The questionable "art" of baton twirling will not be discussed, except, that it might be said there is no justification for making it the responsibility of the band director.)

Since the concert band originally developed out of the marching organization, its literature was, for a long time, a mixture of marches and transcriptions of lighter orchestral pieces. Today, there is also a large and growing repertoire of original concert works for this medium, and these should supply the core of literature to be studied, supplemented for variety by marches, transcriptions, and arrangements of other material, including show tunes.

Stage Band. Since the late 1950's, there has been a tremendous growth in stage band activity throughout the country. Today, there are several thousand stage bands (a term denoting a combination dance band and jazz band) performing in our secondary schools. Some of these have even reached semi-professional standards, performing at well-known festivals. In previous days, there was little acceptance of such groups in the school program as anything other than social activity. Even now, there are many educators who believe that the stage band leads to careless playing, poor tone quality, and faulty intonation. It has been proven, however, that this is not a destructive force at all. If a student's tone quality is poor, or his intonation faulty, the fault lies only with his teachers and in the student's own inherent abilities—not with the music he is playing. Chances are that this student is the one who will play badly in any group. In truth, the best stage band musicians are usually the top performers in the concert band as well.

The stage band has a number of educational values: it fosters creativity through the use of improvisation; it introduces unusual and somewhat difficult rhythms that might not be met in other music except that which is too difficult; it encourages the student through his responsibility to carry an independent part (due to the individualistic nature of this type of performance); it offers a good format for increasing sight-reading skills; it promotes the student's sense of tonal balance because of the small size of the group; and, in short, it can develop all the usual skills acquired in any performing group.

The stage band, then, should be a part of the music program because of its educational value, not just its social value. Two rehearsals a week are desirable, preferably during school time, but during afternoons if they cannot otherwise be scheduled. Membership in the group should be selective and limited to those who are also enrolled in the concert band or orchestra.

Small Ensembles. In addition to these groups, there is also a need for small ensembles, scheduled during free study periods when prospective members of an ensemble are available, during a regularly-scheduled time block, or after school. These groups, which not only introduce students to a different type of literature but also develop skills on a more individual basis, might include a string trio, quartet, or quintet; a woodwind quartet or quintet; a saxophone quartet; a brass quartet, quintet, or sextet; a percussion ensemble; and many other small combinations. Naturally, preferred time should be given first to those ensembles for which a large body of literature has been written.

CONTENT IN PERFORMANCE CLASSES

The course content for each of the vocal and instrumental groups should serve the students as both performers and listeners. In the process of learning to interpret the music, there should be an attempt to advance appreciation from the consumer's standpoint—through attention to form, style, the relationship of parts, the background of the music, and its composer and his period. There is no time, of course, for extended digressions from performance itself, but directors should be urged to fill in breaks in rehearsals with historical and stylistic information in short, pointed comments. When this is done regularly, the effect upon the students will be directly reflected in their performance and will carry on into their lives as listeners. In addition, rehearsals should be designed not only to create certain interpretations of selections, but also to develop technical facility in performance. Attention should be given to the fundamentals of breathing, tone quality, and articulation (fingering, bowing, diction), and to the skills of sight reading and ear training.

Each of these groups should have opportunities for performance before the school or general public. One important principle needs to be kept in mind here: any public performance should be a culmination of regular class activities; rehearsals should not be viewed only as preparation for a particular performance. These two ideas are not really in opposition to one another, but there is a slight difference between them.

Consider, for example, the Christmas or winter concert, which is a common program in many communities: Although this may be a good time to present a concert from the standpoint of placement in the school year (it is not so good in the sense that it is a busy time for most people, and a large audience is sometimes difficult to draw), often, too much time is devoted to the preparation of Christmas or seasonal music alone. This may include fine music, but some schools, with limited rehearsal time, must spend most of the fall term preparing the Christmas program, which is way out of proportion to the time devoted during the rest of the year to other literature.

In order to overcome this problem and yet retain the Christmas concert, if one is wanted, it would be advisable to involve as many organizations as possible in the program. Though a full concert would be presented, each group would be responsible for only a few seasonal numbers—the weaker groups doing one or two selections, the better ones doing four or five at the most. In this way, only a part of the rehearsal time will have been spent in preparation for this particular event, allowing for a balanced study of literature in the fall as well as the rest of the year. Furthermore, when the Christmas program is over, a group will not be starting from scratch, having had its repertoire reduced to nothing. It will have made progress in a certain number of selections that are still appropriate for a concert in February, in the spring, or whenever one is needed.

In this sense, rehearsals are not the requirement of a successful performance so much as a performance is the requirement of successful rehearsals. Herein lies the difference between professional and educational programming.

BALANCE AND CREDIT IN MUSIC CLASSES

Balance in the Music Curriculum. Two basic types of courses have been discussed here: performance and non-performance classes. Although it is not always obtained, a balance between the two (and between courses for general students and those with special musical interests) is very important. In many school systems one can find a complete reversal of principle in moving from the elementary to the secondary level; while the core of the elementary music curriculum is the general music program, in the upper grades many schools emphasize only performance groups, under the mistaken notion that this constitutes refinement. In reality, it advances only one phase of musical experience and curtails other areas of musical growth, interest, and participation for a large body of students.

The provision of band, orchestra, and chorus is necessary, but there is also a vital need to *offer* (whether required or not) music classes through the twelfth grade that serve the wide and varied needs of all students, not just one need (performance) of one particular group. The fact that music classes are seldom required in the secondary school, at least beyond the eighth grade, accounts for the limited variety of such courses offered in a curriculum that yearly increases the number of required subjects a student must take. Within this limited scope, the wide recognition that comes to a performing group through public performance, and the immediate public support that results, accounts to a considerable degree for the emphasis given to vocal and instrumental activities. The attention of the general public to performing groups is natural, but it should not be interpreted as a placement of prime value on only one aspect of music education. Aside from sports activities, perhaps no other courses in the school display student achievement before the public as much as bands or choruses. Yet, the need and value of most other courses are not questioned. Most schools, for example, offer student performances of plays, but this does not remove from the curriculum the study of dramatic literature in English classes. There is still a need to investigate the works of great playwrights from approaches other than performance alone. The same is true in music. The difference lies in the fact that one course is required and the other is not.

Required study, however, should have no direct bearing on how a music curriculum is balanced. Requirements have never met, and never will meet, all the varied needs of any student body, because each student has different needs. If a music program is to serve some of these needs as best it can, it is essential to maintain both a balance between types of courses and a balance within courses of each type.

It is not uncommon to find imbalance even within the area of performance. Sometimes the success of a chorus leads to still more concentrated effort in developing the choral program, while the orchestra and band are overlooked. Such attention has often centered on the band program, too. The director of a program—especially one who is also involved in teaching a performing organization—needs to view carefully each aspect of the secondary music curriculum, not only in terms of its individual importance but also in terms of its relationship to all other parts, to assure a proper distribution of weight.

Credit for Music Courses. Credit for music should be granted on the same basis that it is given in other subjects. Usually, a course which meets four or five times a week (depending on the type of school schedule) is considered a major subject and receives one unit of credit. A half unit is ordinarily given to a subject meeting two or three times a week. If this is the procedure in the school, it should be applied to music classes. When music meets as many times as a full-credit subject but receives only half the credit, the implication is that music is only half as important as other subjects. This may very well be true for certain students; but then, it is also true that physics may be only half as important as French, economics only half as important as typing, or math only half as important as music, depending upon the needs and interests of individual students. Still, if the credit for physics, French, math, and other subjects is standardized, the policy regulating credit should extend to the entire curriculum.

Sometimes outside preparation is required for the approval of credit. This is a meaningless standard since the establishment, for a group, of minimum time spent has no relation to achievement by the individual. One student doing no homework may achieve more than another who does two hours of homework in a subject. Similarly, specific material covered does not relate to student capacity and is an equally meaningless requirement for credit. Is the student who works to full capacity, but covers less ground than another, to be denied credit? Still, some schools persist in maintaining the homework requirement. If this is so, it can be argued that students in performing groups should qualify for credit because of their outside practicing. It is irrelevant that some students do not practice. Some students don't do their biology homework, but that does not negate the establishment of credit for the biology course.

In most secondary schools, credit in music is not required for graduation; this in itself is not disturbing since a strong argument can be presented for not *requiring* credit in most subjects. What is disturbing is that many schools *do not accept* music credit toward graduation. Furthermore, a survey made by the NEA has revealed that a third of all secondary schools do not allow students to enroll in music courses unless they maintain a minimum grade level in required subjects. According to the survey, this was the policy of 18.4 percent of large schools (over 1,000 enrollment), 44.4 percent (!) of medium-sized schools (300 to 999 students), and 35.8 percent of small schools. What right has any school to say that because a student does not achieve in certain areas, he should be denied the opportunity to achieve in other areas? This is exactly what the ruling amounts to.

Existing practices regarding what is accepted for credit and accepted toward graduation reflect not simply local administrative policies, but even more the ridiculous, nationwide acceptance of the "Carnegie unit," which measures time spent and content covered—but has little to do with evaluating achievement.

The Carnegie unit was originally designed for the purpose of defining a "college," one part of the definition being that a college was an institution that demanded of its students the prior completion of high school work amounting to fourteen credits. (This has since been raised to sixteen units, a unit being the measure of a year's study of an academic subject.) Oddly enough, the reason for identifying these colleges was to allow their faculties to participate in a retirement plan of the Carnegie Foundation for the Advancement of Teaching. Through the committee on college entrance requirements, the unit came to exert tight control over the high school curriculum — something which it was not really intended to do.

According to the NEA survey, 27.7 percent of large schools and 12.5 percent of medium-sized schools offered a kind of major in music, usually requiring enrollment in a music course for each of three years. Some schools required that the entire three years be spent in a performing group! These "majors" allowed between two and six credits toward graduation. For non-majors, small-sized and medium-sized schools allowed mostly one or two credits toward graduation, and a good number allowed no credit. Large schools, on the other hand, allowed mostly two to four credits, while 12 percent set no limit. However, regardless of policy, the necessary units required in other subjects limited the number of music credits that could be acquired.

Properly, a student should graduate when the school has provided all it can offer him for his particular needs and he has achieved to his best ability the objectives of those offerings — not when he has accumulated so many units of credit in specific courses. When the unit principle of credit is replaced (this is a long way from realization, though there is considerable opposition to the present system), the entire secondary school curriculum will benefit. As long as it is in force, however, the best course for music education to pursue is a demand for equal credit recognition, in whatever form it may be.

SPECIAL ACTIVITIES

Every high school has a number of special activities, such as clubs and committees, which meet outside of school time. Although these are often thought of only as "enjoyment" programs, they do serve important educational purposes in the curriculum (and enjoyment is a big factor in learning).

Clubs. There are several worthwhile types of clubs that can be sponsored. Performance clubs are suitable for small numbers of students who are interested in ensemble experiences of a sort that cannot be scheduled as part of the regular music program. A contemporary vocal quartet, a small jazz combo, a folk music club, or any ensemble of a classical nature that cannot be worked into class time can meet at regular intervals after school to draw students into musical activity. A small listeners' club can also be organized to make monthly trips to hear concerts and other musical programs in the area.

For greater student participation, a music club of a general nature can be organized to give monthly programs featuring students and guest performers. One high school in the Boston area organized such a club with 500 student members. Some of their monthly meetings were devoted to concerts by school groups, variety programs by individual members, and special concerts of original student compositions. Other meetings featured professional musicians. Figures such as Leonard Bernstein, Lukas Foss, Richard Rodgers, jazz artist Herb Pomeroy, and members of the Boston Symphony Orchestra have appeared before the club through the courtesy of the American Federation of Musicians.

Musical Competitions. Throughout the country many festival and competitive activities are operated by regional and state music teachers associations. These are usually of two types: regional festivals in which entire groups from a school may participate, and selective district and state performance groups, for enrollment in which individual students audition.

Festivals can be both advantageous and wasteful. They are worthy, naturally, when they lead a group toward higher musical achievement. A problem of some festivals is the excessive concern over voting for first-place, second-place, or third-place positions, whereas minor consideration is given to the educational values that should be concomitant with the competition. As a result, ill feelings may arise between groups and constructive criticism may be wanting in the judges' remarks. The better festivals have taken on a broader basis of adjudication, using more general ratings that can be shared by a number of groups, and offering suggestions in areas where improvement can be made.

It should be possible for the participating groups to hear performances by each other. Sometimes this is not arranged, with the result that an individual group is gaining no more than it could if it simply gave a performance by itself at its own school. Furthermore, it is also possible that too much time may be spent in preparing required selections for the festival, thus precluding the experience of a greater variety of music at the school. The results must be worth the time involved in bringing the performance about.

If, however, the educational aspects of the festival are upheld, participation can be of considerable value. It can set higher standards of performance, and both students and teachers alike can receive useful criticism in regard to the strengths and weaknesses of their presentation.

Selective district and state organizations provide excellent opportunities for specially-talented students to participate in performances of a calibre that is not usually possible in the local high school. Participation in these should become accepted practice in every successful school program. However, the work within the individual system should come first, and no student should be allowed to audition unless he is a contributing member of his own school organization.

Generally, when a student has been accepted for one of these performance groups, he is given the music to learn before meeting with the guest conductor for a brief period of rehearsal (ordinarily two or three days with the full ensemble). If a school sends students to audition, it should only be with the provision that the school's music teachers will work with the selected students in preparing the program. Many students arrive at the group rehearsals without having learned their parts, and valuable time is lost in covering what might have been done in the home town. This is an obligation that the music supervisor should recognize before involving his students.

Musical Shows. A number of music educators still frown on the production of musical shows in the schools, feeling that the time spent on such a presentation could be put to better use in learning other music. This would be true in those instances where the entire school choir is enlisted and required to prepare the show during their regular school rehearsal periods. However, when a special cast is selected through auditions (open to the whole school, not just the music students), and when rehearsals are held afternoons following the regular school program, the whole venture can be of high value. There is good and bad music in every area of musical activity, and the good examples of each are worthy of study. Therefore, as long as the educator is discriminating in his selection of a show and is capable of proper direction, only good might come from a school musical.

First of all, it introduces the students to a different type of music than they are exposed to in band, chorus, and music class — an exciting blend of several of the arts (music, drama, dance, scenic design). Through active involvement, the students learn much more than they could ever grasp by simply hearing a cast recording in a general music class. When it is done well there is something about a theatrical production that offers the cast and production staff an aesthetic experience unlike any other. The school show also provides an unusual opportunity for both instrumental and vocal students to work together on music that can be quite demanding.

One may often hear or read comments to the effect that singing or playing show music disrupts what the teacher is trying to accomplish in performance skills. This is completely false, unless, of course, the teacher aims for or accepts less than he demands in his other performance groups. The best performers in the pit band are generally those who also hold first chairs in their school orchestras and concert bands. And from a vocal standpoint, style has nothing to do with proper techniques of vocal production. The director who teaches his cast members to sing with a different technique (not style, now) in a show than in a classically-oriented chorus would appear to know very little about the voice.

Selection of the proper show involves four main considerations: a complementary balance between a good book and a good score, the suitability of available students to the dramatic and musical demands of casting, the cost involved, and the problems of staging. No show should be chosen simply because of its music. A show can be truly successful only if it has a good plot, dramatic construction, and believable characters, in addition to a good score. Unfortunately, the two areas do not match their values too often. Secondly, no show should be chosen that cannot be appropriately cast, both dramatically and musically. The participating students derive aesthetic satisfaction only to the degree to which the rehearsals and performances rise. Third, in estimating cost, the director must consider royalties, rental of scripts and orchestration, scenery, costuming, lighting, publicity, and other items. It is always better to do an artistic job with a less costly show than to cut expenses on a more demanding production and lose some of the dramatic effect in staging. Finally, there is staging to figure in the choice. Some modern schools have elaborate theatre facilities, with a great deal of fly space, lighting equipment, and so on. Others can handle shows with only one or two scenes. Musicals generally have a large number of scene changes that must be handled quickly, as opposed to the straight dramatic play which normally involves one to three settings. There are ways to simplify scenic demands, but still the problem is one which may require a decision against producing a certain musical.

Perhaps only that school which has produced an *artistically* successful musical show (many are successful financially or in community approval; artistic ones are few) can appreciate the important place this activity can rise to in the music program. But then, that statement is equally true of each facet of the music curriculum.

The value of everything discussed in this chapter and the preceding one lies not in the concept but in the action!

5

Relations with the Administration

No supervisor can do his job alone. It is essential to the success of the school program that he establish solid working relations with the administration, the teaching staff, and the community as a whole. Otherwise, in spite of the finest plans he may have for the music curriculum, he is apt to find himself facing one difficulty after another because of an indifferent administration, disinterested classroom teachers, and an uninformed public.

The most frustrating problems often occur in working with the administration. This is because the members of the music staff are specialists, whereas those in administration are generalists. Although both are hopefully working toward the same ends, the generalist must view the music program as only one part of the total curriculum, not as the entire field of his operation. Working together on common ground, but from two different vantage points, the music supervisor and the administrator have to create a cooperative attitude toward developing the best possible program —not so much through a system of give-and-take by which both may lose ground, but through mutual interest in a common goal.

The supervisor's key to dealing with the administration, as with any other group, is in human relations — doing things to recognize and uphold the integrity and self-respect of others. This means, first of all, being friendly and courteous, and showing an interest in others by calling them by name, talking with them about their own work, and helping them personally with various services. It also means being available when needed, being prompt and efficient, and providing extra help in making the other person's work better and easier. Listening to the ideas and opinions of others, giving them credit for their contributions, avoiding an authoritative approach, and using all the other elements of "winning friends and influencing people" are techniques which the experienced supervisor has learned to use continually in his relationships with the various groups he works with.

The late professor Marshall Stearns once related an appropriate story of a conference at which a famous musicologist told his colleague Charles Seeger: " 'You know, I don't hate jazz; I think it's probably very important and it certainly deserves serious study. The trouble is that all the jazz

81

people treat it as holy, holy, holy!' To this Seeger replied: 'Well, now don't you consider the area of classical music in which you specialize as holy, too?' 'Ah,' said the musicologist, 'BUT IT IS!' " [1] This anecdote illustrates a type of attitude found in many fields where a man is entirely devoted to his work. Actually, there is not a single music director or teacher I know that feels his subject is the only one to consider in the curriculum. There are many, however, that unintentionally create this impression in their talks with administrators. Naturally, the supervisor who does not keep in mind the administrator's other concerns is going to make problems more difficult.

PRINCIPLES OF HUMAN RELATIONS

There are several basic principles of human relations that should be kept in mind in administrative work. First of all, the supervisor should develop his ideas completely before presenting them. When someone gets a good idea, it is human nature to want to talk about it. The wise supervisor, however, will keep it to himself until he has analyzed it thoroughly and considered every possible objection. Otherwise, all sorts of questions will be raised that cannot be answered, and despite the enthusiasm the creator feels for his plan, it can be easily defeated. Before submitting a plan to the person in authority — whether it is to a superintendent, principal, or school committee member — it is good to solicit the ideas of co-workers who will be involved in carrying the plan through to completion. If they find defects in it, the holes can be plugged before making the important presentation. Furthermore, by bringing others into the planning, the supervisor will overcome objections his staff might raise later in implementing the plan.

With the idea fully developed, the supervisor can then select the best time to talk with the administration. The administrator who is tired, hungry, or disturbed about something else is not the easiest to persuade. It is better to wait until he is relaxed, unhurried, and in a leisurely mood. This by itself, of course, does not guarantee success. The administrator will still have to be sold. If he has different ideas, no matter how right the supervisor's idea or plan may be, opposition will only help to close the administrator's mind further.

Convincing anyone to adopt an idea requires an understanding of the other person's point of view and a realization that differences of opinion may exist only in the means of accomplishing a goal rather than in the goal itself. Merely presenting one's side will not always work, but showing a willingness to understand the other's *will* help to open his mind. This

---

[1] Marshall W. Stearns, *The Story of Jazz.* (New York: Oxford University Press, 1956), p. xi.

means that the supervisor should make known any of the apparent and potential disadvantages of his plan, in addition to the advantages. As long as the advantages outweigh the possible drawbacks, and as long as the idea is determined the best possible solution to a problem, the honesty in this approach can increase confidence in the supervisor's integrity. Selling the idea requires a complete statement of the basic points; it does not mean long, boring, or extraneous detail, however, nor excursions into musical terminology that may only confuse the general administrator. Neither should over-enthusiastic statements or promises be made about a plan. It is far better to understate and let the administrator be surprised and pleased by exceptional results.

In some cases, a plan for action may have to be brought before a group of administrators, such as all the elementary school principals. When this is necessary, the supervisor should consult as many of them as possible beforehand to sell them the idea individually, get their reactions, and make them feel they are an active part of the music program. Then the plan may be taken before the entire group. Approaching the group "cold" will usually result in less stable relations and, quite often, either defeat for the plan or qualified acceptance. On occasion the supervisor may have to appear before the school committee to sell his program or present changes or additions he wishes to make. Here, as with the principals, it is advantageous to see individual members first before presenting a case to the entire board. However, they ought not to be approached without the approval of the superintendent.

PROBLEMS AND PROCEDURES

Cooperative endeavor of the sort outlined here can lead the music director to solutions to many problems. Among the basic ones on which he and the administration will have to work are the following: (1) agreeing on the scope and content of the program needed to meet the formulated objectives; (2) determining the extent of the supervisor's duties and responsibilities in relation to the rest of the staff; (3) providing adequate time to carry out the program; (4) providing enough personnel to carry the specialists, and other personnel; (6) providing for teacher growth through program; (5) promoting cooperation among classroom teachers, music an in-service program; (7) working out schedules for the supervisory staff so that all schools and grades will be covered and all teachers will be served; (8) providing the necessary materials and equipment; (9) working out a means of circulating materials; (10) providing space for filing and storing music, equipment, and other materials; (11) working out a satisfactory budget; (12) providing the supervisor with clerical help for routine, non-musical jobs; and (13) providing for evaluation and re-planning.

It is important to the effectiveness of his work that the supervisor establish definite procedures by which the work is to be done. In conference with the superintendent, he should determine to whom he is responsible and with what authority he is charged. It is best, for example, to consider the principal and music director as being on the same level of authority, since the director's job is system-wide and does not confine him to working with a single building administrator. The director should be directly responsible to the superintendent.

Responsibilities of special-area supervisors, operating under the music director, must also be determined. If an elementary music supervisor is only a consultant, the basic procedure will be that the teacher solicits help through the principal who, in turn, invites the supervisor to the school. More favorable is a situation where the supervisor is free to enter the school regularly to observe, teach, and implement ideas; and here, an exact relationship with the principal has to be determined. In dealing with the special projects of an individual school and its teachers, the supervisor naturally has a direct responsibility to the building principal; but in carrying out system-wide policies, the supervisor also has a direct responsibility to the director of music. To maintain good relations, the special supervisor should report to the principal on first entering the school, to see how things have been going, to inform him of current plans, and to get his consent. The principal should be consulted before any changes within the school are made. On leaving, the supervisor might stop again at the principal's office to report what has taken place. Keeping the principal informed will keep him on the side of the music department.

In working with the superintendent the director has to follow procedures of a different sort. Each system, for example, will have certain recognized steps for filing reports, purchasing equipment, and so on. These must all be acknowledged. The director must also provide all the information necessary to support and justify the organization of his program and the budget it requires. It is only fair that the superintendent have something substantial to present to the board of education. To be able to work cooperatively on the organization of the program and its financing requires that the supervisor keep the superintendent informed at all times: that he discuss long-range plans and problems regularly so that sudden curriculum and budgetary needs will not appear without warning.

The superintendent may be kept informed not only by personal meetings, but also through written reports of various kinds. These may include short notes on current problems, reports on the progress of the in-service program, estimates of possible budgetary needs as they occur, and summaries of the supervisor's work, by the month and the year. Monthly reports should include information on visitations, workshops, conferences of various kinds, performances, special events, and new ideas being developed. In addition the yearly report may include a general survey of the year's work, progress made, problems that have occurred and are likely to occur, possible solutions for these problems, and other recommendations. It is also good for the supervisor to provide a copy of his basic schedule, for the superintendent and others on the staff, so that the nature of his work and the organization of his program can be easily seen (and, of course, so that he can be reached immediately whenever he is needed). Such a schedule may not be available from the supervisor who has a limited staff and must be continually in and out of his office answering calls to various schools. He should nevertheless always leave word of where he is going and what time he expects to return.

The administrative problems facing the supervisor are ones which do not have single, absolute answers. Each school system is unique and solutions can be arrived at only by analyzing the special circumstances of the system. Some general suggestions can be offered, however, in two particular areas—scheduling the curriculum and providing proper physical facilities.

SCHEDULING

In tackling the scheduling problem the music director needs a knowledge of the total curriculum in operation, the general philosophy and objectives behind it, and the structure and general activities of the main areas within it. He can then interpret the music program and its needs in terms of the total curriculum, and can help schedule with an understanding of all the problems involved.

A tight schedule should not push the music program outside the school day. It is a legitimate part of the curriculum and therefore should be scheduled within school hours. The fact must be recognized, however, that there is a limit to the length of the school day and to the number of subjects a student can take within this time. Because of this, there is a tendency on the part of administrators to want to schedule only certain, limited activities. And one of the main problems the supervisor may have at the secondary level is in convincing the administration that time must be allowed for more than performing groups — that these should, in fact, be supplementary to a strong general music program. Here is revealed the importance of planning objectives and processes cooperatively with the administration. When the supervisor works *with* the administration in giving the program direction, balancing the offering, and providing for sequential instruction, there is less conflict later over what needs to be scheduled and why. The only problem is *how* to do it.

Elementary Schools. In the elementary school, the matter of scheduling the general music program rests primarily with the classroom teacher, since he or she teaches all the subjects in the self-contained classroom and knows best how to set up a workable format. It remains the responsibility of the director to see that sufficient time is allotted to music. The elementary supervisor, too, can easily establish her schedule of visitations with the individual teachers.

However, there may be problems in arranging time for instrumental and choral instruction outside the classroom. Grouping by grade level on each instrument (or for choruses) is generally the most convenient system and it does not result in too much variation in ability. Grouping by level of accomplishment, on the other hand, is more disruptive of classroom procedure since it is likely to cut across grade levels, with varying numbers of students being taken out of fourth, fifth, and sixth grade classes at the same time. A great deal depends on whether beginning instruction is offered in more than one grade, and on the size of the school. In the small school, for instance, grade-level grouping may result in the availability of too few students, and a practical-sized ensemble may only be obtained by combining students in two or three grades. In the large elementary school this is not apt to be a problem. In either case, full-group rehearsals require the availability of all students, regardless of grade. Time for this is best determined by the principal, who, if a large number of students are involved in music, may wish to establish some sort of simultaneous activity period for non-performing students.

It is helpful when classroom teachers vary their schedules to cover subjects at different times of the day in successive weekly patterns. In this way, a student leaving for band or chorus is not likely to miss the same classroom subject each week. Although some teachers like to do this simply for the change of pace, others feel it is a necessity to stay with a specific routine. If this is so, it may be possible for the music teacher to rehearse on a rotational basis, so that a student would not be out of the classroom at the same time of the day for each rehearsal. For example, imagine an instrumental teacher who has separate classes of clarinets, trumpets, trombones, percussion, saxophones, and violins meeting three times a week, as well as two full rehearsals. On a rotating schedule, his classes could be set up so that the instruments each meet at different times of the day in successive rehearsals, as indicated in the chart below.

M	T	W	Th	F
Clarinet	Saxophone	Trumpet	Trombone	Percussion
Trumpet	Trombone	Percussion	FULL	Violin
Percussion	FULL	Violin	Clarinet	Saxophone
Violin	Clarinet	Saxophone	Trumpet	Trombone

In situations where these classes meet fewer times during the week, a rotating system can be established from week to week. For example, a teacher who has several instrument classes in a given school, but teaches them only on Mondays (since he covers other schools on other days), could change the order of the classes from week to week on a pre-determined monthly schedule. The same amount of time would be given to each class, but students would come each week at a different time:

1st Monday	2nd Monday	3rd Monday	4th Monday
Clarinet	Trumpet	Violin	Percussion
Trumpet	Percussion	Clarinet	Violin
Percussion	Violin	Trumpet	Clarinet
Violin	Clarinet	Percussion	Trumpet

Secondary Schools. In the junior high school, general music classes are sometimes scheduled in blocks of eight or ten weeks, meeting daily in some cases or once or twice a week in others. This type of policy should be avoided since it does not allow for the gradual development throughout the year of changing voices, nor does it provide sufficient time for the teacher to identify the needs of individual students. Furthermore, with long breaks of musical inactivity, cumulative experience from year to year is difficult to establish. It is much better for the junior high school class to be scheduled as a regular subject meeting throughout the year. In other matters of scheduling, junior-high music courses are generally similar to those in the senior high school, since they are usually elective at both levels.

Need for more periods. It is interesting that the eminent educator James B. Conant, in his study of the American high school, stated that "all students should be urged to include art and music in their elective programs." [2] He also suggested that students with special ability and interest in a course such as music theory might do well to take it in place of a second language. Quite often, the difficulty in letting such students take a special music course arises from having too few periods in the school day. A seven- or eight-period day serves the students' interests much better than a six-period day in allowing for individually-tailored schedules. In fact, when Dr. Conant made his first study in 1958, he found that most of the academically-talented students who did not report having two or more years of art or music were in schools harnessed by the six-period format.

In schools where more than six periods is not practical, some administrators have found a workable plan in a rotating schedule wherein classes meet only four days a week instead of five. This allows a student to take seven different classes during a week of six-period days, or six

---

[2] James B. Conant, *The American High School Today.* (New York: McGraw-Hill Book Co., 1959), p. 48.

classes in a format of five-period days. Whether a student is taking four or five major subjects, he is still able to work in electives in this system.

M	T	W	Th	F
1	6	X	3	2
2	1	5	4	3
3	2	6	5	4
4	3	1	6	5
5	4	2	1	6

M	T	W	Th	F
1	7	5	4	2
2	1	6	5	3
3	X	7	X	4
4	2	1	6	5
5	3	2	7	6
6	4	3	1	7

The blocks above marked "X" are generally used as homeroom, study, or activity periods. (These diagrams do not indicate lunch periods, which may be scheduled between two blocks or as an extension of a given period.)

Basic principles. Regardless of the number of periods or the classification of students to be scheduled, there are some basic considerations that can aid the music director in working with the administration in scheduling. First of all, in the case of elective-selective groups where auditions are required for membership, the director should have his staff hold auditions and submit the names of the selected students early — before programming for the following year begins. A student cannot very well ask his guidance counselor to sign him up for the special chorus if he has not had an opportunity to audition or has not been informed of his acceptance. For these selective groups, the guidance department should be requested, as a means of checking, not to register students unless their names are on the membership list submitted by the music department.

When the enrollment for all classes is known — for both general and special groups, performance and classroom subjects—arranging the periods may begin. The music classes should be scheduled during periods that are free of other one-section courses so that a choice between the two will not have to be made. This includes not only special courses for which there may be only one period allotted, but also single sections of certain levels within multi-class courses. For example, there may be a number of senior English classes offered in different periods, but only one "honors" section of senior English. The student who is scheduled for honors English, which meets at the same time as orchestra, would be unable to take both. It is often impossible to avoid some conflict between single-section courses, especially in the large high school which offers many subjects; however, it should still be possible to re-schedule conflicts with single-section courses in which music students are involved, since the number of students affected is generally small.

Another recommendation is to schedule the largest groups first; and if a choice must be made between band and orchestra, it is probably best to schedule the orchestra first, since this group includes all the basic instruments. A student who plays violin and is required to take a course that meets only at the same time as orchestra could not be transferred to band. But by placing such a course opposite band instead (if there is no other solution), a student playing a band instrument could probably still fit into the orchestra.

Using study periods. Some schools have classes meeting only four out of five days a week, but without a rotational system as indicated above. The fifth classroom period is turned into a study or extra-help period. These fifth-day study periods, coming during the same periods for all students, may be used to schedule some music groups for two or three meetings a week. A glee club, for example, might meet during the study classes of the first, third, and fifth periods, or a woodwind ensemble during studies in, say, the second and fourth periods:

M	T	W	Th	F
A	A	A	A	Study
B	B	B	Study	C
C	C	Study	C	B
D	Study	D	D	D
Study	E	E	E	E
F	F	X	F	F

M	T	W	Th	F
A	A	A	A	Glee Club
B	B	B	Wood-wind	B
C	C	Glee Club	C	C
D	Wood-wind	D	D	D
Glee Club	E	E	E	E
F	F	X	F	F

The same plan allows for sectional rehearsals of a group which meets in full ensemble during the odd study periods:

M	T	W	Th	F
A	A	A	A	Full Orchestra
B	B	B	Percussion	B
C	C	Strings	C	C
D	D	Full Orchestra	D	D
E	Wood-winds	E	E	E
Brass	F	F	F	F

M	T	W	Th	F
A	A	A	A	Basses
B	B	B	Tenors	B
C	Full Chorus	C	C	C
D	D	Full Chorus	D	D
E	E	E	Full Chorus	E
F	Altos	F	F	F
Sopranos	G	G	G	G

Another use of study periods is to supplement, on a more individual basis, the rehearsals of groups meeting during regular study blocks. For example, a student who is enrolled in band during one block may have a study-hall block at some other period of the day. During this time, the student could be allowed to practice; or if a certain number of students are available in studies at the same time, small ensembles like a string quartet, percussion ensemble, or madrigal singers might be arranged to broaden their experience.

Alternate rehearsals. Whenever it is impossible to schedule band and orchestra in separate periods, or whenever the orchestra has to draw on band musicians to fill out the instrumentation and these students are unable to schedule both classes, the following plan may be of some use. The band and orchestra can be scheduled for the same period, meeting on alternate days. During football season, the band might meet three times a week, on Monday, Wednesday, and Friday, with the orchestra rehearsing on Tuesday and Thursday. After football, the schedule could be reversed to allow the orchestra more time. On orchestra days, those band members who are not involved can do small ensemble work or have a study period. On full band rehearsal days, the string players from the orchestra can either do ensemble playing or have more personalized study on their instruments. This requires, of course, more than one rehearsal hall in order to maintain both groups in the same period.

Although this plan is offered as a solution to a problem, it is not recommended when each group can be scheduled separately. The disadvantage here is that an organization needs 200 minutes or more of rehearsal time a week in order to make significant progress, and neither organization in this set-up is allowed that much time. Regardless of the fact that students may be having music five days a week, having them alternate from band to orchestra on successive days cuts into the full ensemble time of each group and disrupts rehearsal continuity.

Extended periods. Another possibility, when an orchestra has to draw on band musicians, is to schedule band and strings during the first or last periods of the day in extended time blocks that make use of time before or after school hours, immediately preceding or following the rehearsal periods. During these extension blocks, the orchestra or full band may be pulled together. (See diagrams on page 92.)

In each of these "extension" plans, every musician in both band and orchestra is scheduled for the regular school period, but not for the time before or after school. During the extensions, string players will not come early or stay late on band days, nor will non-orchestra students be present for other rehearsals. Although this approach has its merits, the main objection to it is that it places music partly in out-of-school time. There is nothing wrong with extra afternoon or before-school rehearsals just before a concert or in preparing for a show, but regular classes, if they are to be justified in the curriculum, should be entirely on school time. I would prefer, therefore, a plan similar to the above which makes use of

	M	T	W	Th	F
Before school	Band	Orchestra	Band	Orchestra	Band
First period	Band / Strings	Band / Strings	Band / Strings	Band / Strings	Band / Strings

or

	M	T	W	Th	F
Last period	Strings / Band	Band	Strings / Band	Band	Strings / Band
After school	Orchestra		Orchestra		Orchestra

or

	M	T	W	Th	F
Before school	Band	Orchestra	Band	Orchestra	Band
First period	Wind Ensemble / Orchestra / Full Band	Strings / Wind Ensemble	Orchestra / Full Band / Strings	Wind Ensemble / Orchestra / Full Band	Strings / Wind Ensemble / Orchestra

lunch periods instead of out-of-school time, especially if the rehearsal comes *before* the student has lunch.

By this method, the students are scheduled for the full period immediately before or after lunch periods, with an extension into the first or last lunch for convening the full ensemble   (See diagrams pages 94-95.)

Lunch-time rehearsals. Some schools schedule their rehearsal groups during lunch periods only.   (See diagrams at the right of page 95.) Although this system may allow groups to meet more often, allow more students to participate, and make it possible for a student to be in more than one group, there is a major disadvantage in the short length of the lunch periods. It is true that some teachers can accomplish more in meeting a group daily for a short period than two or three times a week for a full period. Nevertheless, there is a great deal of pressure involved in a 20-, 25-, or 30-minute lunch period that does not allow much time for setting up and storing away instruments, nor for enlarging rehearsal content into the area of "appreciation" through the use of related recordings and discussions of style.

Flexible schedules. Out of the new thinking taking place in education has come a trend toward having subjects meet for different amounts of time per week (rather than equal-length periods) and toward more flexibility for independent study. This is a logical concept since every subject does not require equal time to be taught. A schedule constructed on this approach can allow more opportunity for students to take music. For example, courses such as industrial arts, laboratory science, art, and music could meet for double periods a couple of times a week, providing sufficient time for setting up and putting away equipment and materials, and allowing more flexibility for electives. Instructional time in this system is approximately equal to single periods meeting five times a week.

Per.	M	T	W	Th	F
1	Math	Math	Math	Math	Math
2	History	Chorus	History	Chorus	History
3	P.E.		P.E.		P.E.
4	Lunch Open	Lunch Open	Lunch Open	Lunch Open	Lunch Open
5 6	Physics	Language	Physics	Language	Physics
7	English	English	English	English	English

Another system that allows more time for students to elect music or other subjects is based on the premise that the amount of learning that takes place does not necessarily reflect the amount of time spent in

	Band	Strings	Band	Strings	Band	Strings	Band	Strings	Band	Strings
Before lunch										
First lunch	Orchestra		Band		Orchestra		Band		Orchestra	
Second lunch										
Third lunch										

or

First lunch	Strings	Strings	Strings	Strings	Strings
Second lunch	Orchestra	Orchestra	Orchestra	Orchestra	Orchestra
Third lunch	Orchestra	Orchestra	Orchestra	Orchestra	Orchestra
After lunch	Band	Band	Band	Band	Band

or

	Orchestra	Orchestra	Orchestra	Orchestra	Orchestra
Before lunch					
First lunch	Strings / Band	Strings / Band	Strings / Band	Strings / Band	Strings / Band
Second lunch	Band	Band	Band	Band	Band
Third lunch					

Period 3	Lunch A	Band	Band	Band	Band	Band
Per. 4	Lunch B	Orchestra	Orchestra	Orchestra	Orchestra	Orchestra
Per. 5	Lunch C	Chorus	Chorus	Chorus	Chorus	Chorus
Period 6	Lunch D	Glee Club	Glee Club	Glee Club	Glee Club	Glee Club

classes. Therefore, academically-talented students may be allowed to enroll in two courses during the same block of time, alternating courses from one day to the next. This frees the student during another period to take an elective course—possibly music.

In the various plans presented here, most of the illustrations have been based on scheduling instrumental groups, simply because orchestras may have to draw on members of the band. However, the same ideas can be applied to scheduling vocal organizations. In fact, the music director should strive for a scheduling system that removes conflicts between groups in each area. The orchestra player should not be denied an opportunity in choral music by having every group rehearse at the same time. If one chorus has to meet during the period he is in orchestra, he should be able to join another vocal ensemble scheduled at another time.

In a high school that is marked by a pro-music administrative attitude and an enthusiastic student body which has received a solid musical education in the lower grades, a strong program can be worked out. The three schedules on pages 97-99 have been devised, from a rather idealistic viewpoint, to indicate the scope of a music program that is possible in a large, musically-interested high school employing three teachers. The schedules, to be sure, are difficult ones for the teachers, since they allow free periods only at lunch time. However, realizing their impracticality in regard to the work load, as well as the fact that very few schools could manage such a plan, they are given here for two purposes: to point out that there is more to a substantial high school music curriculum than simply a chorus, orchestra, or band, and to reveal some of the possibilities for scheduling a full program.

Scheduling is one of the most important tasks the director faces. Everything he stands for in music education depends on his ability to work with the administration in devising a sensible and flexible schedule. What use, after all, is the careful planning of objectives or the acquisition of necessary instruments and other equipment unless students can be scheduled for classes in which these ideas and materials are put into meaningful action?

PLANNING MUSIC FACILITIES

Administrators in every school system have to cope with the difficulties of building new school facilities from time to time. Some school districts, in fact, face this problem of space and increased enrollment every year. Part of the music supervisor's job consists of acting as a consultant in planning the music facilities of new buildings or in renovating older facilities. Of course, the actual designing will be in the hands of

TEACHER I: INSTRUMENTAL MUSIC

	Monday	Tuesday	Wednesday	Thursday	Friday
1	String Class	Wind and Percussion Ensemble	String Class	Wind and Percussion Ensemble	String Class
2	Beginning Band	Beginning Band	Beginning Band	Beginning Band	Beginning Band
3	Brass Class	Percussion Class	Brass Class	Percussion Class	Brass Class
4	Advanced Band	Advanced Band	Advanced Band	Advanced Band	Advanced Band
5	FREE	FREE	FREE	FREE	FREE
6	Orchestra	Orchestra	Orchestra	Orchestra	Orchestra
7	Instrumental Ensembles	Stage Band	Instrumental Ensembles	Stage Band	Instrumental Ensembles
8	Woodwind Class	Intermediate Orchestra	Woodwind Class	Intermediate Orchestra	Woodwind Class

TEACHER II: VOCAL MUSIC

	Monday	Tuesday	Wednesday	Thursday	Friday
1	Voice Class I (Section A)	Girls' Glee Club	Voice Class I (Section A)	Girls' Glee Club	Voice Class I (Section A)
2	Advanced Chorus	Advanced Chorus	Advanced Chorus	Advanced Chorus	Advanced Chorus
3	Chamber Singers	Chamber Singers	Chamber Singers	Chamber Singers	Chamber Singers
4	Voice Class II	Piano Class I	Voice Class II	Piano Class I	Voice Class II
5	FREE	FREE	FREE	FREE	FREE
6	Vocal Ensembles	Boys' Glee Club	Vocal Ensembles	Boys' Glee Club	Vocal Ensembles
7	Beginning Chorus	Beginning Chorus	Beginning Chorus	Beginning Chorus	Beginning Chorus
8	Voice Class I (Section B)	Piano Class II	Voice Class I (Section B)	Piano Class II	Voice Class I (Section B)

TEACHER III: GENERAL AND SPECIAL MUSIC CLASSES

	Monday	Tuesday	Wednesday	Thursday	Friday
1	Music Theory I	Music Theory I	Music Theory I	Music Theory I	Music Theory I
2	Advanced General Music (Section A)	Music Literature	Advanced General Music (Section A)	Music Literature	Advanced General Music (Section A)
3	Music History And Appreciation (Section A)	Music History And Appreciation (Section A)	Music History And Appreciation (Section A)	Music History And Appreciation (Section A)	Music History And Appreciation (Section A)
4	Comparative Arts	Comparative Arts	Comparative Arts	Comparative Arts	Comparative Arts
5	FREE	FREE	FREE	FREE	FREE
6	Advanced General Music (Section B)	FREE	Advanced General Music (Section B)	FREE	Advanced General Music (Section B)
7	Music History And Appreciation (Section B)	Music History And Appreciation (Section B)	Music History And Appreciation (Section B)	Music History And Appreciation (Section B)	Music History And Appreciation (Section B)
8	Music Theory II	Music Theory II	Music Theory II	Music Theory II	Music Theory II

an architect, but the architect has to know in detail what is needed, and to provide this information the music director must know what should be considered. It is not enough to say, "We need a band room, chorus room, and general music room, plus a music office"—not unless the director will be satisfied with rooms that are too small to rehearse in, rooms with poor acoustics or without facilities for storage of equipment.

Here are some of the things the director should keep in mind when he is analyzing his particular program and its physical needs:

1. What is the exact nature of the work to be done in each room?
2. What is the expected enrollment of classes, including anticipated growth over the next ten or fifteen years? In the case of performing groups, what would be the maximum number of students desired?
3. What are the needs for music classrooms, rehearsal halls, practice rooms, listening rooms, a music office, a music library, a uniform storage room, an instrument storage room, concert facilities, an auditorium and stage, dressing rooms, and a recording studio? Which of these are needed? How many? Must there be facilities for simultaneous rehearsals?
4. Where should these rooms be located in relation to themselves and to the rest of the school?
5. What equipment is needed — chalkboards, music boards, projection screens, speaker systems, special chairs, permanent or movable risers, basic school-owned instruments, audio-visual equipment, music stands, podiums, bulletin boards, storage and filing cabinets, sorting racks, special office equipment?
6. What is needed in the way of lighting?
7. What are the problems of temperature control in relation to performance and instrument storage? Will a humidifier be desirable for the instrument room?
8. What are the acoustical needs? In which rooms will proper sound insulation obviate room connection of sound-conducting media such as pipes, walls, beams, doors, and so on?

Each of these questions requires an answer if the music director expects facilities that are going to serve his needs. Although each school will differ in its physical plant requirements, there are again some basic thoughts to keep in mind in every situation.

Location. The music complex is usually placed in the school's "noise wing" along with industrial arts classrooms. This is fine as long as the sound of shop machinery does not penetrate music rooms where acute listening must take place. Those who isolate rehearsal halls so that the sounds of the music department do not disturb other classes often forget that students in music rooms should not be disturbed either by other sound sources.

All the music rooms should be in a single unit, with rehearsal halls near to the auditorium for easy access. A corridor, however, should separate the auditorium and music facilities to provide sound-insulation. Storage areas should also be located adjacent to the rehearsal halls so that there will be minimum movement of equipment. Since equipment sometimes goes out of the building, such as for football games or exchange concerts, there should be an outside entrance and loading platform. This or some other entrance will also make it easier to reach the music rooms for night-time activities when the rest of the school will be locked.

Rooms. In rehearsal halls, the MENC recommends an allowance of twenty to twenty-four square feet per student for instrumental groups, and 400 cubic feet per performer for proper acoustics. When separate facilities are provided for band and orchestra, the architect should design a room with less reverberation for the band than for the string ensemble. For choral groups using chairs on risers, fifteen to eighteen square feet per student is recommended. The ceilings here do not have to be as high as in instrumental rooms, but they should still be higher than in regular classrooms.

Practice rooms for individual students should be fifty-five to sixty-five square feet in size, while those designed for small ensembles require at least 120 square feet. Non-parallel walls in these rooms will help reduce the reflected sound.

General music classrooms should be arranged with a lot of storage space and provisions for basic items like staff-lined boards and listening equipment.

Stages. The planning of an auditorium stage is a subject to which the supervisor is apt to give less concentrated thought until the time comes to make use of the facility. Then, all kinds of problems become obvious. A proper stage requires wide doors opening into the backstage area to allow passage of not only musical equipment but large, bulky scenery. Ample storage space away from the wings will give performers and stage crew more room to work and wait during performances. For scenery, there should be ample fly space and rigging, with a grid a little more than twice the height of the proscenium arch. Unless this last item is observed, scenery cannot be adequately raised out of sight of the audience. A lighting board is preferably placed on the side nearest the dressing rooms, and from the same point there should be an audio communications hook-up to the orchestra pit and to the lighting loft. In addition to providing a good acoustical design, a proper sound amplification system should also be installed.

The orchestra pit also needs to be acoustically treated, not only to subdue sound but also to maintain correct balance and quality of tone. The pit should be out of sight of the audience, sunk into the floor and running the length of the stage and about fifteen feet in width. Separating the audience and the orchestra is a partition, descending about five feet from the auditorium floor into the pit and rising to the level of the stage floor opposite. This allows the front row of the audience, a couple of feet behind the partition, to clearly see the stage but not the orchestra.

Seats in the auditorium ought to be raked for clear vision, with the front row situated so that occupants can see over the floor of the stage as well as the pit partition. Front-row spectators should never have to look up over the stage apron, but should be able to see the stage floor clearly. Often this is not possible unless one sits farther back in the hall at a higher level.

A number of schools try to cut costs by combining the auditorium with other facilities. This results in a combination auditorium and cafeteria (cafetorium), a combination stage and music room (with a partition between it and the auditorium), or a combination stage-gymnasium. All of these are objectionable from the standpoint of good music facilities. So, too, are rehearsal halls designed to accommodate both vocal and instrumental ensembles, and the use of classrooms designed for purposes other than rehearsal.

By referring to the MENC publication[3] on music plant facilities, and making it available to administrators and the architect, the music director can save himself from a number of problems that arise in poorly-planned music rooms.

---

[3] Charles L. Gary, ed., *Music Buildings, Rooms and Equipment.* (Washington, D.C.: MENC, 1966).

6

Relations with the Teaching Staff

The music director works principally with two groups of teachers —
those who are employed to teach or supervise music activities, and those
who are general classroom teachers, involved in teaching music along with
many other subjects. For the moment, we will be concerned with the
special teachers on the music staff. (Many facets of working with classroom teachers, as well as music teachers, will be covered in Chapter 8.)

FULL-TIME PERSONNEL

Obviously, to construct a good philosophy of music education and to
outline a sequence of valued activities is not enough to guarantee a successful program. The vital link that holds this chain of ideas together and
brings plans to their full realization is the teacher. Thus, considerable
thought must be given to the selection of teachers who will meet the
program's needs.

Selecting Music Personnel. In the end, the hiring of a teacher is usually
done upon the recommendation of the music director to the superintendent, who in turn makes a recommendation to the board of education as a
matter of formality. But there are several important steps that precede
this. The music director must first determine who is needed to accomplish
the stated goals, and what qualifications will be required. Theoretically,
a good music teacher is a good music teacher, but practically this is not
always so. Everyone has his strengths and weaknesses, and no one can
be expected to know everything about any one field. A teacher who has
been highly successful in developing high school vocalists will not necessarily excel in teaching instruments to beginning students in the elementary
grades — even if he has a working knowledge of the instruments and has
studied elementary children and methods. Although a teacher might be
quite knowledgeable about many different areas of music education, in
practice he will probably find his forte in just a few types of activities.
This is a fact that must be considered in deciding what type of teacher
is needed. Sometimes, an administrator will hire a teacher with a strong

background in junior high school general music classes and then put him in charge of the high school orchestra and band. Perhaps the teacher will do a good job, but how much more valuable he would be in the junior high school!

Having the knowledge of the type and background of the teacher needed, the music director can then begin an active solicitation of candidates. University placement services are an important first step in this process, but outside contacts with other people in the music field may furnish valuable leads. Teachers' agencies can also be consulted if other sources fail.

In soliciting through a placement service, the following information should be furnished: (1) the name and location of the school system; (2) a description of the position that is open, including the types of classes, activities, responsibilities, desired results, and general working conditions; (3) a salary schedule; (4) general requirements for the job, including degree(s), experience, specialties, and type of background; and (5) the name, address, and telephone number of the person to whom application should be made. This may be supplemented by a brief calendar of the school music year, types of musical activities, distinctive characteristics of the music program, and a description of the community.

In some instances, when an opening must be filled immediately, it is necessary to interview each candidate as he applies. When there is time, however, it is better to accept applications, transcripts, and recommendations until a weighable number of credentials has been received; review them; and then arrange interviews with the preferred candidates. If a top prospect applies, of course, he should be called in without delay, before he is committed to a contract elsewhere.

Hiring a teacher is a two-sided operation. Many employers think only of the chance *they* may be taking in accepting a certain employee, but the *employee* is also taking a chance on a job that may not prove to be a good move. The music director, then, should not only look for a good teacher, but also present to the candidate an accurate picture of the position and the school system so that the teacher can determine whether the job is one in which he would be happy. For in any situation, the unhappy employee is one who will do less than his best work. At the interview, opportunity should be given to the candidate to ask questions about the opening, the music program as a whole, the school system, the community, and so on. It is only fair, too, that he be able to see a part of the program in action so that he can obtain a better view of the situation. In a summer interview this is not possible, but he can at least be given a tour of the school plant, including an inspection of music facilities, equipment, and materials.

At the interview, a representative from the superintendent's office, and preferably the principal of the building in which the teacher will be working, should be present to work with the music director in determining the applicant's qualifications. Here, it is perhaps best to start with the teacher's previous experience, putting him at ease by asking him to describe activities he is familiar with. Then the conversation can be directed toward the type of work involved in the opening he has applied for. Whenever possible, the candidate's own teaching philosophy — particularly in relation to the specific job — should be drawn out for comparison with the philosophy of the school system and the music program. All three must be compatible. It is important to assess the prospect's understanding of children and teen-agers, his knowledge of music, and his theories about specific classroom practices. Often, it is valuable to pose a particular teaching problem to the candidate to see how he would handle it. The interview should also be interspersed with conversation about non-teaching, non-music subjects — not to uncover opinion or knowledge, but to gain insight into his personality, for a "whole person" is being hired, not a departmentalized specimen who separates himself from all else when he enters the classroom. At the end of the interview, it is a courtesy to the candidate to inform him of when he will hear a decision.

The final selection, before going to the board of education, should be a joint decision by several personnel, although the music director should have veto power over even a majority preference when he is confronted with a prospect whom he does not feel is qualified. Among the major items to consider in selecting a teacher are the following:

1. *Personality and attitude.* Regardless of how knowledgeable a candidate may be in regard to music, education, and students, unless he has a warm, receptive, pleasant personality, and a willing and respectful attitude, he will find the going difficult in front of students and in working cooperatively with the rest of the staff.

2. *Professional experience.* The teacher with fifteen years of experience is not necessarily better than the teacher with one or even none. Nevertheless, a reputable standing in the field and a successful background in those areas which the position involves are most desirable.

3. *Education and training.* The applicant must be certified, of course, or be ready to pass certification requirements. But college degrees are not always representative of the teacher's qualifications. Potential lies only in the individual's character, not in credentials of minimum knowledge, nor in the holding of advanced degrees which may or may not be an indication of achievement. It must also be realized that a master's degree from one institution may not be worth a baccalaureate from another with higher standards.

4. *Capacity for growth.* This is a difficult thing to measure, particularly during the course of a short interview, but it is perhaps the most

important factor in determining a person's value. The teacher's over-all attitude and past achievement beyond required performance are valuable clues to his potential.

5. *Interest*. The applicant's interest in the job is also very important. Few people can do outstanding work when they do not have high interest in the work they are doing. It is true, not only in education but in all fields, that the really successful person is the one who has a compelling interest in his work, is happy in his work, and has made his work an important part of his life. True success does not rest only on tangible achievement; it is, to a great degree, an inner, personal quality.

6. *Musical knowledge*. It is sufficient to say that a teacher must know far more than the amount he teaches. He cannot, as the old saying goes, be reading one chapter ahead of his students.

7. *Musical talent*. The music teacher needs to possess skills at least to the degree necessary for the specific position. However, the greater his musical talent, the more sensitivity he will transmit to his students.

8. *Understanding of students*. This quality needs no explanation. Obviously, one must understand those with whom he works in order to communicate meaningfully.

9. *Organizational ability*. One of the constant problems of competent teachers is not what to teach, but what *not* to teach. The teacher is faced with the situation of providing as comprehensive an education as possible in a limited amount of time. He necessarily must be able to organize his work, select only the best materials and the choicest experiences, present his subject in the most easily understandable manner, and be able to plan carefully for developmental growth.

10. *Recommendations*. Both personal and professional references should be considered in selecting a teacher, but these should not always be taken seriously. It is often difficult to distinguish an honest account of past experience from a sincere, but misrepresentative account. A knowledge of the person writing the letter of reference is really necessary for a true evaluation of its contents, but this is rarely possible.

11. *Other interests and abilities*. Generally, the person with knowledge, ability, and capacity to grow is one who has a wide range of interests and a certain range of talents outside of music.

Orienting the New Teacher. The first step in orienting a new teacher is to review the job he has just accepted. This includes general matters such as making sure he understands contract provisions, salary, increments, benefits, options or requirements for course work, policies regarding absence and leave, and procedures and relationships among personnel. Concerning actual teaching activities, he should be informed of his exact responsibilities and duties, told of any possible problems that he may have, and given a more detailed inspection of facilities, materials, and equipment.

In some cases, there might also be an understanding that the teacher might be re-assigned at a later date, after an evaluation of the situation. This may be due to the teacher's particular needs or talents that become apparent after a certain length of time; it may be due to a balancing of the work load, or to new plans that are put into operation. Whatever the reason, it is important that the teacher know of this possibility before he signs his contract. In no case should a teacher be transferred to another building or another position without mutual consent. Although the school may be legally justified in taking such action against the teacher's will, it is unfair and ethically improper to change a teacher from the position for which he signed a contract, unless, of course, he is being released from service altogether.

The music director can also help to orient the teacher by introducing him to members of the staff and various groups in the community, helping him to get settled in the community, and putting him in touch with local professional organizations. As soon as possible, he should be brought into program planning, committee work, and participation in the in-service program.

Working with Teachers. Aside from professionally-directed meetings with teachers (to be discussed in the "in-service" chapter), the supervisor will have numerous opportunities to work with teachers in a more personal manner. By "personal," reference is still made to individuals in their teaching capacities rather than as private citizens, but also in regard to their general well-being and professional advancement, rather than to specific teaching activities. For example, the supervisor may notice certain things that can be done to improve working conditions and raise morale. He should express his interest in the teachers' needs and take whatever action he can to improve conditions. These include providing the best available materials, making classrooms and teachers' rooms attractive, and working for well-equipped music rooms.

Working in pleasant surroundings will increase the morale and efficiency of the teaching staff. Other considerations, however, can also serve to build the confidence and morale necessary for a successful program. Keeping this in mind, the music director ought to:

1. Consult teachers before taking action on anything that will involve them, perhaps even a minor affair to which the teacher would be expected to offer no opposition. Consultation is more a courtesy than a formality, and it will unconsciously uphold the teacher's sense of self-importance.

2. Listen to the teachers' own proposals for improving the teaching situation. They, after all, are the ones who are face to face with the

actual problems involved in teaching. If anything is to work, they are the people who ultimately will make it work; their talents are needed in planning as well as in execution.

3. Respect the contributions of individual teachers, show confidence in their abilities, and let them know they are doing a good job. Criticism is too often a fault-finding act instead of a carefully-weighed judgment. Praise is criticism too, and in certain instances this is the very thing that will lift the individual to new heights. If a person is praiseworthy, chances are he does not need someone else to dwell on whatever faults he does have. He may very well know just what they are, and may need only encouragement and recognition of his achievements to make him tackle his shortcomings.

4. Avoid an authoritarian attitude in helping teachers and in planning work with them. Helping teachers begins with a realization that they must recognize their own teaching abilities. There is little to be gained in setting down invariable doctrines implying that the supervisor always knows best. There is much to be gained, on the other hand, by leading the teacher toward the discovery of new techniques, different procedures, and better concepts through open discussion, experimentation, an introduction to new materials and teaching ideas, observation of other teachers, or perhaps suggested reading in professional literature.

5. Use the special talents of each teacher. Each person has something different to offer, and unless his talents are utilized, a teacher can lose his self-identity. It is important to make each staff member feel "special," not only in his daily routine, but also in occasional special assignments — putting him in charge of a project, having him lead a workshop for classroom teachers, making him a resource coordinator for a special unit, or involving him in experimental research.

6. Encourage informal relations and be interested in topics other than music, including teachers' activities outside the school. Informal association offers many opportunities for encouraging a teacher's growth through professional organizations, participation in regional and state associations, enrollment in courses, and personal musical performances in the community.

7. Be available, and answer requests immediately. Teachers need to know that the supervisor is there to offer assistance, not just to preside over them.

8. Remember teachers' names and use them; a name is the mark of all a person is, and to forget it or disregard it is to ignore the person.

Evaluating Teachers. The evaluation of a teacher's work involves four basic steps: (1) determining whether the teacher is in need of improvement; (2) pinpointing the exact area in which help is needed; (3) realizing the cause of the problem; and (4) determining what can be done to improve the situation.

The problem may be caused by the teacher's method of instruction, by environmental conditions, by the materials used, or by the structure of the curriculum itself. It may even be due to an outside influence in the life of the teacher. In any case, it is important that the teacher be encouraged to evaluate his own work. Through the cooperation of the entire staff, a check list may be drawn up by which this can be done.

Items for the director to consider include the teacher's understanding of students and their needs; attention to individual needs; ability to adjust to situations; use of experimentation; recognition of student interests and ability to communicate in terms of those interests; control of class; rapport with class; clarity of objectives; appropriateness of materials and methods; knowledge of subject; methods of planning and organizational ability; success of experiences in terms of student growth; encouragement of students; personal relationships with administrators, fellow teachers, and students; willingness to offer extra help to students and colleagues; breadth of interests; personal qualities such as appearance and the use of the voice; and self-criticism.

Some of the devices used in evaluation are observations and interviews, activity check lists, questionnaires, written reports, personal data sheets, rating scales, tests, and tests of pupil growth. However, a fair evaluation of a teacher's work involves more than an examination of the teacher himself. It involves the actual observation of the learning situation — that is, the teacher in action with the pupil. Only in this way can conditions for improvement be defined.

PART-TIME PERSONNEL

Many of the principles discussed in the previous section can be applied in work with part-time personnel as well. Nevertheless, there are also special matters to consider in working with two particular groups — professional musicians and student teachers.

Professional Musicians. Many systems — especially larger ones — employ professional performers on a part-time basis as instrumental instructors at the elementary and junior-high levels. There are two advantages in this practice. First, these musicians can teach individual and class lessons that may not be sufficient in number to justify the hiring of full-time personnel. Since they are actively involved in careers as performers, the musicians do not have to rely solely on their part-time teaching salaries, although they often depend on teaching to supplement their performance income. Their employment allows the school to offer instruction of a sort that might not otherwise be possible, due either to the number of classes involved or to the availability of qualified, full-time instrumental instructors. Secondly, this practice allows the school to employ brass specialists, woodwind specialists, string specialists, and percussion specialists. In some systems, where performer-teachers are not on the staff, a music teacher may find himself giving instruction on instruments with which he himself has had little or no experience.

The use of professional performers naturally gives rise to special problems. Because of the inconsistency of professional rehearsal and performance times, the supervisor may occasionally encounter conflicts with school activities. At the beginning of employment, the supervisor must establish that the teacher's performance duties will not interfere with classes. Scheduling as many classes as possible during the morning session will alleviate most conflicts. It is also wise to avoid programs that require the part-time teacher's presence during evenings. If the teacher handles only private and class instrument lessons, while a full-time music teacher directs the activities of performance groups, there should be no need for the performer-teacher to be present for instructive purposes other than at regular class times.

This does not imply that the part-time teacher should by any means be isolated from the rest of the music program. It is important to bring him into the planning of instruction in his own area if possible, particularly in meetings with other teachers. The part-time teacher who is involved in planning and feels a part of the total program is likely to do a better job. Furthermore, this may provide the only opportunity he has to communicate with other music personnel in the school. Such communication is important psychologically in developing his interest and sense of self-importance in the program; it is also important from the practical standpoint of breaking down the concept of teachers and performers as separate groups. Every effort should be made to prevent a feeling of "professional" superiority or inferiority on the part of any staff member. Each member should rightfully be identified as a "professional musician," regardless of his prime concentration on either teaching or performing. It is not necessary to bring the part-time teacher into all staff meetings. Of importance to him are meetings that deal with his particular teaching area, and these should be scheduled with respect to his other activities.

The supervisor must also guard against placing the teacher in a situation that will compromise the Code of Ethics established jointly by the musicians' union and the music education profession. Employment by the school does not release the performer from his obligation to the union, and requests to perform (through the school) must be weighed carefully to determine their educational or entertainment status.

Since the part-time teacher is employed as part of the school program, he should be paid only by the school. Some school systems have established a procedure by which students pay the teachers on a weekly or monthly basis for their lessons. This is to be avoided because it removes the instruction from its proper place in the total tax-supported educational program. Private, individual fees should be replaced by a direct salary, established and paid by the board of education. Finally, because of the performer's position on the school staff, he should not be allowed to promote the sale of instruments through his classes when he has any direct involvement in the sales.

Student Teachers. When it is practical, a school system should involve itself in the preparation of future educators by accepting student teachers into its classrooms. This is part of the local system's responsibility to the profession. Unfortunately, there are some schools that look upon their proximity to a teachers' college or university as an opportunity to meet their personnel needs without the expense of hiring certified teachers. The music director should not allow student teachers placed in his program to be assigned to classes for which there are no regular instructors.

Having accepted the responsibility of assisting in the training of teachers, the music director needs to cooperate with the college supervisor in planning the student-teaching program in his community. It is important that everyone involved know and agree on policies to be followed. Working with each participating "critic" teacher on his staff, the music director can determine the most effective means of orienting a student teacher to the school, launching him in his first teaching experience, and guiding him toward the acceptance of full responsibility for a class. The student, for example, should meet key personnel in the school and know their function; be informed of any administrative policies or procedures that involve him; be introduced to the resources available and to the location of facilities; and learn of the educational and general community background of students he will be teaching.

Since the participating college may not have a sufficiently large staff of supervisors to visit student teachers regularly, an extra budren may be placed on the local director and his staff to help the students. Even with regular, frequent visits by college personnel, the student teacher needs guidance, assistance, and understanding from the local department. The music director, at the outset, might caution his own staff to guard against putting the student in a position where he is caught between the college supervisor and the cooperating teacher. From the latter, the student frequently hears that he should forget the philosophical theories he learned in college and deal with practical ideas; from the former, he is still pressured by idealistic concepts. Each view, of course, is false by itself; both the practical and the idealistic are necessary to balance education and to make teaching both immediately effective and purposeful in a larger sense.

It is best to consider the student teacher's position in terms of the opportunities he may be given to become involved — to analyze the teaching situation, to plan, to teach, and to analyze again the whole operation. The student should not simply be placed in front of a class and told to take charge. Rather, he needs to teach his classes *in cooperation with* the regular teacher. He will observe some classes, assist in some of the planning work of the critic teacher, teach portions of class periods, and in many instances teach classes for full periods. In no case, however, should the student be thought of as replacing the regular teacher. The teaching responsibility should be shared.

Before the student starts to teach, the cooperating teacher must be sure that both the student teacher and the class are prepared. Before this moment arrives, the student will have been introduced to the class, will have had the opportunity to observe the class, and will have assisted the regular staff member in his own teaching before the group. The cooperating teacher should also discuss the student's plans for his first lessons and review them with him before the actual teaching takes place. This will assure the student of more opportunity for success. While the cooperating teacher may, and should, offer suggestions, his primary purpose should be to guide the student teacher in developing his ideas. During the student's early teaching, it is best for the regular instructor to remain in the classroom, principally as an observer and participant in class performance, but also to assist when called upon. In no case should the critic teacher interrupt with any suggestion or comment that will lower the student teacher's status in the classroom. Later, when the student teacher has gained his confidence and that of the pupils, the regular teacher may absent himself on occasion.

Time should be made available, soon after a lesson is taught, for a conference between the regular teacher and the student to analyze the work. The less participation there is by the college supervisor, the more time there should be for conferences with local personnel.

7

Relations with the Community

In recent years, the functions of public relations have come to play an important role in the life of business operations. The business of education, with approximately fifty million young people actively engaged in some stage of its training program, must deal in public relations like any other concern.

With his colleagues in other departments, the music supervisor should realize that his work is not confined to the classroom alone; for the educational process relates to all times, to all activities, and to all people, and should be carried on with the understanding and cooperation of the total community. The community, after all, comprises the total body of stockholders in this business. The supervisor's relations with the general public are apt to be closest, and at the same time most informal, in the small community. Regardless of the size of the school system, however, public relations in some form are bound to take place for either better or worse — through both formal and informal practices — and the successful supervisor needs to be both aware and in control of these activities.

In order to develop an effective public relations program, the music educator must concern himself with two main processes — that of understanding the community and its needs, and that of keeping the community informed. The first requires a knowledge of the socio-economic structure of the community, of its businesses and industries, its racial and national groups, its attitudes, its intellectual and cultural climate, its social and recreational facilities, and its educational resources—anything that may have a bearing on the school curriculum. The second requires knowledge of how to inform the people of the purposes, values, conditions, needs, and activities of the music program.

Following these two lines, one of relating the community to the school and the other of relating the school to the community, we can define several purposes of the music department's public relations program:

1. To interpret to the public what is going on in the music program and why.
2. To obtain the public's interest in the program.
3. To obtain the public's confidence in the work that is being done.

4. To obtain the public's support in continuing and improving the program.
5. To develop an awareness of the place of music in education and its role as an integral part of human activity.
6. To develop the concept of community partnership in the educational process.
7. To evaluate the school music program in terms of the needs of the community.

The first step for the supervisor to take is to recognize the community with which he is dealing. The most obvious segment of the public, of course, is composed of the parents of school children — not only the parents of pupils active in the music program, but also of non-music students. We must also be concerned, however, with those citizens who are not parents. These people are still taxpayers who support the school system financially, and they are needed to take an increased interest in the schools, supporting them in other ways. Whether parents or non-parents, citizens may assume several other roles in the community, becoming members of groups with which the music supervisor ought to be concerned. Among these groups are private music teachers, professional musicians, and the music industry, including music publishers, music dealers, and those in specialized services; civic and social organizations and institutions, including the church, business clubs, women's organizations, and fraternal bodies; and finally, those involved in the communications media — the press, radio and television.

Once the supervisor knows whom he is working with, he has three main approaches to take in establishing good public relations: (1) a person-to-person or group-to-group approach; (2) the use of mass media; and (3) the education of the community through adult programs.

PERSON-TO-PERSON AND GROUP-TO-GROUP

The contacts that the supervisor has as an individual, either with other individuals or with groups, are the most direct lines to good relations between the school and the community. It should be realized first of all that the relationship of the teacher to his students in the classroom is the basis of good community relations. A poor music program cannot be covered up by clever publicity, whereas good teaching will create its own advertising. If students are pleased with a program and with their experiences in the classroom, they will transmit their feelings not only to their parents but also to non-music students. Furthermore, the high school student will remember these experiences when, just a few years later, he becomes a taxpayer and is in a position to support further the music program.

In many cases it will be the comments of the student alone which will influence the opinions of parents (and other members of the community, too). However, there are other ways in which the music teacher can reach parents individually. Such occasions as "choir night" or "band, night" can serve to acquaint parents with the program by having them spend an evening at a special rehearsal. A similar occasion may introduce parents to the activities of a general music class, in which case the parents themselves can assume the roles of students. Although these "nights" may be held by the music department alone, frequently they are part of a larger "back-to-school night" in which the whole school participates. National Education Week is often chosen as an appropriate time for these meetings.

Another way of informing parents is by means of a letter sent home with students or through the mail. Such a letter may explain certain facets of the program, point out its objectives, solicit suggestions, and so on. To be effective it should be as conversational as possible, adopting a "you" approach that will indicate to the parent that the program is designed to meet individual needs.

On the occasion of concerts or special programs, invitations may be sent to important figures in the community. Parents, of course, are most likely to attend since their children are participating, but other influential people would undoubtedly show some interest if they were to receive an individual invitation. Obviously, this cannot be too extensive lest it exceed it usefulness. Its usefulness has been proven, however, and for this purpose, a music director may keep a select file of names and addresses, including musical and cultural leaders, business notables, church officials, social leaders, and important political figures, including the mayor. Many of these people will not have time to attend, or else will not wish to make the time, but the receipt of an invitation can still build good will.

Opportunities for the music director to speak before a club or other organization should also be considered whenever his schedule allows it. An address should be kept informal, avoiding vague educational terminology, and should be related to the interests of the particular group to which the director is speaking. A demonstration (other than by a performing group, which will be discussed later) can do much to create a warm atmosphere and rapport with the audience. One such demonstration may be a motion picture of activities in the school music program or of community music activities. Films for this purpose have been made inexpensively, and they may be done with imagination and interest, without requiring professional aid.

Parents Organizations. The Parent-Teachers Association is not an active organization in every school or school system, but where it is, several opportunities exist for the music educator. The PTA may view the supervisor's services to them in terms of leading the group in a song to open a meeting, serving on the entertainment committee, or perhaps providing entertainment for the group. More important, though, he can request that a meeting of the PTA be devoted to the music program, in which case he may speak to the group, answer their questions, offer demonstrations of typical activities and of materials being used (a demonstration of new materials is particularly good since it indicates that the program is being kept up to date), and conduct performances by students.

In many communities there are also parents organizations especially associated with music groups. These may be known as the Band Parents Club, the Choir Parents, or perhaps the Music Boosters Club. Too often, one of these groups functions only in a financial capacity, as in raising funds for equipment for the band. It is more important that it provide the interest, enthusiasm, and support that is necessary for good school-community relations. Equipment, uniforms, robes, and so on are legitimate educational items and should therefore be purchased by the board of education — not a parents club. When a club buys these things, the parents are simply paying twice, since they have already been taxed for the school budget. If the club must be looked to for financial support, it should be only for equipment that is beyond the means of a normal budget allowance, in which case purchases may be considered in the same regard as the contributions any interested citizen is entitled to make to a school. However, this aid should be supplementary only and should not replace the school music budget. Furthermore, one performing group should not be given any advantage over another by a boosters club, unless it is specifically a band club or a choir club.

The parents club is most effective when it serves as an advisory group to the music department, encourages pupil participation in musical activities, and supports musical events sponsored by the school. Members may also help with publicity for performances and may serve as chaperons and drivers on trips. Generally, in speaking to such a group, it is best to point out the benefits that will derive for the individual student rather than for the band or chorus as a whole. Parents are interested in the good of their own child as a member of the band, and only secondarily in the band itself.

The Professional Music Community. Although parents are generally the director's principal community contacts, other groups are directly concerned with and affected by his work. Among these are three segments of the professional music community: private teachers, professional musicians, and members of the music industry. Unique factors are to be considered in the director's dealings with each.

Private music teachers. The school program is sometimes felt by private teachers to deprive them of students. When the school music director encounters this feeling, he should point out that it actually results in more students taking music seriously, more students wanting outside instruction, more musically-intelligent and -sensitive pupils for the private teacher, and students who will be willing to devote time to practicing at home.

One of the ways of cooperating with private teachers, and at the same time encouraging students, is to offer school credit for private instruction. This involves the establishment of standards for qualifying the teachers and means of evaluation. In the first instance, standards may be set by the local school authorities, based on such considerations as training, degree, teaching experience, or an examination or demonstration. In some states requirements are established by the state board of education, which may also issue permits or certification for the private teachers. A particular program of instruction may also be determined by school authorities or worked out between them and the teachers.

An evaluation of the student's work may be based on several factors. First, there should be a report from the private teacher which includes the number of lessons taken, the amount of practice time required, the technical progress achieved, a list of materials studied, and finally a grade on the quality of the pupil's work and performance. The frequency of such a report should be determined by the school. Secondly, there may be a report from the student himself as to the amount of time he has given to practicing; or this may come from his parents, along with a statement of his attitude toward home study. These reports should be submitted either to the school principal or to the director of music, and turned over to an examining committee at the end of the semester. The board that examines the student's performance for a final grade should be composed only of school personnel.

In helping parents select a private instructor, the school music teacher ought to avoid recommending just one person. It is better to suggest two or three names from which the parents and the pupil together can make a final choice. It goes without saying, of course, that in no instance should one discuss with parents the work of a private teacher in such a way that it could harm that individual's professional reputation. Finally, better relations may be promoted if the private teacher is encouraged to take part in planning and leading community music programs.

Professional musicians. In 1947 the American Federation of Musicians, the American Association of School Administrators, and the Music Educators National Conference jointly worked out a code of ethics, which was published by the MENC under the title "For Understanding and Cooperation Between School and Professional Musicians."[1] One year after it was set up, the code was renewed, and it has been reviewed periodically since then. In effect, it establishes the areas of performance in which school and professional musicians may participate.

The field of entertainment should be left to the professional musician. This includes community activities not organized for educational purposes (parades, festivals, ceremonies, games, etc.); functions related to private and public enterprises; any occasions that are partisan or sectarian; and functions of clubs, societies, and civic and fraternal organizations.

The field of music education includes school functions; community functions that are organized for educational purposes; educational broadcasts; civic occasions that are of such breadth that participation by school groups will not infringe upon the rights of professional musicians since the occasions enlist the cooperation of all persons; benefit performances in instances where professional musicians would also donate their services; recordings for educational purposes that are limited to use by students and teachers; and any occasion upon which agreement is reached cooperatively by school authorities and representatives of the musicians union.

The music industry. Relations with music publishers are frequently strained by school personnel, often unknowingly. A good association begins with the simple operation of ordering music in a direct and easily understood manner; this means, to include in the order the exact identification of publications, the exact number of copies wanted, the exact instrumentation in the case of a band or orchestral work, and so on. A business handbook published by the MENC offers suggestions to the teacher in this line.[2] When ordering music "on approval," it should be remembered that copies are not sent free but only for examination. If the material cannot be used, it should be returned immediately; if it is kept, a charge may be expected.

The main source of difficulty with publishers is the copyright law. Many articles and books have been written on it, indicating that it is too involved to deal with here at length. Copyrighted materials may not be duplicated by the teacher in any way, whether typewritten, mimeographed, projected on a screen, or by some other means. Furthermore, a composition that is not in the public domain may not be re-arranged for a special performance by a school group without the written permission of the publisher. Usually, if a published version in the medium required is not available, a publisher will offer permission, providing a copy of the arrangement is submitted. It should be understood that of works in the

---

[1] Now titled "Music Code of Ethics" (pub. #323-10242), a single copy of this publication may be ordered free from the MENC through NEA Publication Sales, 1201 Sixteenth Street, N.W., Washington, D.C. 20036.

[2] "Business Handbook of Music Education," prepared by the Music Industry Council (pub. #321-10450); a single copy is available free from the MENC.

public domain, only the original versions, or versions on which the copyrights have expired, may be reproduced or altered. Current published arrangements of publicly-owned compositions carry their own copyrights which must be observed.

The process of purchasing materials and equipment from local dealers is usually determined by the school board on recommendation from the music department. Consequently, bids by individual dealers may be submitted on specifications that are made available. In other cases, purchases from local dealers should be equalized whenever possible, as long as quality of goods is maintained. A teacher should not solicit parents of students in his classes to purchase instruments through him at discount prices. Neither should he accept commissions from a dealer, manufacturer, or distributor for recommending a particular piece of merchandise. This is not to say, of course, that the music teacher or director should not aid parents in the selection of instruments by suggesting certain brands that he feels are superior. Such help is perfectly all right.

The supervisor may also have dealings with members of the community who are involved in special music services. There are companies, for example, that will tape record school performances or make recordings from one's own tapes. Others include uniform manufacturers and suppliers of sound equipment. In regard to recording services, the director must once again keep in mind the copyright law. Unless a composition or arrangement is in the public domain, it must be cleared for recording. If the work has previously been recorded with the copyright owner's approval, simply notifying the owner of intent to record is sufficient. But if it has not been recorded before, permission from the copyright owner must be obtained. Secondly, these records should be used only by teachers and students. Selling them to the general public, even to raise money for educational purposes, is not legitimate unless royalties are paid. Such an occurence can cause trouble not only for the school but possibly for the recording company as well, since some of these custom record producers are not licensed to make discs for commercial use. In addition, selling records of school instrumental groups might constitute competition with professional musicians, a matter determined by their distribution.

Public Performances. In many cases, the non-parent in the community forms his only impression of the school program when he sees the half-time show at a football game, the band marching in the Memorial Day parade, or perhaps a performance at an all-city music festival. The public performance, then, is one of the most direct means of reaching the community. There are several types of performances for which the music director may plan. First, of course, are the school events, including games, concerts, spring musicals, and assembly programs that are open to the public. There are also city events, including festivals and parades, and inter-community programs in which a band or chorus from one city may perform in a joint concert with a group from a neighboring community. The latter category may also include exchange programs with communities out of the state. An exchange involves considerable planning, in addition to working out schedules for performances, since the band (or other group) must make travel arrangements, find accommodations for the few days it stays in the cooperating community, and make arrangements for receiving and housing the exchange group in its own home town. Whenever such a program can be arranged, however, it provides a fine opportunity for the performing organization — and one of which the local community will take note.

Relations between a group and its audience, in any of these situations, naturally depend on the quality of performance. Since good performance, and what it involves, goes beyond the scope of this book, it is sufficient to state that no school group should be scheduled for a performance when it is doubtful that a good performance can be achieved in time. A band, for example, that has spent most of the fall months preparing for football games would do well to reconsider performing in a Christmas concert if it has only two or three weeks to rehearse its concert material. Holding a winter concert in late January or early February might be a better choice.

A few other matters of presentation may be considered here. The director should not feel it is necessary to program everything that a group has studied since its last performance. If a program is too long, no matter how good it may be, the audience is apt to leave with somewhat less enjoyment than if it goes away wanting more. In overseeing the structure of a program involving several organizations, the tastes of the audience should be considered, but they should never be allowed to dictate the selection of a program; for the performance is, first of all, for the benefit of the students involved, and high standards must be maintained. The emphasis should be on quality, with those elements of "show" being incidental. It is quite possible to include music that will suit everyone without using inferior material, for in providing for variety, excellent material can be found regardless of whether the director is looking for classical, popular, folk, or theatre music. (This is a matter, of course, about which the supervisor should check with his staff throughout the year, rather than at concert time.) It is desirable to arrange the order of the music in such a way that unfavorable comparisons between selections are avoided. It may also help if the program, or portions of it, is focused upon a single theme. If this is the case, the supervisor will have to plan further in advance so that the teachers involved will have time to select and prepare music that is appropriate to the theme. It can seldom be worked out from the typical potpourri that a group may have ready at any given moment.

To increase the audience's appreciation, program notes may be provided, and in informal concerts the numbers might even be announced. If space allows, the printed program can also be used to call the public's attention to other phases of the school music program and to future events. This should be done inconspicuously and artistically, however, without detracting from the evening's presentation.

Performances for Civic and Social Organizations and Institutions. The possibilities of performance for civic and social groups in the community are quite extensive. Among the organizations that may wish such an event are business and professional groups, including the Rotary, Kiwanis, and Lions; fraternal bodies, such as the Masons and Elks; youth-oriented groups, like the YMCA, YWCA, CYO, and boys' clubs; the Chamber of Commerce; women's organizations; churches; and charitable institutions, such as hospitals, orphanages, and homes for the aged. The last category is particularly receptive to performances by small choral groups during the Christmas season.

The professional associations provide opportunities for the music supervisor to contact a good cross-section of the business community. Since the meetings of these businessmen are often tightly arranged, their schedule as well as that of the school should be considered carefully. Generally, this type of organization prefers a performance by a group rather than by a few individuals.

Civic organizations, being established for the betterment of the community, are quite receptive to performance by students. Furthermore, they include many prominent citizens. Women's groups, too, frequently influence the cultural interests and development of a town.

With any of these groups, there needs to be an understanding that school organizations must necessarily limit their appearances because of the preparation required and because of other obligations, especially to the student. Whenever an invitation is turned down, it should be done graciously with an explanation and a statement that an effort will be made to accommodate the organization in the future. Respecting the code of ethics with professional musicians will automatically relieve the school of a number of community requests since many invitations to perform are for entertainment purposes only.

Because of the traditional feeling that most church choirs contribute little to the quality of music heard in a city, relations with church musicians must sometimes be handled carefully. Students should be encouraged to contribute to the musical services of the churches of their choice, and the music teacher may offer his own assistance whenever appropriate. Sometimes, performances by an entire school group can be arranged, but these should not be attempted unless the performance is non-sectarian. In such an instance, important contacts can be made.

THE MASS MEDIA

It has been stated that the best form of public relations is personal contact, but such contact is generally limited to association with private teachers, professional musicians, church musicians, a few music dealers, and members of civic and social organizations. As important as these people are, they form only a very small segment of the population of a community. The rest of the people must be reached through the mass media and adult education programs. The latter, again, reaches only a limited public; consequently, while direct contact with individuals and groups may be the best line of relations, the mass media must be considered the most important in reaching the total community.

School Publications. There are four types of school publications that can serve to inform the public of the music program. In some school systems a newsletter is sent home to parents three or four times a year to explain certain phases of the school curriculum. Although this type of publication allows a very limited amount of space for any one subject (usually the entire paper is only four or six pages long), the music department may contribute a few paragraphs on a specific activity to solicit the parents' interest and support. Considering the space, it is best to promote a single activity rather than the entire music program or even an entire area of it.

At the high school level, student newspapers may include notices of music activities and reviews of concerts. Although the circulation is generally limited to the student body, there have been numerous instances in which a small high school paper has received wide distribution.

A third publication that a school system may issue is the annual report or survey. If the scope of the report is school-wide, the music department should definitely be included. Although this type of publication is apt to be statistical, the fact remains that newspaper editors are often more receptive to annual reports than to many other types of school news.

A fourth possibility for the music department is the curriculum guide. Although this is intended for use by school personnel, a guide sometimes has distribution beyond the local community and may create, at least among the educational profession, a certain impression of the school music program. (See Chapter 9 for details on planning this type of publication.)

Local Newspapers. There are three main things to be considered in issuing news releases to the local newspapers: knowing beforehand what the editor might be interested in, writing the release in a manner that will get attention, and submitting the manuscript in the right way at the right time. Many music directors mistakenly feel that those things which interest them in their program will automatically interest everyone else; yet, these same directors frequently overlook activities and achievements which are good news items. In preparing a news release or in looking for the subject for one, the supervisor must ask himself what will appeal to many people with many different primary interests. Generally, the proven ingredients of stories that have news interest are those which are either new or novel (that is, a turned-about situation), are related to famous people, have a direct effect on a group of people, pertain to the future, involve conflict, or are funny. Among the items that may have local interest, the supervisor might look for the following:

1. Concerts and musical shows.
2. Trips.
3. Pupil achievements.
4. Achievements of the teaching staff.
5. Honors awarded to teachers or to the school music program.
6. Ratings received at festivals.
7. Participation of school groups in outside-school events.
8. Success of alumni in the music field.
9. Additions or alterations in the physical facilities of the music department.
10. New techniques or materials being used.
11. Experimental teaching programs being tried.
12. School music activities that can be tied in with news events.
13. Results of annual surveys or reports.
14. Adaptation of national surveys and reports to the local program.
15. Formation of committees for important projects.
16. Attendance of local school personnel at state and national conferences or conventions.
17. Participation of members of the music staff in professional organizations and in local community projects.
18. Tie-ins with national organizations, such as the Ford Foundation or MENC projects.
19. Local conferences on music.
20. Important meetings affecting future plans.
21. Speeches by members of the music staff.

The community may be interested in some of these items at various stages of their development, as well as in completion. When a major performance is in rehearsal, for example, a "dead spot" in public relations may be avoided by informing the newspapers of significant progress — but only if it *is* significant. This will serve to publicize the event and create public anticipation. However, these items must be chosen with care. Too many insignificant releases sent to the editor will only cause disinterest and make it more difficult to have important news releases accepted.

Some editors want a written release submitted, while others prefer to have the facts so that a staff writer can prepare the story. However, unless you receive specific instructions from an editor for a specific occasion, it is best to write the release yourself. The newspaper staff can always rewrite the story if it wishes; and if it does not have the time, it may still use the original.

The release should not be written in a formal style. "Talking" the story will create the best effect. The lead paragraph, and if possible the lead sentence, will include all the main facts which answer the six questions: what, who, when, where, why, and how? The order of these is best determined by the individual story, but "what" (involving "who"), "when," and "where" should always be answered before "why" and "how" are considered. Following the lead, the release should be written in "inverted pyramid" form, meaning that each paragraph is more important than the one which follows it. This allows the story to be cut after any paragraph to fit the space available in the newspaper, while a complete story is still retained. Paragraphs should be no longer than fifty words if possible.

Editors like to have as many names as possible (and practical) in a release, since this increases the chances that the average reader will see the name of someone he knows or knows of, thus increasing reader interest and circulation. A review of a concert, therefore, should include more than a list of compositions that were performed. In running through the performances, there ought to be sentence variety and use of phrases other than "was played by"; otherwise, the release could very well be replaced by the printed program. It may help to put in interesting sidelights pertaining to the compositions, the audience, and so on, which, although not directly concerned with the actual performance, will attract attention.

If a picture is submitted for publication, a 5" x 7" or 8" x 10" glossy photograph is preferred. Editors have an aversion to formal, staged pictures, such as those of the 75 members of the band or chorus on the front steps of the school. A photo of four or five students (some standing, some seated; a few active, the rest watching) is much more likely to be used. Always write a caption for each picture submitted, making it brief, but including the names of the participants and what they are doing. Do not write the caption on the back since it could make an impression on the glossy side of the photograph and since the back will be pasted to a layout board. The caption may be typed on a separate sheet of paper and numbered with a corresponding number on the back of the photograph. It is a good idea, however, to put the school's name on the back of the photo with a rubber stamp that will not make an impression; then, if the picture is separated from the copy, it can be easily identified.

When the release is prepared for submission, the writer's name and address, or that of the school, should appear in the upper left-hand corner of the page. If an outside source has provided the information in the release, that source should be listed under the writer's address. On the right-hand side there should be instructions for publication; for example, "For immediate release" or "Release Sept. 24th." The body of the release should naturally be typed and double-spaced on 8½″ x 11″ paper, and should begin about one-third of the way down the page, leaving room for a heading or printing instructions to be written in by the editor and his staff. It is best to confine the story to a single page, but if it is longer the pages should be numbered and the word "more" should be typed at the bottom of the page. At the close of the release, the end may be indicated by "End," "30," or "#." Pages should never be coupled together, but a "slug," or identifying heading, should appear at the top left of each successive page. It is important that a paragraph be complete on one page, even if an extra-wide margin must be left at the bottom to avoid starting one that cannot be finished. The reason for this is that the release will be cut up into "takes," which are distributed to different linotype operators for composition. A handy place to cut up the release is at the end of a page, so that if a paragraph is continued from one page to another, part of it is apt to be set into type by one compositor and part by another. This can result in lost sentences, misplaced lines, or incomplete phrases, unless the paragraph is complete on one line.

A news release should be sent to the city editor unless the paper is large enough to have several sectional editors. In that case, the particular news slant of the story will determine whether it should be sent to the city editor, the music editor, the feature editor, the education editor, the Sunday editor, or someone else. The day on which a release is submitted may have a definite effect on whether or not it is used. The supervisor should study his local paper to determine the days when there is heavy or light advertising. Heavy advertising means more news and feature space and consequently more chance of having the story accepted. Do not send a release so that it reaches the editor's desk on Saturday, since papers on this day are very thin. Advertising is saved for a large Sunday newspaper. If an editor receives a story on Saturday, he will most likely hold it over until Monday, and in the meantime something more important might come in that will force the school release into the wastebasket. Stories for the Sunday paper should be specifically marked as such and should be on the editor's desk by Friday noon at the latest. Generally, Friday (because of a slender paper the following day) and Monday are also good days for advertising.

A news release should be sent to all the newspapers in the city. If weeklies are published, the story should reach them early in the week, while submission to the dailies should be held until two days before the weeklies appear. If it is sent earlier to a daily paper, that paper may print the story before the weekly newspaper goes to press, in which case the weekly might drop the story as "old news." If the story is of state or national interest (as when a student wins a substantial award, or the school program is aided by a national foundation), copies of the release may also be sent to the local offices of United Press International and the Associated Press.

National Publications. The music supervisor who has built a solid local program generally has something to say that will be of interest to other teachers throughout the country, or will have a command of musical knowledge that may be of interest to some segment of the general musical audience of the nation. If he is able to write effectively, a national publication in the educational or musical field may be interested in an article by him. The relation of national publications to public relations in the local community may seem remote, but there are two reasons why it is not. First, if the article mentions the local school system, there will be national attention, no matter how slight, drawn to the music program. Secondly, whether or not the article is on music education, the music supervisor, as author, is placed in a position that commands local attention. The impression this makes on the community is favorable to the school regardless of the topic of the article (that is, as long as the topic is favorable), for a good portion of the public will think that the school music program must be important if it is taught by someone whose ideas are published nationally.

Radio and Television. In addition to the use of radio and television for spot "community-service" announcements, there are a number of possibilities for programs involving school groups. Radio stations, for example, may be interested not only in concert programs, but also in broadcasts of music festival events that include several communities, in interviews with school music personnel and students concerning musical issues either directly or non-directly dealing with the school program, or in musical programs narrated by students or a music teacher. Television is well suited for both small ensembles and large groups, and both might even be considered for the same program. Whereas radio stations tend to use school groups on weekends, TV stations can frequently schedule such programs during the week, in the early evening, when airtime is not tied up by network affiliations.

In approaching a station for a possible broadcast, the music supervisor should present definite ideas to the program director and should take along a tape recording by which the students may be auditioned. A program director is generally interested in local talent, including school talent, because of its drawing power; but if he approves the broadcast, he may not have time to prepare a script. It will be up to the supervisor to prepare one for his approval. In selecting material for presentation, it must be remembered that a radio or TV audience is much larger than any audience that hears a school concert, and therefore its background and musical interests are more varied. Furthermore, for a television production, something visual needs to be planned; simply standing and singing can be done just as well for the radio. If the script includes narration, make it simple enough to be understood by the ear alone. Remember that the audience is not reading the script, in which case longer words and more complex sentences might be permissible. Choosing simple but very descriptive words will help.

Since it is necessary to time the program exactly, the program director should be consulted as to the amount of time, excluding commercials, introductions, credits, etc., that will be allowed. When the script involves talking, the supervisor should time how fast he talks and write at the bottom of each page the time it takes to read that far. Then, if the presentation is for radio, as he reads he can check this time against the studio clock to determine whether he should speed the delivery or slow down. Marking the script for emphasis and pausing will also eliminate a good deal of stumbling. Finally, to avoid unnecessary sound, the script should be typed on non-crinkly paper, and the pages should not be attached.

If the performance is taped for television, the procedure will be handled, of course, by the station. However, if it is taped for radio at the school, it is best not to use the final concert performance. Instead, taping sections in rehearsal will eliminate mistakes and audience disturbances.

PROGRAMS OF COMMUNITY INVOLVEMENT

A community music program, involving adult education, is of considerable value to the school music curriculum. Not only does it provide for post-school participation in musical activities, but also it can establish a proper musical climate, develop the creative abilities of the community, raise the community's standards of music appreciation, and promote a more intelligent music public that will take greater interest in the school program.

The Community Music Council. In towns and cities of over 5,000, it may be profitable to form a community music council to coordinate the efforts of existing agencies and organizations. Such a council can provide for an interchange of ideas in developing the cultural, recreational, and civic life of a community, and it can work to promote musical activity in the home, church, industry, and other centers of community life. Furthermore, by coordinating the activities of its member agencies, duplication and conflict can be avoided.

The council should represent a cross-section of the community. Therefore, many people should be called upon to offer guidance in planning: the superintendent of schools, school music supervisors, civic club representatives, the chamber of commerce, church officials, the mayor's office, the director of the city recreation department, youth-centered organizations, women's clubs, veterans' groups, fraternal bodies, and so on. It may be best to establish several main committees to concentrate on special areas; these might include committees on city-wide interests, church music, school music, and adult education. In working out a central calendar of musical events, activities can be correlated not only within the framework of the music program, but also with other cultural and educational programs of the community.

Among the activities which a community council is likely to promote are music festivals, formal concerts, community-wide performance groups, industrial music activities, performances for lodges and clubs, organized concert series, joint concerts with school groups, and musical shows produced in cooperation with dramatic groups.

Adult Education Programs. A community program of adult education in music, which may be organized under the direction of a council or by the school department, is important to the school program because it increases the community's sensitivity to all musical activity and creates an awareness of the need for a strong music program in the schools. The music supervisor may be actively involved in adult education as an instructor of evening and weekend classes or as director of performing organizations.

Classes might be held either in school buildings or in private buildings, such as those owned by councils or the YMCA. Among the most popular classes are those in general music appreciation, the appreciation of music theatre, piano instruction, and in recreational instruments such as the guitar, accordion, or ukulele.

In addition to classes, choral and instrumental performing groups, both large and small, can be organized. A community band, orchestra, and chorus may form the nucleus, but depending on the size of the city there may also be instrumental ensembles, barbershop quartets, and other groups. Whenever his time permits, the music supervisor would profit by participating and offering assistance in the direction of these organizations. However, he should not assume leadership as a conductor unless invited to do so by the participating members. When a group is just being organized, it may be possible to negotiate with the school in the use of music, although a band or chorus should purchase its own music as soon as possible. Depending on the resources of the city and the nature of the organization, a group may be sponsored by a civic organization or by a particular industry; it may be financed by the city recreation department; or it may be self-sustaining through dues.

Whatever its main cultural purpose may be, a community concert series is also a form of adult education that will lend support to the school program. It is often organized by an outside association and established locally by subscription, although the series may be built around local and regional talent rather than national artists. In either case, a concert series can make an important cultural contribution to the community and aid the music supervisor in his work, with comparatively little expense to sponsors.

Another means of educating the community in music is through exhibits and displays. These may be arranged at the library or in local stores so that the public can see pictures and a story of either a phase of the school music program or of some prominent musical figure or activity. A music dealer would probably be willing to set up a display in part of his store window, if it is designed so that it not only creates an interest in the school program but also motivates the passer-by to go into the store. Displays should focus on a single idea that can be grasped in a glance, while detail may be provided to the side or at the bottom. An open exhibit (one that is not encased) may include baskets containing reading matter to be taken. This need not be confined to a discussion of school music; it may be educational material prepared by the music department, such as lists of recommended records and books.

Finally, the music supervisor can promote adult education by encouraging the collection of recordings and books on music at the public library and, if the library is a sizable one, by encouraging its use for talks and chamber performances. The supervisor might also speak to the local music dealers and book shops about stocking music magazines and books. Since music magazines are seldom carried in any but very large music stores, those that do stock them usually find that they sell.

Community Participation in the School Program. A public relations program may be considered successful when it not only interprets the school's activities to the public but also receives the public's support in return. One form of support which can solidify relations is that in which members of the community are brought into the school to contribute their musical talents. Local performers may appear as soloists with school organizations, or members of national groups in the town may be called upon to speak on the music of their homelands. Professional musicians can also be invited for assemblies and music club programs through the Music Performance Trust Fund of the AFM. This fund, which is established by a percentage of recording royalties, pays professional musicians for educational and charitable performances.

When the music supervisor attempts to reach the public by contact with individuals and organizations, by the use of mass media, and by educating the people in their appreciation of music and their awareness of the musical needs of the community, the public relations program of the music department should prove successful.

8

The Effective In-Service Program

When a supervisor steps into a new position he is faced with an immediate problem. He will want to set up the program which he feels is best for his particular community, but at the same time he will have to work with the music staff under the existing program until he can implement whatever changes are desired. The processes of helping teachers through an in-service program and developing the curriculum must go on at the same time.

The first step, naturally, is to analyze the program that is underway to determine what there is to work with. Then, while recognizing the good that has gone before, the supervisor should begin immediately to build anew upon the strong features of the program. Regardless of whether new curriculum proposals can or should be started right away, teachers will need help. So, as soon as possible, an informal staff meeting should be called to meet each group with which he will be working, to find out what problems are most pressing at the moment, and to gain the staff's cooperation in planning a program of service. It should be made clear at the outset that the supervisor is willing to help in any way possible, but that he is also in a position to learn from others and is therefore open to and in need of suggestions.

At an early conference with his music teachers, some decisions should be made and plans put into operation. With the cooperation of the staff, problems may be singled out for group action. The individual problem will determine to some extent the procedures that must be taken. Some of the techniques that may be decided upon to provide for teacher growth and improve the learning situation are: (1) classroom visitation by the supervisor; (2) observations by teachers; (3) conferences with individual teachers; (4) demonstration lessons; (5) teachers meetings; (6) grade-level meetings; (7) committee studies on curriculum development, and participation in formulating school policies; (8) workshops; (9) bulletins and other course guides; (10) guided experiments with new materials or procedures; (11) committee surveys of student needs, attitudes, interests, etc.; and (12) guided reading in the professional library.

The in-service program should not be planned by the music supervisor alone. There are two major reasons for using cooperative effort in its design. First, through group participation there will be far more ideas offered, much more imagination used, and a much greater awareness of problems evidenced than any one person can call forth by himself. Secondly, by participating in the planning, teachers will be more willing to accept the program, will be more aware of its purposes and values, and will be more cooperative in its operation.

Cooperative planning can begin by having the teachers organize and sometimes preside at meetings in which the program is drawn up. The teachers may draw up a list of problems which should be considered, and may elect committees to determine how they should be handled. These committees can make reports to regular staff meetings on the plans of action which they have devised. Perhaps the best way to start is to work with the teachers and administration in developing a statement of philosophy and what they hope to accomplish. From here, work may be organized at first to study those problems which are recurrent. Flexibility in the program can be encouraged by allowing some of the teachers to experiment with new materials or techniques; their experiences may then be reported to the entire staff for further use.

The teachers should be given the opportunity to work on phases of the program in which they are most interested. These will usually be areas in which they have been most successful. Recognizing the special abilities of each member of the staff can do much to increase the effectiveness of group planning.

When committees are formed, their functions should be precisely defined. The group should realize its relationship to other groups and the limitations of its operations. It is not necessary, of course, to form a new committee for each problem that arises; existing groups may still be used as long as responsibilities are spread fairly. In certain instances, committees may also solicit the aid of students and parents. When solutions are suggested, they should be presented to the entire staff for consideration before a final decision on action is made. Group decisions, rather than those of the supervisor alone, are to be worked for whenever possible. In order to get things moving early, however, the supervisor will probably have to make some tentative decisions until the group is organized.

VISITATION

A visit to the classroom by supervisors is one of the basic techniques employed in the in-service program, and is made by the director as well as by an elementary music supervisor or the music consultant in charge of a certain area of instruction. The latter two will generally cover only the elementary classes, while the director will also take in classes taught by members of the music faculty at the secondary level. In the elementary school, where it is customary for the classroom teacher to handle the daily music work (in addition to regular lessons with a music specialist), a supervisory visit may be on a regularly-scheduled basis, unannounced, or made at the call of the teacher.

Unannounced appearances should be avoided since these tend usually to make the teacher apprehensive. Although there is nothing wrong with on-call visitation, the program should not rest on this alone, since counsel is rarely sought by the teacher who really needs it. Some sort of regular schedule should thus be arrived at.

During one of these visits, the supervisor may do the actual teaching himself or observe the classroom teacher in action. If the supervisor teaches, the classroom teacher will have the opportunity of seeing a number of techniques applied to a real situation. On the other hand, an observation by the supervisor will provide him with some idea of where the teacher is in need of help. For this purpose, it is handy to have a check-list to mark during the course of the observation. However, jotting down marks in a book can be quite distressing to the teacher, unless she knows beforehand and approves of what is being done. At some time before the observation, preferably in a group meeting with all the teachers involved, the form of the check-list may be worked out. The teachers' own ideas can then be incorporated in it. Generally, the list will cover problems pertaining to singing, reading, directed listening, class response, motivation, and so on.

A classroom observation sheet might include a check-list similar to that given below. On the front side of the sheet are specific items related to the various activities the supervisor is likely to observe. Some of these items apply only to the teacher's musical understanding and skills, some only to the students', and others apply to both. Therefore, two columns are provided (marked "T" and "S") for reference to either the teacher's or the students' work. In these columns the supervisor can write the numeral one, indicating "excellent work"; the numeral two, indicating "good or competent work"; or the numeral three, indicating that he can make some suggestion for improving a particular item. To the right is a column for more specific comments and suggestions if necessary. This part of the list is for checking during the observation.

On the reverse side of the sheet are general items relating to lesson organization, teaching, and class response. These can be checked in just a few minutes *after* the lesson has been completed. With such a detailed list, it is obvious that all the items on both sides cannot be checked, nor would all be applicable to any one lesson. To comment on everything or even a major portion would require that the supervisor give more attention to the list than to the lesson. This is not the purpose, however. The check-list is simply a time-saving guide to enable the supervisor to comment on anything he feels deserves attention.

CLASSROOM OBSERVATION SHEET

School _____ Teacher _____ Grade ____ Date _____

Key: 1 — Excellent
     2 — Good
     3 — Make suggestion for improvement

	T	S	Comment
Singing Activities			
Procedure in teaching new song			
Use of pitchpipe			
Class response			
Correct pitches			
Correct rhythms			
Tone quality			
Expressive singing			
Sureness in part-singing			
Balance and blend			
Use of accompaniment			
Other _____			
Playing Activities			
Choice of instruments for accompaniment			
Use of piano			
Use of bells			
Use of flutes			
Use of Autoharp			
Use of percussion instruments			
Other _____			
Listening Activities			
Listening objective			
Clarity of presentation			
Class response			
Identification of elements			
Choice of recording			
Other _____			
Reading Activities			
Main objective			

Clarity of presentation
Class response
Application of symbols to
  sounds
Naming key
Naming meter
Naming notes
Use of syllables
Use of numbers
Other _____

Other Activities
Creating melody
Creating accompaniment
Dancing
Free movement
Other _____

Reverse side or second evaluation sheet:

General Observations

Organization of Lesson   *Comment*
Purpose of lesson (nature of
  musical learning)
Length of lesson
Relation to other lessons
Variety in lesson
Use of familiar material
Use of new material
Continuity in lesson
Level of material
Suitability of selections
Teacher's understanding of
  material
Use of audio-visual aids

Teaching
Motivating factors
Clarity of presentation
Accuracy of presentation
Application of materials
Amount of "doing" rather
  than "talking"
Awareness of individual and
  class problems

Need for restful activity
Need for physical activity

Class Results
Class interest and response
Involvement of entire class
Musicality of performance
Success of class performance

Strong points: Weak points:

During a visitation, a supervisor should focus his attention on three main things: teacher, learners, and materials being used. Each of these areas is covered in the sample observation list above. In regard to the teacher, classroom observation may be combined with other knowledge to evaluate the factors in an individual teacher's growth. These are generally environmental, personal, mental, morale, and learning factors. The organization of a lesson, the materials used, and the attitude and response of the class may indicate specific changes which the supervisor will want to suggest.

CONFERENCES

Individual conferences with teachers may result from a visitation by the supervisor or may be called for especially by the teacher herself. The conference might then center around a need which the supervisor has detected, or it may be based on a reaction that has arisen from the teacher's own observations or discussions in meetings. When the need is sensed by the teacher herself, the conference is likely to be more fruitful.

In such a conference, it is much better for the supervisor to point out to the teacher strengths rather than weaknesses. This will help to build her confidence, and the supervisor can still help her to improve the weaknesses without calling attention to them. Above all, the supervisor must be tactful; otherwise, the conference can do more harm than good. By giving credit where it is due, by offering positive, constructive suggestions, and by being professional in every respect, a proper attitude may be achieved.

It is important to create within the teacher a desire to be helped. This can be brought about by helping her to analyze and evaluate her own teaching. A guide may be drawn up for her to use after teaching a music lesson in order to evaluate herself. This might include such questions as the following:

1. Did the lesson have a definite purpose? What was I trying to do?
2. Did my plan achieve its objectives? If not, what was wrong with it?
3. Were the materials used effective?
4. If something did not go over, did I try a different approach?
5. Did the class respond favorably?
6. How could I have reached those that did not respond?
7. Was the lesson enjoyable?

The teacher might suggest other questions that can be added to these.

By the end of the conference, the supervisor should have offered some definite suggestions for teaching or provided some useful resources. A follow-up conference or visitation of some sort should be scheduled at the same time to check on progress.

OBSERVATIONS AND DEMONSTRATIONS

Having a teacher observe a music lesson can sometimes put across concepts that are more difficult to understand in written or spoken form. The observation may be of the music supervisor during one of his classroom visits, but it may also be of other teachers in the school who are doing particularly good jobs with music instruction. Sometimes it is possible for an outstanding teacher to take over another's class for the music lesson until such time as the regular classroom teacher feels capable of handling it herself. Intervisitation may also extend beyond the immediate school to other schools in the system. It might also be arranged for a group of teachers to observe a class in a neighboring system where significant work is being done. Field trips to concerts, music lectures, special clinics, and conferences are other possibilities for observation of music activities.

Teachers may also take advantage of special demonstrations of audio-visual aids and new materials. Demonstrations should be based on the needs of a particular group of teachers, and a survey should be taken to see what materials they want most to see demonstrated. This may be done with the entire staff of a school or it may be focused at a particular grade level throughout the system. In some instances, it is profitable to simulate actual classroom conditions, whereas in other cases a demonstration under ideal conditions is best to make certain procedures clear.

When a teacher has revealed particular talents with the item to be demonstrated, it is useful to have *her* present the program rather than the supervisor. In this way, other teachers will see that they are probably not incapable of doing the same thing. Regardless of who conducts the demonstration, though, the supervisor should not feel that what is obvious to him in a presentation will automatically be clear to everyone watching. Some sort of outline or check-list of what is presented should be provided for the teachers to follow. Following the demonstration, there should be time allowed for group discussion to clarify any points necessary. In addition, provisions should be made during the meeting, as well as after the demonstration has been given, for the teachers to actually try their hand at the same thing.

Some of the more common subjects of demonstration clinics are the use of audio-visual materials, such as the phonograph, tape recorder, and correlated filmstrips and recordings; instruments, such as the Autoharp, Tonette, bells, and rhythm devices; and the issuance of new materials, such as music book series or recordings.

BULLETINS

During the course of conferences, teachers' meetings, and visitations, the supervisor will perhaps notice that certain problems more than others are faced by a number of teachers. He may wish to consider such problems in the form of a bulletin that offers suggestions. However, bulletins need not deal only with problems. They may be used as references to source materials, to clarify policies and aims, announce a series of meetings or special music programs, suggest possible units of study, recommend new materials and how to use them, and any number of items. If, for example, an elementary teacher uses some special materials, a bulletin on their use could be prepared for other teachers who might be able to apply the same approach. Sub-titling such a bulletin "As used in Miss Jones' 3rd grade class" could make it of special interest to the other teachers, who would recognize the fact that these materials had proven successful for one of their own associates.

To be effective, a bulletin should be given special treatment to distinguish it from the ordinary announcement or notice. Otherwise, it may not be read. First, it should be fairly short and limited to one major item. It should make specific points, and be arranged in semi-outline form for quick reference by teachers. The format should be informal but attractive, with a lively style and an interesting title. If it is concerned with a matter of lasting importance, it may be desirable to have the bulletin printed by an inexpensive form of lithography, rather than to have it mimeographed.

Although it is not always possible when the circulation of a bulletin is wide, it is best to distribute it in person, for then the teacher is apt to pay more attention to it. Teachers should be encouraged to file these bulletins for future reference, and to suggest subjects for future bulletins. If the paper is well organized, these bulletins later may be of considerable use to the supervisor and the staff in compiling an instructional guide.

PROFESSIONAL LIBRARY FOR CLASSROOM TEACHERS

One of the supervisory offerings that seems to be most welcomed by teachers is the provision of a professional library within the school. Although most systems maintain a library at the central office, this is of little use to the teacher who does not wish to travel to that office or to wait for the circulation of a particular book. A small selection of literature is therefore quite useful within the individual school. Some book topics which teachers might like available are:

1. Instruction in piano chording and playing the Autoharp.
2. Background information on music.
3. Resource units.
4. Lists of recommended recordings and correlated materials.
5. Music terminology.
6. Suggestions for teaching different phases of the music program.

In addition, music periodicals and children's books on music may also be provided.

With a professional library in the school, the supervisor may then suggest specific readings for self-help during a conference with a teacher or in bulletins dealing with special problems.

TEACHERS' MEETINGS

Monthly or bi-monthly faculty meetings are established procedure in most school systems, often with school being in session for only half of the day or cancelled entirely. After general conferences between building principals and their staffs, there are usually department meetings, allowing the supervisor to gather all of his music personnel together. In special cases, the music faculty can also convene during the afternoon of a regular school day, if other activities permit. Many such teachers' meetings, unfortunately, are called together with a purpose but without organization. Consequently, they tend to become rather boring, and teachers do not look forward to them with any interest. Meetings can be organized, however, with interest and effectiveness by applying a few simple considerations, such as the following:

1. *Planning the meeting.* A meeting should be called together with a definite purpose in mind — something the teachers themselves consider of importance. In fact, the teachers themselves may help choose the topic through a planning committee, membership in which should be changed frequently. Once a topic has been chosen, an agenda of items to consider should be drawn up, duplicated, and circulated to the staff before

the meeting is held, in order that they may have time to formulate some ideas on what is to be discussed. By using a planning committee, the supervisor may make suggestions, but his ideas will not be imposed on the group.

Of course, in the case of a pressing need or a last-moment situation demanding immediate attention, the supervisor can take one of the following steps: (1) take time from the planned agenda to bring up the matter; (2) if the new problem requires considerable time for discussion, postpone discussion of the other topics until the next scheduled meeting; or (3) if neither the new problem nor the planned topics can be postponed, call an additional special meeting for one of the next few days.

2. *Setting up the meeting.* The meeting should be held in a room with an informal atmosphere, comfortable furniture, and flexible arrangement. A classroom is not suitable. The arrangement should be such that no person is isolated from the rest and that each teacher is in direct view of everyone else. A pad of paper and pencil should be provided for each person, with a blackboard for the leader if necessary. Since thoughts flow and decisions are made more easily when tension is relieved, coffee might be provided and smoking permitted. In addition, the time of the meeting should be other than after school, except in emergencies, as this is not a very creative time of the day. Usually there are provisions to release teachers for special meetings, and a special series of meetings on curriculum building may even be scheduled for the summer, immediately after the closing of school.

3. *Conducting the meeting.* Although the supervisor is generally the chairman of a meeting, this is not always necessary. If an individual teacher has been working on a particular problem, the director could contribute ideas just as well from the sidelines, letting the teacher conduct the procedure. However, as chairman, the supervisor can facilitate the effectiveness of the meeting in several ways. First, he should be certain that the purpose of the meeting is clear in everyone's mind, that the group knows where it is at present and where it is trying to go. A relaxed atmosphere should be set, in which the members feel both free and responsible to contribute. It is up to the chairman to decide which ideas are worth further discussion; however, he should not try to cut anything short by giving a single answer to a problem. The group ought to be allowed to do its own thinking.

The supervisor can help the flow of discussion by keeping the main points before the group, by summarizing thoughts, drawing relationships, and keeping the group on the topic. When the discussion wanders to an interesting and important area, it can be put up to the whole group to decide which line to follow for the moment. It is important that terms be defined so that everyone is dealing with the same thing. When a point needs clarification, the director should ask for such, since others may also be confused about the meaning. Contributions that cannot be accepted fully ought to be challenged, although the director must be careful to respect minority viewpoints. In fact, whenever the chairman is aware of them, ideas that are not adequately presented should be slated for further discussion.

It is best to draw out all ideas first — impractical or not — before the "how" of any problem is approached. These may be noted on a blackboard for everyone to keep in view. By watching the faces of members who have not spoken, the supervisor may be able to detect a certain reaction that indicates the individual has something to offer. (The same technique, of course, may also indicate signs of boredom, thus suggesting different steps to be taken.) When everything is out, it is a good idea to restate the problem and the possible solutions to see if some agreement can be reached. Final decisions must not always be made immediately; however, it is best to take some action before the end of the meeting, even if it is only to refer the problem to a committee for further study. If a committee is needed, members should be chosen for their particular capabilities in regard to the stated problem. The committee should be small enough for an exchange of ideas, and an agenda for their work (including when they must make a report) should be provided.

4. *Following the meeting.* Immediately after the meeting, an evaluation should be made to determine what worked, what did not work, and what should be done next time. Secondly, a written summary, of what was discussed and subsequent steps that are being taken, should be circulated to everyone who was present at the meeting.

WORKSHOPS

Workshops provide opportunities for teachers to see in action many techniques that the supervisor may have talked about in conferences. Teachers should contribute to the planning of a workshop so that it will serve an interest that has arisen out of their own experiences. The specific needs for such a meeting may be determined through individual conferences, by the circulation of a questionnaire, or through a need which the supervisor has observed in his rounds. Once a specific need has been determined, it must be decided for whom the work will be planned. It may, for example, be designed for a particular level, for all teachers in a specified area of the curriculum, for a single school, or for teachers at a given level throughout the school system.

A committee can then proceed with arrangements for time and space, clearing the project through the proper channels (the administration, of course, should be in on the planning), and checking for conflicts with other activities. The same committee may also work on promoting the workshop so that there will be a good turn-out.

The next step is in working out the actual content of the workshop and its procedure. Materials should be determined, including not only those to be used in the demonstration, but also outlines for the teachers to follow. Here, it should be remembered that teachers who take time to attend a workshop (usually in the afternoon after school) are interested in specific ideas they can put to work in their classrooms. This is no place for talking, but for *doing*. Therefore, some provision should be made for making the audience *participants* in the work, through singing, playing rhythmic accompaniments, etc. It may even be desirable to have a capable teacher do the actual teaching involved, with assistance from the supervisor or any others who are needed. Professional people from outside the system may also be called in, for a fee, if they offer unique talents. This, in fact, might create the extra interest that is needed to put the workshop over.

Time should be allowed, following the presentation, for group discussion and experimentation with the materials used. Within a few days, the committee should evaluate the work that was done and determine what follow-up assistance is necessary. A second, brief questionnaire, with space for general comments and suggestions, may be circulated to the participants to aid in the evaluation.

9

Implementation and Development of the Curriculum

Once a curriculum or any part of it has been designed, it must be put into operation; and once in operation, it must be molded, improved, and constantly remodeled to serve the changing needs of changing students. This means selecting appropriate teaching materials for each type of experience; providing resource ideas, teaching aids, and guides for the staff; and developing means of evaluating both the students' achievements and the success of the program as reflected in their achievement.

CURRICULUM GUIDES

Although there are a number of means by which the supervisor will seek to implement the program he and his colleagues have drawn up, one of the more popular devices is the curriculum guide. A course of study, naturally, may be worked out at various levels of the school program, with a syllabus outlined for individual courses, but the curriculum guide (with suggestions for teaching) is especially practical at the elementary level for use by classroom teachers and music specialists alike.

The guide may be set up under the direction of the supervisor, but it is important that the committee include more than supervisory personnel. A classroom teacher to represent the primary grades and another for the upper elementary level (or better still, one for each grade) can contribute many suggestions of use to teachers that the supervisor might not otherwise think of. However, once the materials have been accumulated for the guide and their organization decided upon, the actual writing should be done by one person rather than a committee. This will serve to unify the style and readability of the text.

Curriculum guides vary in format, depending upon what the committee feels should be included. Generally, its contents will include the following items:

1. A statement of the aims and objectives of the music program.
2. A visual plan showing the scope of the program and the sequence of instruction.

3. Implications for the music teacher of the physical, emotional, and mental characteristics of students at various ages.

4. A list of desirable experiences and anticipated learnings in different areas of the program and at different grade levels, arranged to provide for sequential growth. This may be presented in individual graded sections, or it may be in one place in cross-chart form.

5. Suggestions for teaching activities of various kinds.

6. Lists of resources, including songs in book series, recordings, films, instruments, etc.

7. Suggestions on how the teacher can evaluate her work in class. (This may include a check-list similar to the one discussed in Chapter 8.)

In the resource section there are many ways of organizing materials. An excellent procedure is to devise certain categories of experiences within the basic areas of singing, playing, and listening — experiences in reading skills, listening skills, creating accompaniments, using melodic and rhythmic instruments, exploring harmony, and so on. In addition, songs and recordings may be listed according to selected classifications, with a parallel structure maintained through sections for each grade. In this way, materials can be arranged to represent a definite plan for developmental growth within each area and each specific type of experience. For example, resources may be listed under:

Mood (calm and restful; light and happy; sad, mournful, or melancholy; fun-filled and humorous; mysterious; bright and active; triumphant and rejoiceful; boisterous and mischievous)

Type (programmatic, descriptive, absolute)

Aural concepts (fast and slow, high and low, loud and soft, legato and staccato)

Musical forms (binary, ternary, rondo, suite, march, overture, theme and variations, etc.)

Dance forms (minuet, waltz, gigue, polka, tango, ballet, country, interpretive)

Instruments (to represent sections and individual instruments of the band and orchestra)

Voice types (soprano, contralto, tenor, baritone, bass, chorus, duets, trios, quartets)

Special days (Hallowe'en, Thanksgiving, Christmas, etc.)

Related subjects (music about animals, toys, the sea, times of the day, seasons, vehicles)

Composers

Special units (the home, the community, America, foreign countries, etc.)

Some guides include information for administrators as well, on planning, designing, and evaluating activities, and on providing needed time and resources. There may also be materials specifically for the classroom teacher to help her understand the components of music and develop her musical skills. Information on the use of the pitchpipe, playing the Autoharp or Song-flute, organizing a listening lesson, or teaching a song in parts can prove very valuable to the teacher who has had little background in music. Curriculum guides are also quite useful at the junior-high level for general music classes. Here the resources are usually organized in special units.

Since guides are compiled for reference over a long period of time, they should be attractively laid out and published to withstand wear. Many are simply mimeographed and bound in a spiral column. However, since the document will be issued in quantity, an inexpensive form of lithography can produce a printed work of better appearance for relatively little cost. Although printing will depend on the budget available, reproduction by the multilith process is well worth the expense, and is much more suitable than a mimeographed product.

SUPPLEMENTARY BULLETINS

As good as a curriculum guide can be, it will not cover everything that the teacher needs to teach music. From time to time the supervisor will realize there are certain problems that require special techniques and procedures that could not be covered in the guide. Situations will occur, too, which could not possibly be anticipated, and a teacher may request information that will be of value to the entire staff. The supervisor may want to supplement the guide with resource lists compiled for special units or with results of experimental studies that have been underway. For these purposes and others, special bulletins may be issued. Bulletins of a lasting nature should be carefully prepared and duplicated, and provision should be made for assembling them in a collection. Then, these may be consulted not only for day-to-day occasions, but also at a time when the curriculum guide is being revised. Some of the topics for such bulletins might be:

1. Understanding the basic aims of the music program.
2. Special techniques for teaching singing.
3. Helping the uncertain singer.
4. Assembly singing.
5. Special techniques for teaching music reading.
6. Understanding rhythm.
7. Class projects in writing songs.

8. What makes musical experiences creative ones.
9. Teaching songs in parts.
10. Suggested procedures for the listening lesson.
11. How to use instruments to accompany songs in classes.
12. How to play the Autoharp.
13. Choral techniques.
14. Rehearsal techniques.
15. Conducting for classroom teachers.
16. Keyboard exploration in the primary grades.
17. Special instrumental techniques.
18. Source materials for special units.
19. Recommended basic repertoire for elementary classes.
20. Recommended new materials and how the teacher can use them.
21. Guides to special programs and broadcasts.
22. Preparation for festival events.
23. Recommended units for general music classes.
24. Syllabus for instruction on individual instruments.
25. Syllabus for a music theory course.
26. Syllabus for a music history and appreciation course.
27. Suggestions for special seasonal programs.
28. Techniques for small instrumental repairs.
29. Lists of materials in the music library.
30. Recommended children's books on music.
31. Lists of audio-visual materials.
32. Evaluation forms.
33. Music interest surveys.

SELECTING TEXTBOOKS

The selection of textbooks requires, first of all, the consideration of what is needed in terms of what must be done. Secondly, the students' ability to understand the material must be considered, and provision must be made here for individual differences. The content must be of permanent value, providing both balance and variety so that it is adaptable to a number of situations; and the organization of material — its arrangement and the convenience with which special content may be located — should be taken into account. The supervisor will also want to consider the attractiveness of its make-up, the interest of its literary style, its clarity, and durability.

The selection of a basic music book series for the elementary schools and for general music classes in junior high involves a good deal of thought and investigation. In recent years, revised editions and new series have presented many interesting and generally fine programs for developing musical skills through graded material. These have been written and compiled around certain philosophies of music education, which the director will want to examine to find the program best suited to his needs. Unfortunately, despite good intentions, fine teaching suggestions, and attractive layouts, there is a major fault in most of the available series: the use of dull, contrived musical material to introduce certain concepts or experiences such as scalar patterns, melodic jumps of a particular interval, music to correlate with George Washington's birthday, etc. The lack of really interesting, musical, and aesthetic tunes, that relate to students' needs, abilities, and interests (in terms of style and of text) at each grade level, is a pressing concern for music education. Some series editors have tried to overcome this problem by including specially written songs which are often as poor as older material; others have relied heavily on folk music, the quality of which is just as variable. The supervisor, then, must study the books carefully to determine which has the best music as well as the desired approach and philosophy.

In evaluating a series, the following factors should be considered:

1. General philosophy of the series as a whole.
2. Selection of song literature.
   a. Balanced amount of folk music.
   b. Music by great composers.
   c. Music by contemporary composers and in modern idioms.
   d. Songs for use in units.
   e. Singing games and action songs.
   f. Well-known traditional material.
   g. Religious music, such as chorales and spirituals.
   h. Music of the popular idiom.
   i. Music related to student interests at each grade level.
3. Opportunities to develop special skills.
   a. Use of proper vocal ranges and appropriate tessituras.
   b. Material suitable for a variety of vocal activities.
   c. Intelligent approach to music reading, with graded materials.
   d. Songs to sing in harmony.
   e. Parts to conserve tenor voices in junior high books.
   f. Rhythmic material.
   g. Songs lending themselves to instrumental applications.
4. Provision for instrumental performance.
   a. Use of chord symbols for the piano.
   b. Regular piano accompaniments.
   c. Autoharp accompaniments.
   d. Rhythmic and melodic accompaniments.
5. Correlation with listening lessons.
   a. Lists of related compositions.
   b. Material on composers.
   c. Material on types and styles of music.
   d. Information on instruments.
   e. Special units.

6. Special aids for the teacher.
   a. Organization of teacher's edition
   b. Suggestions for teaching different songs.
   c. Help on scales, key signatures, etc.
   d. Background material on songs.
   e. Recordings for use in teaching songs in the books.
7. Appearance and durability.
   a. Inclusion of pictures, poems, etc.
   b. Use of color.
   c. Ease in handling.
   d. Clarity for reading.
   e. Good binding.
   f. Good paper and printing.
   g. Durable covers.

Selecting texts for special courses such as music history and theory at the high school is a still more difficult task. Of the small number of books written for this area and level, most are weak in content and organization. Others, written primarily for college use, tend to be too comprehensive or technical. The particular arrangement of the course in each school — the desired chronological or unit approach — will automatically eliminate many books that follow a different procedure. Others may be of use only in certain parts. Until appropriate material is made available, the individual director may deem it wiser to use no textbook in class at all, but to stock the school library with a variety of specialized books for related reading assignments.

There are fewer problems in choosing instruction books for class instruments. In reviewing this type of material, the following items need consideration:

1. Information and pictures on assembling the instrument.
2. Information on the care of the instrument.
3. Pictures showing clearly the correct handling of the instrument, hand positions, embouchure, and posture.
4. Material on the principles of tone production.
5. An explanation of notational symbols, staves, and musical terms.
6. Fingering charts.
7. A logical, sequential arrangement of learnings, with well-paced progression to more difficult skills.
8. Clear directions and use of markings for fingering, phrasing, bowing, etc.
9. Musical and melodic interest of exercises and tunes.
10. Inclusion of music for ensemble performance.
11. A functional, clear layout.

SELECTING MUSIC

Music for instrumental and vocal groups should be selected by the teachers in charge of directing these organizations since they know best what the students' capabilities and needs are. Nevertheless, orders for music will be placed through the music supervisor, and at that time the supervisor should check to see that the selection is balanced. A variety can be achieved by using both secular and sacred works; folk, popular, and art music; a cappella and accompanied pieces in the case of vocal music; and selections from different periods of music history.

With the vast amount of music available today in all the basic vocal and instrumental media, there is no need for any teacher to use music of inferior quality in a blind attempt to find something that appeals to his students. There is good music of many types, and when selections are combined in a balanced variety, the interests and taste of every student can be reached. This does not mean that the repertoire should be confined to the works of the classical masters. Equating the term "good music" with the classical field in an absolute sense is wrong and may explain why teachers who only occasionally select something outside this field to please their students often choose poor examples. There is no such thing as good and bad music in an absolute sense. Aside from the matter of personal taste (*i.e.,* what is good to one person may not be so to another), these terms are only valid in a comparative sense, and then only *within* each basic type of music.

One should not look for the same things in listening to classical music as in listening to jazz or folk or popular. Each type has its own tradition of accepted practices, and each requires a different set of criteria. The elements of good jazz, in other words, are not the elements of a good classical sonata. In selecting music, the teacher needs to familiarize himself with the standards in each field. He should also keep in mind the intended purpose of each work, since he cannot expect music to be what the composer did not intend it to be. (Music written to accompany a tap dance, for example, is better music in that area than a Beethoven symphony.) From this standpoint, it is possible to find both good and poor music in each basic category: classical, popular, jazz, folk, theatre music. And the good in each field is worthy of study. The supervisor, then, requires a knowledge of many types of music so that he can oversee not only a balanced representation of styles, but also a good selection from each style.

In regard to choosing music from different historical eras, the present period deserves more consideration than it has received. The fact that many courses in music history never reach beyond the beginning of the twentieth century reflects an attitude that is too prevalent throughout music education programs. Contemporary music is often overlooked in schools, partly because teachers do not know enough about it themselves, sometimes because they may not know how to judge it, or because there is so much other music of great worth that they feel there is no need to bother. There is a great deal of fine music of the twentieth century, however, and much of it by American composers. It deserves a place within the school curriculum. Unfortunately, many schools limit a representation of the current scene to selections from musical comedies.

The supervisor can promote contemporary music in several ways. He can call to the attention of his band, orchestra, and choral directors, music that is of worth to their groups. He may even schedule a concert, including all these groups, devoted entirely to contemporary writing. Several selections may be chosen for festival performances, and works by regional and university composers can be solicited (and whenever possible, commissioned).

Recordings of newer works should be stocked in the library for use in general music classes, and bulletins on their styles, composers, forms, and so on, can be prepared for circulation to teachers. One of these bulletins may be simply a listing of recommended contemporary works.

Although a number of contemporary works are beyond the capabilities of school performers, there are nevertheless a number of compositions that are interesting, challenging, and playable. Some, in fact, are easier to play or sing than they appear and sound.

ENRICHING INSTRUCTION

Audio-Visual Aids. The use of multi-sensory aids can increase the effectiveness of music teaching in a number of ways. First, they can create interest and stimulate response simply by being a "change of pace" and preventing the learning situation from becoming routine. Secondly, they can increase the ways in which a student can perceive what is being taught. For example, if a chart with a melodic pattern is placed before a student who is playing a set of bells, he will experience that pattern in three ways: by seeing it in notation on the chart, by seeing the relation of the notes on the set of bells, and, of course, by actually hearing what the pattern sounds like. By approaching something through several forms of sensory perception, the student's understanding will be much more concrete. Furthermore, what the student may miss in a presentation by one method, he may grasp through the use of another aid. Audio-visual aids serve the function of turning words or verbal descriptions into meaningful experiences.

Aids such as FM radio, television, and recordings can introduce the student to programs of types of music that would otherwise be beyond his capability. The tape recorder can be used for any number of ideas, from making special arrangements for class use to taping supplementary lessons for the classroom teacher, from adding accompaniments for singing to letting the students hear their own performances for self-evaluation, and from taping short sections of works in close sequence for comparison and contrast to recording demonstration material for the in-service program. (It must be remembered, however, that tape recording is a form of reproduction, and therefore taping must be done within the limits of the copyright law.)

More care must be taken in selecting a tape recorder than in choosing most audio-visual equipment, for the typical home recorder which many schools use is not of high enough quality to record music without distortion. Specifications to look for include an instant stop switch, sound-on-sound (for adding parts without erasure of previously-recorded material), speed selections including 7½ inches per second (ips) (3¾ ips is too slow for recording music; 15 ips is used by professionals for better fidelity), at least two magnetic heads (for recording and playback), output jacks for speakers and headphones, input jacks for microphones (and if desired, an input to record from non-microphone sources), and a frequency response of at least 30 to 16,000 hz $\pm$ 2 db. This last item is important. The human ear is capable of hearing sounds ranging from 16 hz to 20,000 hz, but the upper frequencies are lost except to very young ears. For musical purposes, it is important to have a recorder that can record the fundamental pitch of the lowest note on the piano (about 27.5 hz), as well as the overtones (up to about 15,000 hz) that give identifying timbres to instruments. Since the ear is unlikely to hear variations in sound levels of three decibels louder or softer, $\pm$ 3 db is a good specification on frequency response; $\pm$ 2 db is better. It is important, too, to select quality microphones and speakers; a recorder with good frequency response is of little value when the microphone being used only records to 7,500 cps. Similarly, poor speakers will limit the sounds heard no matter how good the recording is.

The advantages and uses of most audio-visual materials are obvious and need not be stated here. Some of the more common aids which the director may want to use are:

Records and phonographs (with three or four speeds)
Tape recorders
Pre-recorded tapes
FM radio
Television
Motion pictures

Filmstrips
Still pictures (instruments, composers, musicians)
Photographs
Charts (scales, keys, tonal and rhythmic patterns, note values, the
     keyboard, periods of music history, seating plans, etc.)
Slides
Opaque projections
Overhead transparencies
Chalkboards
Music staff boards
Display and bulletin boards
Three-dimensional models (orchestra, band)
Books and magazines on music for children

It is important that quality equipment be used. It is far better, for example, to spend a little more to purchase an even-running phonograph that will reproduce sound faithfully than to pay less for an inferior machine so that something else may be purchased along with it. Bulletins on the care and use of such materials should be circulated to the teachers, and a formal procedure for distribution should be established.

Closed-Circuit Television. Educational television today is no longer limited to broadcasts by professional non-commercial stations. In recent years there has been a rapid development in the use of closed-circuit television within the schools. Studios, set up in high schools or in separate buildings, are now broadcasting regular and special programs to classrooms throughout school systems. There are numerous possibilities here for music education. On a regular schedule, a basic grade-level program by a music specialist can be broadcast to each elementary classroom weekly, either as a central activity or as supplementary material. There may also be special programs as occasions arise, broadcast to selected schools or to the entire school population.

The closed-circuit studio makes it possible to present performers who are unable to go into a number of schools personally; it can show models that cannot be taken into the classroom and can magnify materials too small for practical classroom use; it can simplify instrumental demonstrations designed to interest students in beginning instruction by making the demonstration a one-time operation; and it can present concerts by the high school chorus or orchestra for the lower grades, or share the talent of special elementary groups with their peers in other schools.

From the standpoint of the elementary school program, closed-circuit television is perhaps best used to teach basic music appreciation lessons to a number of classes at the same time. Some of these, if well planned and produced, can be put on video tape for repeated use. Since the TV teacher lacks personal contact with the students during the presentation, the advisability of lessons requiring simultaneous performance in the classroom (teaching a song, for example) is questionable. This is a type of activity that requires the teacher to be with the students to guide them in their singing. But programs about composers, types of music, music of other countries, and demonstrations of instruments and voices can all be presented effectively, with follow-up lessons in the individual rooms.

Television, then, is not a substitute for personal contact; it is only an aid to supplement the teacher's work in the classroom. It does, however, save valuable time in presenting certain types of experiences to large groups of students, and is a fine outlet for student performance within the school.

Integration and Correlation. Both integration and correlation play a part in the enrichment of the learning process. Integration is the process by which music takes on meaning for an individual in relation to other facets of his life. Music can be an integrating factor by increasing a person's cultural perspective, making him sensitive to various emotions, developing his awareness of aesthetic experiences, and by other means. It should not be confused with "correlation." While integration concerns the inter-relationships within the person, correlation refers to the relationships between different subject matter.

Correlation may be between music and another subject, such as science (as in studying the properties of sound) or history (for example, music about the Napoleonic Wars, Abraham Lincoln, or Billy the Kid); or, it may be between several aspects of music itself (*singing* a sea chantey and *listening* to a description of the sea in Debussy's *La Mer*).

Music should always be taught in such a way that it is an integrative force. Correlative teaching, on the other hand, may be profitable in some cases and inadvisable in others (when relationships are contrived). Many classroom teachers like to teach units in which they can relate work they are doing in two or more subjects, and in junior high school, unit work within the general music class is commonly found. The supervisor can help in this line by suggesting areas in which units may be done, or by providing resource materials when a teacher is doing a special project.

In the lower grades, units are usually built around the home and immediate community; in the fifth grade it is typical to study America, and in the sixth grade, other countries. Special resources may be supplied to the teachers in order to relate music to these areas. Within music itself, work can be organized around types of music, styles, dance forms, compositional forms, instruments, moods, countries, composers, performing media, and so on.

While units that involve other subjects are quite interesting, the supervisor should be certain that music is not used simply to teach the other subject or that other subjects are continually used to teach music. Music does not need science, health, or social studies to be of value; correlation should serve to increase musical understanding rather than stand as an excuse for it.

THE TESTING PROGRAM

The need for evaluation has been mentioned several times previously. Objective tests are one means of evaluation, but they should not be used, as the sole criteria. Evaluation must take into account objectives, opportunities offered for all students and for exceptional students, methods of the program, and the accomplishments of the students. The truest evaluation is that which measures behavior changes; consequently, a standardized objective test cannot do the whole job. Frequently, questionnaires and surveys involving the students and their parents, and concerning the students' musical interests outside of school, can be of considerable value.

The objective musical aptitude test, however, can be of use in determining the native musical abilities of students, which may be considered in selecting students for certain groups or in selecting instruments for individuals to study. These should be used along with other means of testing since their reliability is variable. The aptitude test generally covers areas such as tonal memory, melodic taste, rhythmic recognition, and discrimination in pitch, intensity, volume, and timbre. The most widely-used of these include:

Bentley Measures of Musical Ability (1966), Ages 7-12.
    October House, Inc., 134 East 22nd Street, New York 10010.
Conrad Instrument-Talent Test (1941), Ages 7-adult.
    Mills Music, Inc., 1619 Broadway, New York 10019.
Drake Musical Aptitude Tests, Forms A and B (1957), Ages 8-adult.
    Science Research Associates, Inc., 259 East Erie Street, Chicago 60611.
Gaston Test of Musicality (1957), Grades 4-12.
    Odell's Instrumental Service, 925 Massachusetts Street, Lawrence, Kansas 66044.
Gordon Musical Aptitude Profile (1965), Grades 4-12.
    Houghton Mifflin Co., 110 Tremont Street, Boston 02107.
Kwalwasser-Dykema Music Tests (1930), Grades 4-12 and adults.
    Carl Fischer, Inc., 56-62 Cooper Square, New York 10003.
Kwalwasser Music Talent Test (1953), Form A: grades 7-adult; Form B: grades 4-6.
    Mills Music, Inc., 1619 Broadway, New York 10019.
McCreery Elementary Rhythm and Pitch Test (1936), Grades 4-8.
    Lyons Band Instrument Co., 223 West Lake Street, Chicago 60606.

Pan-American Music Aptitude Test (1942), Grades 4-8.
　　Pan-American Band Instrument Co., 1101 East Beardsley
　　Avenue, Elkhart, Indiana 46515.
Seashore Measures of Musical Talent (1960), Grades 4-adult.
　　The Psychological Corporation, 304 East 45th Street, New
　　York 10017.
Tilson-Gretsch Musical Aptitude Test (1941), Grades 4-12.
　　Fred Gretsch Mfg. Co., 60 Broadway, Brooklyn, New York.
Wing Standardized Tests of Musical Intelligence (1961), Grades
　　4-adult.
　　National Foundation for Educational Research, The Mere,
　　Upton Park, Slough, Buckinghamshire, England.

Achievement tests are also available to measure a student's growth in musical knowledge, skills, and appreciation. These cover topics such as notation symbols, note values, keys, recognition of meters, pitch discrimination, and melodic recognition. Some of the tests available are:

Beach Music Test (1939), Grades 4-college.
　　Bureau of Educational Measurements, Kansas State Teachers
　　College, Emporia, Kansas.
Colwell Elementary Music Achievement Tests (1965), Grades 4-12.
　　Follett Publishing Co., 1010 W. Washington Boulevard, Chicago
　　60607.
Farnum Music Notation Test (1953), Grades 7-9.
　　The Psychological Corporation, 304 East 45th Street, New
　　York 10017.
Jones Music Recognition Test (1949), in two parts: elementary-
　　junior high, senior high-college.
　　Carl Fischer, Inc., 56-62 Cooper Square, New York 10003.
Knuth Achievement Tests in Music (1966), two forms for each of
　　three levels: grades 3-4, 5-6, 7-12.
　　Creative Arts Research Associates, 30 Cedro Way, San Fran-
　　cisco 94132.
Kwalwasser-Ruch Test of Musical Accomplishment (1927), Grades
　　4-12
　　Bureau of Educational Research and Service, State University
　　of Iowa, Iowa City, Iowa 52241.
Providence Inventory Test in Music (1932), Grades 4-9.
　　World Book Co., 313 Park Hill Avenue, Yonkers, New York.
Strouse Music Test, Forms A and B (1937), Grades 4-college.
　　Bureau of Educational Measurements, Kansas State Teachers
　　College, Emporia, Kansas.
Watkins-Farnum Performance Scale (1954).
　　Hal Leonard Music, Inc., 64 East Second Street, Winona,
　　Minnesota.

SELF-GROWTH

There is one other major factor to consider in curriculum development — the supervisor himself. Just as an in-service program is provided to enable teacher growth, the supervisor should set up his own self-service program so that he may grow in his profession. For unless his concepts and abilities develop, his curriculum cannot develop. He can do this, first, by taking an active part in professional organizations at the local, state, and national levels. He should not only attend meetings and take note of what occurs, but also offer his services to these organizations, individually and on committees, to contribute to their growth as well as his own.

The supervisor should also keep in touch with the activities and publications of other state and national organizations. The bulletin published by the National Music Council gives accounts of important activities across the country, and this may be used to supplement professional music education journals and other music literature. (See Appendix F for a listing of music periodicals published in the United States.) Curriculum guides and courses of study published by school systems can also contribute to the supervisor's study of techniques and trends.

Study and research may be carried on both within the school system and outside. The supervisor can help keep up to date and do research through university summer sessions and evening courses. Within his own school, action research can be conducted in which pilot programs to test new materials and techniques are set up with the involvement of the teaching staff. The results of such research can be transmitted to the entire staff through guides and bulletins, and to the profession as a whole through teachers' organizations, university seminars, and contributions to professional journals.

Finally, the supervisor should not overlook one of the most obvious and vital means of professional growth — contact with music itself, through concerts, school productions, and actual participation in performing groups.

10

Administrative Duties of the Music Supervisor

The operation of a successful music program involves a complex network of duties in which certain administrative tasks are unavoidable. While the supervisor may find his greatest satisfaction in working directly with teachers and students, he must also function as an administrator to provide the setting in which learning can take place. His duties in this area call for the provision of teaching materials, the maintenance of equipment, the purchase and distribution of new supplies, the filing of records and reports, and the making of a budget.

SUPPLYING THE SCHOOLS

Equipment and Instructional Materials. In order to provide teaching materials competently, the program has to be planned well in advance and its needs must be anticipated. So that demands do not come all at once, large projects should be spaced, and a purchase and replacement plan for constant items worked out over perhaps a five-year plan. A shorter plan, of course, will actually be in operation, but it should be based as much as possible on long-range needs.

Each year at the time of planning the budget, a survey of needs for the following year should be made so that all the known essentials can be ordered at the close of the school term and be available for the opening of school in September. There will naturally be emergency situations and desirable supplementary materials that cannot be foreseen, but if material needs are analyzed in detail, these additional supplies should be few and minor, and perhaps can be purchased during the school year from a miscellaneous or emergency fund. Maintaining a check-list of basic supply categories will help prevent major oversights. This list would include such items as instruments, music for each organization, textbooks, audio-visual equipment, recordings, equipment for music facilities, and storage supplies.

Within schools at each level, some supplies should become standard. Every elementary school, for example, should be stocked with the basic materials listed in Chapter Three, and every secondary school with those items listed in Chapter Four. Among the basics are school-owned instruments of the type that parents and students are not likely to buy. In a new school some of these instruments will have to be provided immediately, but even in the existing school, where basic instruments are already owned, plans should be made for the replacement of instruments in poor condition, the addition of basic instruments required by increased enrollment or the growth of the band and orchestra, and the acquisition of complementary equipment to fill out the instrumentation desired. It would be best to compile a list of all the desired instruments, determine what is needed immediately and which items can be deferred, and then set up a schedule for purchasing the complete list over a five- or six-year term.

On the basis of full instrumentation, school-owned instruments for a band of 40-50 players would probably include one piccolo, one oboe, one bassoon, one alto clarinet, one bass clarinet, one baritone saxophone, three French horns, two baritones, two BB-flat sousaphones, and percussion equipment. For a 60-piece band, add another oboe, bassoon, alto clarinet, French horn, and sousaphone, as well as one E-flat tuba and percussion accessories. For a full band of 75-80 players, increase instrumentation again with one English horn, one contra-bassoon, one bass clarinet, one bass saxophone, one fluegelhorn, one more French horn, two more baritones, another sousaphone, a recording bass, and a string bass.

An orchestra of 30 players should be supplied with the following school-owned instruments: three violas, two cellos, two string basses, one oboe, one bassoon, two French horns, and percussion equipment including a snare drum, bass drum, cymbals, and two timpani. For an orchestra of 50 pieces, add three violas, three cellos, two string basses, one piccolo, one more oboe, one more bassoon, two more French horns, and percussion accessories. For an 80-piece orchestra, the 50-piece group should be enlarged by four more violas, three more cellos, two more string basses, one English horn, one bass clarinet, one tuba, one harp, and more percussion equipment, including additional timpani.

All new supplies that will be housed in a single school should be sent by the manufacturer directly to that building to simplify distribution (unless, of course, the school system has a central processing office and requires a different procedure). An inventory of music equipment in each school should still be maintained in the supervisor's office. In the case of materials to be made available to the entire system, the director can distribute to each school and music teacher a detailed listing of items, with suggested uses and directions for their procurement.

Maintenance. The supervisor's budget should include provision for the maintenance and repair of instruments and other equipment. Instruments need to be overhauled yearly, with a major overhauling after about three or four years. Pianos should be tuned before performances and at least once every six months. Proper storage provisions and the dissemination of information on instrument care to students will help eliminate many repair problems.

A record of repairs should be kept for each instrument, including the type of repair, date, cost, and accumulated costs. Depreciation should also be recorded, for after a certain point it will be less costly to purchase a new instrument than to keep the old one in condition. Depreciation can be figured at 25 percent for the first year, 25 percent over the next two years, another 25 percent over the following three years, and a final 25 percent over the last four years of a ten-year period.

Some minor repairs may be handled by either the supervisor or one of the instrumental directors. For this purpose, essential supplies such as strings, pads, violin bridges, and cleaning and lubricating oils need to be kept on hand. Several instrumental books include sections on repairing, and some of the instrument manufacturers have published repair manuals which are worth having available.

Music Libraries. Although there are certain advantages to a central library of materials, particularly in a large system with two or more high schools, it is much more convenient for each school to have its own music library, which may then be supplemented with materials from the central office. In the elementary school, the library will consist mainly of basic recordings and book series, as well as a small professional library for the teachers. At the junior and senior high schools, there will be more extensive recordings, specialized textbooks, and separate libraries of arrangements for choral and instrumental groups.

These libraries should be catalogued at the respective schools, but a master inventory of music, recordings, and music books throughout the system should be on file in the supervisor's office. New materials coming in should be counted immediately to make sure the order is correct; then, they may be stamped with the school's name, numbered, catalogued, and filed.

For easiest, most efficient use, music ought to be cross-indexed according to composer, title, and type. Cards for this purpose are available from several music supply houses and publishers, or they may be printed by the school. Each card should include the composer's name (and/or the arranger's name), the title of the composition, the medium of performance, the number of copies, the publisher's name, and the acquisition number. Optional information may include the type of accompaniment in the case of choral works, the type of text, the grade of difficulty, the date of acquisition, and the file number if one is used. It is quite useful to keep a record on the back of the master card stating when the music was studied and performed. (If the library is well stocked, there should be enough music for three or four years of study so that a student can complete his experiences in a school without the repetition of material.)

Index cards for the choral catalogue may be made out in the following manner:

Composer Card

> Composer _____ Arranger _____
> Title _____
> Medium _____ Type _____ Copies _____
> Piano Acc. ☐, Piano Reduction ☐, Other Acc. _____
> Grade: Easy ☐,   Medium ☐,   Med.-Difficult ☐,   Difficult ☐
> Publisher _____
> Pub. No. _____ Acquired _____ Order No. _____
> Studied: Performed:

Title Card

> Title _____
> Composer _____ Arranger _____
> Medium _____ Type _____ Copies _____
> Piano Acc. ☐,   Piano Reduction ☐,   Other Acc. _____
> Grade: Easy ☐,   Medium ☐,   Med.-Difficult ☐,   Difficult ☐
> Publisher _____
> Pub. No. _____ Acquired _____ Order No. _____

Type Card

> Type _____ Medium _____ Copies _____
> Title _____
> Composer _____ Arranger _____
> Piano Acc. ☐,   Piano Reduction ☐, Other Acc. _____
> Grade: Easy ☐,   Medium ☐,   Med.-Difficult ☐,   Difficult ☐
> Publisher _____
> Pub. No. _____ Acquired _____ Order No. _____

If band and orchestra cards are kept in separate filing drawers, the same type of format can be used for each. An example of a composer card for an instrumental work follows:

Composer _____ Arranger _____
Title _____
Type _____ Medium _____
Conductor's Score: Full ☐, Condensed ☐, Piano ☐
Parts: Complete ☐, Replacements needed ☐
Publisher _____
Pub. No. _____ Acquired _____ Order No. _____

Performance media need not be indexed separately as long as the music itself is filed by medium, which is probably the most logical and convenient system. Choral works, for example, may be stored under the following headings: unison, two-part, SA, SSA, SSAA, TB, TTB, TTBB, SAB, SATB, and any other combinations that may be used. Within each group, selections may be classified under sacred, secular, folk, popular and musical show, novelty, and special seasonal (e.g., Christmas, Easter) sections, with an alphabetical arrangement by composer or title under each subheading. A similar system may be used for compositions for band, orchestra, and instrumental ensembles.

Filing music in expandable cardboard envelopes in metal cabinets (letter-size for octavo music and marching-band folios; legal-size for the larger instrumental sheets) offers the best protection. Cabinets are expensive, however, and a good number are required to house a sizable library. Many directors, therefore, store music in special filing boxes on open shelves.

Recordings should definitely be placed on shelves in an upright position to prevent warping. Vertical wooden dividers, spaced between every twenty discs, will keep the records straight. There are many systems of filing phonograph records. One of the most efficient is to store them in five basic categories: classical music, folk music, jazz, popular music, and musical theatre (musical comedy, operetta, etc.). Under classical music, recordings are filed alphabetically by composer and then by title. Under folk music, they are filed regionally and then by performer. Jazz recordings and popular music are arranged alphabetically by performer, with anthologies at the beginning of the stack; and musical plays are arranged by composer. With this system, filing numbers are not necessary, as any recording can be located immediately under the name of its composer or performer. (In classical music and theatre music, we generally think in terms of works by certain composers; in jazz and popular music, the performer is the more important figure.)

Each recording should be cross-indexed by composer, title, and topic (type, form, medium). Then, whether the teacher wants something representative of Bach, a recording of Chopin's *Waltz in A-flat,* an example of string quartet music, or an illustration of sonata form, the appropriate material can be identified quickly. Examples of record index cards are the following:

Composer Card

```
Composer _____ Title _____
                                   Teaching
Performer _____ Topic _____
Album  Title _____
Label _____ Record No. _____ Speed _____
Acquired _____ Order  No. _____
```

Title Card

```
Title _____ Composer _____
Teaching
Topic _____ Performer _____
                                    etc.
```

Topic Card

```
Teaching
Topic _____ Title _____
Composer _____ Performer _____
                                    etc.
```

A few sources listing good library materials are given below. (Check Appendix H for full publication data.)

1. Frances Andrews and Joseph A. Leeder. *Guiding Junior-High-School Pupils in Music Experiences* (choral, instrumental, general).
2. Thomas C. Collins. *Music Education Materials: A Selected, Annotated Bibliography* (choral, instrumental, general).
3. Peter Dykema and Hannah Cundiff. *School Music Handbook* (general).
4. Robert Garretson. *Conducting Choral Music* (choral).
5. L. Eileen McMillan. *Guiding Children's Growth Through Music* (elementary general).
6. MENC. *Contemporary Music* (vocal, instrumental).

7. MENC. *Materials for Miscellaneous Instrumental Ensembles* (instrumental).
8. Kenneth L. Neidig. *The Band Director's Guide* (instrumental).
9. Kenneth L. Neidig and John W. Jennings. *Choral Director's Guide* (choral).
10. NIMAC. *Selective Music Lists for Vocal and Instrumental Solos, Vocal and Instrumental Ensembles* (choral, instrumental).
11. NIMAC. *Selective Music Lists: Orchestra, Band, Chorus* (choral, instrumental).
12. William R. Sur and Charles F. Schuller. *Music Education for Teen-Agers* (general, choral).

THE DESK JOB

Records and Reports. Much of the supervisor's administrative work will be written material. Surveys of students' music interests and activities, teachers' problems, and the results of experimental projects must all be worked out on paper for evaluation. So, too, must schedules for day-to-day activities, special meetings and workshops, and major events such as concerts and festivals. (The latter should be planned far in advance, preferably immediately following the previous concert or festival.)

For both daily and long-range work, records must be kept and reports made. The music director's records will include: (1) an inventory and catalogue of all music, recordings, and books; (2) an inventory of school-owned instruments, including a record of model, date of purchase, cost, and repairs; (3) a record of uniforms and robes; (4) results of testing programs; (5) teachers' records; (6) teachers' work loads; (7) enrollment in music organizations and projections of enrollment; (8) agreements with students for the loan of instruments and uniforms; (9) teachers' requisitions for supplies; and (10) purchase orders.

In the loan of instruments and uniforms, cards similar to those below may be of use:

INSTRUMENT LOAN AGREEMENT

Instrument _____ Model _____
Serial No. _____ Value _____
Accessories _____
    I (We) accept full responsibility for any damage to this instrument beyond reasonable wear.
Date _____ Student's sig. _____
                               Parent's sig. _____

Obverse

UNIFORM RECORD

Student's Name _____ Grade _____ H.R. _____
Coat No. _____ Trousers No. _____ Skirt No. _____
Hat No. _____ Sweater No. _____ Vest No. _____
Aiguillette ☐,   Belt ☐,   Boots ☐,   Cape ☐,   Epaulets ☐,
Gloves ☐,   Necktie ☐,   Overlay ☐,   Plume ☐,   Spats ☐.

Reverse

Measurements: Chest _____   Waist _____
          Inseam _____   Outseam _____
          Head _____   Shoulders _____
          Sleeve _____

The necessary reports will ordinarily be indicated by the administration. Monthly and yearly reports should be submitted to the superintendent, as described in Chapter Five, as well as irregular reports on special programs and new projects. Reports to teachers will generally take the form of bulletins (see Chapter Eight). Although written reports to principals are not usually required, they should be offered when there is something important to report, in order to keep a principal up to date on the music activities in his school and gain his support in their operation.

Budgets. Any subject in the school curriculum (as defined in Chapter Three) should be financed by the school. This is not always the situation, however, for in the case of the music department there are two basic ways of financing activities. One is to maintain a school budget that will cover every possible expense of the music department, including even the costs of special activities such as musical shows. Any revenues collected by the music department from concerts and other performances revert to the school system. Theoretically, this is the proper system since the music department does not have to raise any money on its own to finance trips or extra-class activities; everything is paid from the general budget, as it should be to avoid taxing the community twice for school expenses. One disadvantage is that any money collected by the music department is not necessarily used for musical purposes because it goes into the general fund.

A second system, which is quite prevalent in high schools, is to maintain a separate music fund, band fund, or vocal fund, consisting of music revenues. This money is used to finance special projects for the high school groups, and no provision is made in the general budget for these activities. Although this uses money raised by the music department for music purposes only, there is the problem of not being able to offer certain experiences unless the department can provide the money itself. It would seem best, then, to finance through the general budget any activity that is a justifiable part of the curriculum, especially if it has become standard practice and its value has been proven. Particularly objectionable are those music funds which are maintained partly through student fees. In more than 25 percent of secondary schools which offer music courses, students are charged for participating in the program! These fees are charged for instrumental instruction, instrument insurance and repairs, the rental of robes and uniforms (to cover cleaning and repairs), the purchase of scores used in classes, entrance in festivals, and even for *the opportunity to participate in performing groups.* How many of these schools, one may rightfully ask, charge students for instruction in mathematics or for instructional materials used in a history class? Wherever student fees are levied, it is difficult to raise music to its proper place in a public, tax-supported system of education.

In making out the annual budget, the supervisor should be guided by long-range plans as well as immediate needs. Certain items, as in a five-year plan of instrument purchase, will already be projected; other needs, however, will have to be anticipated. With this in mind, the director should have the members of his teaching staff submit their budget needs in advance, considering the total program and their future plans. From this, an over-all budget, including a small emergency fund if possible, can be planned.

It is impossible to stipulate what is an adequate budget for a school system of any given size. Whatever money is needed to implement the desired curriculum is a justifiable budget. The budget which will be submitted for approval needs to be precise and detailed. There should be two general headings: revenue and expenditures. Although a specific form will probably be required by the school system, the supervisor can work out his budget by considering the following subdivisions:

Revenue	*Expenditures*
General budget allotment	Instructional salaries
Performance receipts	Textbooks
Athletic receipts	Instructional supplies
Other receipts	Equipment
	Maintenance
	Special projects
	Miscellaneous

Some funds may be derived from sources other than taxation for the general budget. Although these additional resources may not amount to much, they should be projected in the budget. Included will be expected receipts from concerts, musical shows, and participation in athletic events, and monies received from instrument rentals, program advertising, parents clubs, special sales campaigns, and donations by civic and social groups in the community.

Among expenditures, a large amount will have to go toward instructional salaries, although some schools do not account for salaries in department budgets. Under the classification of "textbooks," the supervisor should include elementary-junior high basic music series, instrumental method books, and special texts for secondary school courses such as general music, music appreciation, or music theory. Books on music for both elementary and secondary reference purposes will normally be purchased out of the library budget or the general budget of each individual school.

Another substantial sum will go toward instructional supplies. In determining the needs for this section, the supervisor should consider music for choruses, bands, and orchestras, festivals and competitions, recordings, classroom "pre-band" instruments, filmstrips, film rentals, charts, still pictures, pamphlets, recording tapes, pitch pipes, music folders, music manuscript paper, testing materials, and other similar teaching supplies.

The "equipment" section of the budget should account for band and orchestral instruments, phonographs, tape recorders and recording equipment, television and radio sets (when used exclusively by the music staff, rather than borrowed from the audio-visual department), tuning devices and electronic equipment, listening equipment, uniforms, robes, music stands, music stand lights, special chairs, risers, podiums, storage racks, filing cabinets, and acoustical shells.

Under "maintenance" there should be provisions for small instrumental repairs, instrument overhauling, piano tuning, insurance on instruments, and uniform cleaning and alterations.

"Special projects" would include monies for students' festival and competition fees, travel expenses to festivals, transportation costs for outside performances and exchange programs, costs of field trips to concerts, royalties and commission fees, clinician fees for workshops, musical show expenses (for royalties, scenery, costumes, lighting, props, special personnel, and rental of rehearsal materials), and costs of experimental teaching projects.

The last category, "miscellaneous," will include office supplies (forms, letterheads, storage boxes and envelopes, music-lined duplicator masters, etc.), printing (concert programs, bulletins, curriculum guides), telephone, professional literature, the emergency fund, and perhaps other items.

So that every possible expense is included, the supervisor should deal with every school individually, considering whatever special programs are in progress there and each phase of the regular program. Then, expenditures can be grouped as above to be double-checked.

Business Transactions. Procedures for dealing with business firms are generally set forth by the board of education. All financial transactions should go through the superintendent's office or the business manager, and special forms should be used for requisitions. In the event that funds must be handled by the supervisor for music productions or small instrumental repairs, books should be kept.

For purposes of ordering, a supply of current manufacturers' and publishers' catalogues should be kept on hand. It is also valuable to be on the mailing list of any company with which business might be transacted. To have his name placed on a mailing list, the supervisor simply has to send a letter stating his name, position, school, address, and interests (choral, instrumental, elementary, secondary, etc.). If new to the job, it would also be helpful to include his former position and school, and the name of the person he is replacing in his current position.

Letters to business firms should be clearly written, as brief as possible, and confined to one subject. A letter covering several unrelated items, such as an order, placement on the mailing list, the return of materials, or a request for information, often is delayed because it must travel through several departments for processing. Enclosing separate sheets for each item, and marked for the appropriate departments, will speed handling. Regardless of the content, a letter should contain full information concerning the supervisor's name, position, school, and address. If an order is being placed, it should also make clear to whom the shipment is to be sent, how it is to be sent, and to whom it should be charged.

In obtaining bids on equipment and in ordering supplies exact specifications need to be given. For example, a solicitation of a bid on instruments should include the model number and name, the quantity, the material and finish, exact size and manufacturing dimensions, the type of mouthpiece, the case, and specific accessories. It would be desirable to have special forms printed for ordering music so that instrumentation, publication numbers, and the number of copies can be checked easily. An example of such a form is given on page 168.

RIDGELAND PUBLIC SCHOOLS

To: _____ Bill to: _____

_____ _____

_____ _____

Requisitioned by _____ Req. No. _____ Date _____
Send via _____ Date required _____

Title _____ Comp./Arr. _____
Publisher _____ Publication No. _____
Orchestra ☐   Band ☐   Other _____

___full score	___1st fluegelhorn
___condensed score	___2nd fluegelhorn
___piano-cond. score	___1st E♭ alto horn
___1st C piccolo	___2nd E♭ alto horn
___2nd C piccolo	___3rd E♭ alto horn
___D♭ piccolo	___4th E♭ alto horn
___1st flute	___1st F horn
___2nd flute	___2nd F horn
___3rd flute	___3rd F horn
___E♭ clarinet	___4th F horn
___1st B♭ clarinet	___1st baritone (treble)
___2nd B♭ clarinet	___2nd baritone (treble)
___3rd B♭ clarinet	___1st baritone (bass clef)
___alto clarinet	___2nd baritone (bass clef)
___bass clarinet	___1st tenor trombone
___contrabass clarinet	___2nd tenor trombone
___1st oboe	___3rd tenor trombone
___2nd oboe	___1st bass trombone
___English horn	___2nd bass trombone
___1st bassoon	___tuba
___2nd bassoon	___E♭ bass
___contrabassoon	___BB♭ bass
___soprano saxophone	___snare drum, bass drum
___1st alto sax	___timpani
___2nd alto sax	___harp
___tenor sax	___1st violin A
___baritone sax	___1st violin B
___bass sax	___2nd violin
___1st cornet	___3rd violin
___2nd cornet	___viola
___3rd cornet	___cello
___1st trumpet	___string bass
___2nd trumpet	___piano
___3rd trumpet	___organ

APPENDIX A

General Educational and Cultural Organizations

As a teacher, supervisor, musician, and researcher, the director of music may find himself in need of information, guidance, or even support that can be obtained from a national organization. Of the many associations serving the general educational and cultural community, a selected number of those which relate most directly to his work and interests are listed here.

Acoustical Society of America, 335 East 45th Street, New York, New York 10017

Adult Education Association of the USA, 1225 Nineteenth Street, N.W., Washington, D.C. 20036

American Association of School Administrators, 1201 Sixteenth Street, N.W., Washington, D.C. 20036

American Council on Education, 1785 Massachusetts Avenue, N.W., Washington, D.C. 20036

American Educational Research Association, 1201 Sixteenth Street, N.W., Washington, D.C. 20036

American Educational Theatre Association, Inc., John F. Kennedy Center for the Performing Arts, Room 500, 1701 Pennsylvania Avenue, N.W., Washington, D.C. 20006

American National Theatre and Academy, 245 West 52nd Street, New York, New York 10019

American Society for Aesthetics, The Cleveland Museum of Art, 11150 East Boulevard, Cleveland, Ohio 44106

Association for Childhood Education International, 3615 Wisconsin Avenue, N.W., Washington, D.C. 20016

Association for Higher Education, 1201 Sixteenth Street, N.W., Washington, D.C. 20036

Association for Supervision and Curriculum Development, 1201 Sixteenth Street, N.W., Washington, D.C. 20036

Association of American Colleges, 1818 R Street, N.W., Washington, D.C. 20009

Association of American Universities, 1785 Massachusetts Avenue, N.W., Washington, D.C. 20036

169

Audiovisual Instruction, 1201 Sixteenth Street, N.W., Washington, D.C. 20036

Council for Advancement of Secondary Education, Inc., 1201 Sixteenth Street, N.W., Washington, D.C. 20036

Council for Basic Education, Inc., 725 Fifteenth Street, N.W., Washington, D.C. 20005

The Council for Exceptional Children, 1201 Sixteenth Street, N.W., Washington, D.C. 20036

Department of Classroom Teachers, 1201 Sixteenth Street, N.W., Washington, D.C. 20036

Educational Communication Association, Inc., 1346 F Street, N.W., Washington, D.C. 20004

Elementary-Kindergarten-Nursery Education, 1201 Sixteenth Street, N.W., Washington, D.C. 20036

Lincoln Center for the Performing Arts, Inc., 1960 Broadway, New York, New York 10019

National Academy of Education, 202 Junipero Serra Boulevard, Stanford, California 94305

National Association for the Education of Young Children, 1629 21st Street, N.W., Washington, D.C. 20009

National Association of Educational Broadcasters, 1346 Connecticut Avenue, N.W., Washington, D.C. 20006

National Association of Secondary School Principals, 1201 Sixteenth Street, N.W., Washington, D.C. 20036

National Catholic Educational Association, 1785 Massachusetts Avenue, N.W., Washington, D.C. 20036

National Education Association, 1201 Sixteenth Street, N.W., Washington, D.C. 20036

National Educational Television and Radio Center, 10 Columbus Circle, New York, New York 10019

National Elementary Principals Association, 1201 Sixteenth Street, N.W., Washington, D.C. 20036

National School Boards Association, Inc., 1940 Sheridan Road, Evanston, Illinois

National Society for the Study of Education, 5835 Kimbark Avenue, Chicago, Illinois 60637

The Society for the Advancement of Education, 1860 Broadway, New York, New York 10023

APPENDIX B

National Music Organizations

The selection of associations in this section has not been limited to organizations concerned only with music education, for the supervisor needs to grow musically in many directions. His individual interests as a musician, scholar, and educator all relate to his work in supervision through actual application to the school program, his work in the community, or the development of his general background and knowledge. A number of these organizations have published materials relating to music education; others have published literature on music in general; and some offer leadership in research or in the unification of professional services.

American Chamber Music Players, 15 West 67th Street, New York, New York 10023

American Academy of Teachers of Singing, 57 Winter Street, Forest Hills, New York

American Bandmasters Association, ABA Research Center, McKeldin Library, University of Maryland, College Park, Maryland; also, 7373 North Cicero, Chicago, Illinois

American Choral Directors Association, c/o MENC (q.v.)

American Choral Foundation, Inc., 130 West 56th Street, New York, New York 10019

American Composers Alliance, 170 West 74th Street, New York, New York 10023

American Federation of Musicians of the United States and Canada, 641 Lexington Avenue, New York, New York 10022

American Guild of Authors and Composers, 158 West 55th Street, New York, New York 10019

American Guild of Musical Artists, 1841 Broadway, New York, New York 10023

American Guild of Organists, 630 Fifth Avenue, New York, New York 10020

American Institute of Musicology, P.O. Box 30665, Dallas, Texas

American International Music Fund, 30 West 60th Street, New York, New York 10023

American Music Center, 2109 Broadway, New York, New York 10023

171

American Music Conference, 332 South Michigan Avenue, Chicago, Illinois 60604

American Musicological Society, 204 Hare Building, University of Pennsylvania, Philadelphia, Pennsylvania 19104

American Recorder Society, 141 West 20th Street, New York, New York 10011

American School Band Directors' Association, 120 Byrd Drive, Fairfax, Virginia

American Society of Composers, Authors, and Publishers, 575 Madison Avenue, New York, New York 10022

American Society of Music Arrangers, 224 West 49th Street, New York, New York 10019

American Society for the Preservation of Sacred, Patriotic, and Operatic Music, 2109 Broadway, New York, New York 10023

American String Teachers Association, c/o MENC (q.v.)

American Symphony Orchestra League, Symphony Hill, P.O. Box 66, Vienna, Virginia

Associated Male Choruses of America, Inc., 1326 West Dartmouth Street, Flint, Michigan

Association of American Choruses, c/o Free Library of Philadelphia, Logan Square, Philadelphia, Pennsylvania

Association of Choral Conductors, 101 West 31st Street, New York, New York 10001

Broadcast Music, Inc., 589 Fifth Avenue, New York, New York 10017

Choral Conductors Guild, P.O. Box 714, Mt. Vernon, New York

College Band Directors National Association, c/o MENC (q.v.)

College Music Society, Mount Holyoke College, South Hadley, Massachusetts

Composers and Authors Guild, 1255 East 24th Street, Brooklyn, New York

Council for Research in Music Education, College of Education, School of Music, University of Illinois, Urbana, Illinois 61803

Delta Omicron International Music Fraternity, 124 Ellis Road, Havertown, Pennsylvania 19083

Hymn Society of America, 475 Riverside Drive, New York, New York 10027

Inter-American Music Council, Music Division, Pan American Union, Washington, D.C. 20036

International Society for Music Education, 1201 Sixteenth Street, N.W., Washington, D.C. 20036

Jazz Arts Society, 16 West 55th Street, New York, New York 10019

Metropolitan Opera Guild, 1425 Broadway, New York, New York 10018

Modern Music Masters, P.O. Box 347, Park Ridge, Illinois

Mu Phi Epsilon, 1139 North Ridgewood Drive, Wichita, Kansas 67208

Music Critics Association, P.O. Box 66, Vienna, Virginia

Music Editors Association, Box 714, Mount Vernon, New York

Music Education League, Inc., 119 West 57th Street, New York, New York 10019

Music Education Research Council, c/o MENC (q.v.)

Music Educators National Conference (MENC), 1201 Sixteenth Street, N.W., Washington, D.C. 20036

Music Industry Council, c/o Harry Wenger, Wenger Corp., Owatonna, Minnesota 55060

Music Library Association, 2121 Broadway, New York, New York 10023

Music Publishers' Association of the United States, 609 Fifth Avenue, New York, New York 10017

Music Publishers' Protective Association, Inc., 460 Park Avenue, New York, New York 10022

Music Research Foundation, 654 Madison Avenue, New York, New York 10021

Music Teachers National Association, 2209 Carew Tower, Cincinnati, Ohio 45202

National Association for American Composers and Conductors, 15 West 57th Street, New York, New York 10023

National Association for Music Therapy, P.O. Box 610, Lawrence, Kansas 66044

National Association of College Wind and Percussion Instructors, c/o MENC (q.v.)

National Association of Jazz Educators, c/o MENC (q.v.)

National Association of Music Merchants, 222 West Adams Street, Chicago, Illinois 60606

National Association of Organ Teachers, 7938 Bertram Avenue, Hammond, Indiana 46324

National Association of Schools of Music, Knox College, Galesburg, Illinois

National Association of Teachers of Singing, 250 West 57th Street, New York, New York 10019

National Band Association, c/o MENC (q.v.)

National Catholic Bandmasters, Inc., 4460 South Austin Street, Milwaukee, Wisconsin

National Catholic Music Educators Association, 620 Michigan Avenue, N.E., Washington, D.C. 20017

National Federation of Music Clubs, Suite 1215, 600 South Michigan Avenue, Chicago, Illinois 60605

National Guild of Community Music Schools, 244 East 52nd Street, New York, New York 10022

National Guild of Piano Teachers, Box 1807, Austin, Texas 78767

National Music Camp, Interlochen, Michigan

National Music Council, 2109 Broadway, New York, New York 10023

National Music League, Inc., 130 West 56th Street, New York, New York 10019

National Opera Association, 2226 Nolen Drive, Flint, Michigan

National Orchestra Association, Inc., 111 West 57th Street, New York, New York 10019

National School Orchestra Association, c/o MENC (q.v.)

Phi Mu Alpha Sinfonia, Southern Securities Building, Evansville, Indiana 47708

Piano Teachers Information Service, Box 3881, Grand Central Station, New York, New York 10017

Piano Technicians Guild, Inc., 512 First Avenue N., Seattle, Washington 98109

Pi Kappa Lambda, Box 2886, University, Alabama

Record Industry Association of America, Inc., 1 East 57th Street, New York, New York 10022

Recording Industries Music Performance Trust Funds, 225 West 34th Street, Room 816, New York, New York 10001

Screen Composers' Association, 9250 Wilshire Boulevard, Beverly Hills, California

SESAC, Inc., 10 Columbus Circle, New York, New York 10019

Sigma Alpha Iota, 1447 57th Street, Des Moines, Iowa

Society for Ethnomusicology, Wesleyan University, Middletown, Connecticut 06457

Society for the Preservation and Encouragement of Barber Shop Quartet Singing in America, 6315 Third Avenue, Kenosha, Wisconsin 53141

United States Army, Navy and Air Force Bandsmen's Association, Inc., 54 Commerce Street, New Haven, Connecticut

United States Youth Symphony Foundation, 441 Washington Avenue, Palo Alto, California

Young Audiences, Inc., 645 Madison Avenue, New York, New York 10022

APPENDIX C

Musical Instrument, Equipment, and Supply Companies

A-Reso Bells, 1133 Seventh Avenue, San Diego, California 92101 (tone bells)

Artley, Inc., 2000 Middlebury Street, Elkhart, Indiana

Baldwin Piano and Organ Co., 1801 Gilbert Avenue, Cincinnati, Ohio 45202

Buescher Band Instrument Co., 225 East Jackson Boulevard, Elkhart, Indiana 46514

CBS Musical Instruments, 1005 East Second Street, Dayton, Ohio 45402 (Rogers drums)

Christlieb Products, 3311 Scadlock Lane, Sherman Oaks, California 91403 (bassoon reeds)

CMI, 7373 North Cicero, Lincolnwood, Illinois (Reynolds instruments)

Conn Corporation, 1101 East Beardsley Avenue, Elkhart, Indiana 46514 (band instruments)

C. G. Conn, Ltd., Elkhart, Indiana (pianos)

Consolidated Band Instrument Service, 5520 North First Avenue, Abilene, Texas (valve oil)

The Cundy-Bettoney Co., Inc., 96 Bradlee Street, Hyde Park, Massachusetts 02136 (flutes, clarinets)

Elkan-Vogel Co., Inc., 1712-16 Sansom Street, Philadelphia, Pennsylvania 19103 (recorders)

The Empire Music Co., Inc., 3216 Forty-fourth Street, S.W., Seattle, Washington 98116 (recorders)

Everett Piano Co., South Haven, Michigan 49090

Fender-Rhodes, 1402 East Chestnut Street, Santa Ana, California (electric pianos)

Fred. Gretsch Mfg. Co., 60 Broadway, Brooklyn, New York 11211 (Grassi saxophones; percussion)

Hammond Organ Co., 4200 West Diversey Avenue, Chicago, Illinois 60639

Hargail Music, Inc., 157 West 57th Street, New York, New York 10019 (recorders)

Harmolin, Inc., P.O. Box 244, LaJolla, California 92038

Wm. S. Haynes Co., 12 Piedmont Street, Boston, Massachusetts 02116 (flutes)

M. Hohner, Inc., Andrews Road, Hicksville, Long Island, New York 11802 (Melodica, harmonica)

Frank Holton and Co., Elkhorn, Wisconsin 53121 (brass)

G. C. Jenkins Co., 1014 East Olive, Decatur, Illinois 62525 (percussion)

Kay Musical Instrument Co., 2201 West Arthur Avenue, Elk Grove Village, Illinois 60007

King Musical Instruments, 33999 Curtis Boulevard, Eastlake, Ohio 44094

Kitching, 505 Shawmut, LaGrange, Illinois 60525 (resonator bells, melody bells, rhythm instruments)

La Voz Corporation, 8484 San Fernando Road, Sun Valley, California (reeds)

G. LeBlanc Corporation, 7019 Thirtieth Avenue, Kenosha, Wisconsin 53141

William Lewis and Son, 7390 North Lincoln Avenue, Lincolnwood, Illinois 60646 (string instruments)

The Lowrey Co., 7373 North Cicero Avenue, Lincolnwood, Illinois 60646

Ludwig Drum Co., 1728 North Damen Avenue, Chicago, Illinois 60647

Lyon-Healy, 243 South Wabash Avenue, Chicago, Illinois 60604 (harps)

Lyons Band Instrument Co., 223 West Lake Street, Chicago, Illinois 60606 (rhythm instruments, drums, xylophones, marimbas, glockenspiels, recorders)

Martin-Freres, 5-9 Union Square, New York, New York 10003 (brass)

The Martin Band Instrument Co., 431 Baldwin Street, Elkhart, Indiana

Mason and Hamlin, East Rochester, New York (pianos)

C. Meisel Music Co., Inc., Union, New Jersey 07083 (string instruments)

Melody Flute Co., Box 276, Laurel, Maryland 20810

National Autoharp Sales Co., Box 1120, Des Moines, Iowa

F. E. Olds and Sons, Inc., 350 South Raymond Avenue, Fullerton, California (brass)

Peripole, Inc., 51-17 Rockaway Beach Boulevard, Far Rockaway, New York 11691 (rhythm and percussion instruments, classroom melody and harmony instruments, glockenspiels, xylophones)

Premier Drums, 825 Lafayette Street, New Orleans, Louisiana 70113

Remo, Inc., 12804 Raymer Street, North Hollywood, California (Weather King drum heads)

F. A. Reynolds Co., Inc., Abilene, Texas (brass)

Rhythm Band, Inc., P. O. Box 126, Fort Worth, Texas 76101 (rhythm instruments)

Rico Corporation, 819 North Highland Avenue, Hollywood, California 90038 (reeds)

St. Louis Music Supply Co., 3711 West Pine Boulevard, St. Louis, Missouri (Rene Dumont saxophones)

Scherl and Roth, Inc., 1729 Superior Avenue, Cleveland, Ohio 44114 (string instruments)

Oscar Schmidt-International, Inc., 87 Ferry Street, Jersey City, New Jersey 07307 (Autoharps)

Schulmerich Carillons, Inc., 9848 Carillon Hill, Sellersville, Pennsylvania (handbells)

Scientific Music Industries, Inc., 1255 South Wabash Avenue, Chicago, Illinois 60605 (classroom instruments)

H & A. Selmer, Inc., 1119 North Main Street, Elkhart, Indiana 46515

Slingerland Drum Co., 6633 North Milwaukee Avenue, Niles, Illinois

Song Flute Co., 630 South Wabash Avenue, Chicago, Illinois

Steinway and Sons, Steinway Place, Long Island City, New York

Story and Clark Piano Co., 7373 North Cicero Avenue, Lincolnwood, Illinois 60646

Targ and Dinner, Inc., 2451 North Sacramento Avenue, Chicago, Illinois 60647 (tone bells)

Trophy Musical Products, 1278 West 9th Street, Cleveland, Ohio 44113 (recorders)

Vibrator Reed Co., Hanover, Pennsylvania 17331

David Wexler and Co., 823 South Wabash Avenue, Chicago, Illinois 60605 (tone bells)

H. N. White Co., Inc., 5225 Superior Avenue, Cleveland, Ohio 44103 (King trumpets)

Wurlitzer, P.O. Box 807, Elkhart, Indiana 46514 (sousaphones)

The Wurlitzer Co., DeKalb, Illinois 60115 (pianos)

Yamaha International Corporation, 7733 Telegraph Road, Montebello, California (pianos)

Avedis Zildjian Co., 39 Fayette Street, North Quincy, Massachusetts 02171 (cymbals)

UNIFORMS, ROBES, DECORATIONS

Academic Church and Choir Gowns Mfg. Co., 1125 North Highland Avenue, Hollywood, California

Award Emblem Mfg. Co., 3435 West 51st Street, Chicago, Illinois 60632 (pins, decorations, awards)

Bale Pin Company, 168 Milk Street, Boston, Massachusetts 02107

Bandribbons, Monmouth, Oregon 97361 (decorations)

Collegiate Cap and Gown Co., 1000 North Market Street, Champaign, Illinois

Commercial Award Pin Co., 608 South Dearborn Street, Chicago, Illinois

Converse Rubber Co., Malden, Massachusetts 02148 (rubber band parkas)

DeMoulin Bros. and Co., 1073 South Fourth Street, Greenville, Illinois (band uniforms, choir robes)

Fechheimer Bros. Co., 400 Pike Street, Cincinnati, Ohio 45202 (band uniforms)

Herco Products, Inc., 53 West 23rd Street, New York, New York 10010 (pins, decorations)

Ireland Needlecraft, 3661 San Fernando Road, Glendale, California 91204 (choir robes)

Edward Morris Jones Co., Box 4174, Philadelphia, Pennsylvania 19144 (pins, decorations)

E. R. Moore Co., 7230 North Caldwell, Niles, Illinois 60648 (choir robes)

Thomas A. Peterson Co., 501 East 33rd Street, Kansas City, Missouri 64109 (choir robes)

Robert Rollins Blazers, Inc., 242 Park Avenue South, New York, New York 10003 (band uniforms)

Saxony Clothes, 925 Broadway, New York, New York (band uniforms)

Springer Fashion Uniforms, 701 H Street, N.E., Washington, D.C. 20002 (choir robes)

Uniforms By Ostwald, Inc., Ostwald Plaza, Staten Island, New York 10301

The C. E. Ward Co., New London, Ohio 44851 (choir robes)

PERFORMANCE EQUIPMENT

Clarin Mfg. Co., 4640 West Harrison Street, Chicago, Illinois 60644 (chairs)

Haldeman-Homme Mfg. Co., 2580 University Avenue, St. Paul, Minnesota (risers)

Howard Products Co., 2625 Marian Lane, Wilmette, Illinois (music stands)

Mitchell Manufacturing Co., 2744 South 34th Street, Milwaukee, Wisconsin (risers and music stands)

The Monroe Co., 353 Church Street, Colfax, Iowa 50054 (risers)

M. Payson Mfg. Co., Box 136, Fairbury, Nebraska (risers)

Perry Products, Box 8156, Portland, Oregon (risers)

Peripole, Inc., 51-17 Rockaway Beach Boulevard, Far Rockaway, New York 11691 (music stands and desks)

Stagecraft Corporation, 25 Belden Avenue, Norwalk, Connecticut (acoustical shells)

Wenger Corporation, Wenger Building, Owatonna, Minnesota 55060 (risers, music stands, acoustical shells)

Wiese Mfg. Co., P.O. Box 72, Davenport, Iowa (music stands)

STORAGE EQUIPMENT

American Educational Music, P.O. Box 126, Fort Worth, Texas 76101 (music storage folders)

Gamble Hinged Music Co., Inc., 312 South Wabash Avenue, Chicago, Illinois 60604 (filing materials)

Instrumental Music Co., 1416 Lake Street, Evanston, Illinois (music storage folders)

Neil A. Kjos Music Co., 525 Busse Highway, Park Ridge, Illinois 60068 (music storage folders, filing boxes)

Norren Mfg. Co., P.O. Box 776, Arcadia, California 91006 (storage cabinets)

S and H Manufacturing Co., 316 Summit Street, Normal, Illinois 61761 (storage and filing equipment and cabinets)

Southern Music Co., 1100 Broadway, San Antonio, Texas 78206 (filing materials)

Wallach and Associates, Inc., Box 3567, Cleveland, Ohio 44118 (storage equipment, tape and record cabinets)

Wenger Corporation, Wenger Building, Owatonna, Minnesota 55060 (storage cabinets)

CHARTS, PICTURES, POSTERS

American Music Conference, 332 South Michigan Avenue, Chicago, Illinois (posters)

Bowmar Records, Inc., 622 Rodier Drive, Glendale, California 91201 (pictures of composers and instruments)

C. G. Conn, Ltd., Elkhart, Indiana (charts)

Educational Music Bureau, Inc., 434 Wabash Avenue, Chicago, Illinois

Electra Publications, Box 70, Selden, New York 11784 ("Sono-Graphs": transparencies and slides)

Carl Fischer, Inc., 56-62 Cooper Square, New York, New York (posters)

The Instrumentalist, 1418 Lake Street, Evanston, Illinois 60201 (pictures)

Keyboard Publications, 1346 Chapel Street, New Haven, Connecticut 06511 (composers' pictures)

Music Journal, Inc., 1776 Broadway, New York, New York 10019 (pictures)

TEACHING AIDS

American Educational Music, P.O. Box 126, Fort Worth, Texas 76101 (metronomes)

Educational Tools, Inc., 198 Meadowbrook Road, Orchard Park, New York 14127 (electric music board)

Franz Mfg. Co., Inc., 53 Wallace Street, New Haven, Connecticut 06519 (metronomes)

E. F. Johnson Co., Waseca, Minnesota 56093 (intonation trainer)

Keaton Music Typewriter Co., 87-A Carmel Street, San Francisco, California 94117

William Kratt Co., 988 Johnson Place, Union, New Jersey 07083 (pitch pipes)

Peripole, Inc., 51-17 Rockaway Beach Boulevard, Far Rockaway, New York 11691 (instrument kits)

Pro Musica Typewriter Corporation, 239 Paterson Avenue, East Rutherford, New Jersey

H. & A. Selmer, Inc., Elkhart, Indiana 46515 (electronic tuner)

Targ and Dinner, Inc., 2451 North Sacramento Avenue, Chicago, Illinois 60647 (electronic rhythm trainer)

David Wexler and Co., 823 South Wabash Avenue, Chicago, Illinois 60605 (music typewriters)

RECORD COMPANIES

Angel Records, 317 West 44th Street, New York, New York

Bowmar Records, Inc., 622 Rodier Drive, Glendale, California 91201

Capitol Records Distributing Corporation, 1750 North Vine Street, Hollywood, California 90028

CBS Records, 51 West 52nd Street, New York, New York

Childcraft Records, c/o Mercury Records, 110 West 57th Street, New York, New York 10022

Children's Record Guild, Greystone Corporation, 100 Sixth Avenue, New York, New York 10013

Columbia Records (see CBS Records)

Decca Records, 445 Park Avenue, New York, New York

Elektra Records, 116 West 14th Street, New York, New York

Ruth Evans (recordings), P. O. Box 132, Forest Park Branch, Springfield, Massachusetts

Folkways/Scholastic Records, 906 Sylvan Avenue, Englewood Cliffs, New Jersey 07632

Golden Records, Simon and Schuster, Inc., 630 Fifth Avenue, New York, New York 10020

Grand Award Record Corporation, Inc., 16 Kingsland Avenue, Harrison, New Jersey

Greystone Corporation, Educational Activities Division, 100 Sixth Avenue, New York, New York 10013

The Jam Handy Organization, 2831 East Grand Boulevard, Detroit, Michigan (records with filmstrips)

Keyboard Publications, 1346 Chapel Street, New Haven, Connecticut 06511

London Records, Inc., 539 West 25th Street, New York, New York 10001

Mercury Records, 110 West 57th Street, New York, New York 10022

MGM Records, 1540 Broadway, New York, New York

Monitor Records, 413 West 50th Street, New York, New York 10019

Music Education Record Co., Box 445, Englewood, New Jersey

Musical Sound Books, Inc., P.O. Box 444, Scarsdale, New York

Period Music Co., Box 134, Pacific Palisades, California

RCA Victor Educational Sales, 155 East 24th Street, New York, New York 10010

Rhythms Productions, 1107 El Centro Avenue, Hollywood, California 90038 (rhythm recordings)

Sing 'n Do Company, Inc., P.O. Box 279, Ridgewood, New Jersey

Vanguard Records, 154 West 14th Street, New York, New York

Vox Productions, Inc., 236 West 55th Street, New York, New York 10019

Westminster Records, 1501 Broadway, New York, New York

Young People's Records, Greystone Corporation, 100 Sixth Avenue, New York, New York 10013

CUSTOM RECORD MANUFACTURERS

The Audio Recording and Manufacturing Co., Inc., 4 New Hyde Park Road, Franklin Square, New York 11010

Century Record Mfg. Co., P. O. Box 308, 26000 Springbrook Road, Saugus, California

Findlay Recording Co., P.O. Box 39127, Cincinnati, Ohio 45239

Fleetwood Custom Recording, 321 Revere Street, Revere, Massachusetts 02151

Ken-Del Productions, Inc., 515 Shipley Street, Wilmington, Delaware 19801

RCA Victor Custom Record Dept., Station B, Box 7031, Dayton, Ohio 45407

Recorded Publications Co., 1575 Pierce Avenue, Camden, New Jersey 08105

Regal Records, 2302 North Going, Portland, Oregon 97217

Vogt Quality Recordings, P.O. Box 302, Needham, Massachusetts 02192

RECORDING EQUIPMENT

Acoustic Research, Inc., 24 Thorndike Street, Cambridge, Massachusetts 02141 (speakers)

Ampex Corporation, 2201 Lunt Avenue, Elk Grove Village, Illinois 60007 (tape recorders)

Califone Corporation, 1041 North Sycamore, Hollywood, California (phonographs)

Concertone, 9731 Factorial Way, South El Monte, California 91733 (tape recorders)

Concord Electronics Corporation, Industrial Products Division, 1935 Armacost Avenue, Los Angeles, California 90025 (video tape recorders)

Garrard Division, British Industries Corporation, Westbury, New York 11590 (turntables, changers)

Martel Electronics, Inc., 2339 South Cotner Avenue, Los Angeles, California 90064 (Uher tape recorders)

Newcomb Audio Products Co., 6824 Lexington Avenue, Hollywood, California 90038 (listening centers, headphones, phonographs)

North American Philips Co., Inc., High Fidelity Products Dept., 100 East 42nd Street, New York, New York 10017 (Norelco tape recorders)

The Perry Co., P.O. Box 7187, Waco, Texas 76710 (listening centers)

Radio Matic of America, Inc., 760 Ramsey Avenue, Hillside, New Jersey (phonographs, listening centers, mobile sound centers)

H. H. Scott, Inc., 111 Powdermill Road, Maynard, Massachusetts (high fidelity and stereo components)

Shure Brothers, Inc., 222 Hartrey Avenue, Evanston, Illinois (microphones, cartridges)

Sony Corporation of America, 47-47 Van Dam Street, Long Island City, New York 11101 (video tape recorders)

Superscope, Inc., 8150 Vineland Avenue, Sun Valley, California 91352 (Sony tape recorders)

Telex Corporation, 9600 Aldrich Avenue, South, Minneapolis, Minnesota 55420 (Telex, Magnecord, and Viking tape recorders)

FILM-FILMSTRIP PRODUCERS AND DISTRIBUTORS

Association Films, Inc., 600 Madison Avenue, New York, New York 10022

Bowmar Records, Inc., 622 Rodier Drive, Glendale, California 91201

Brandon Films, Inc., 200 West 57th Street, New York, New York 10019

Castle Films, 221 Park Avenue South, New York, New York

Children's Music Center, 5373 West Pico Boulevard, Los Angeles, California

Contemporary Films, 267 West 25th Street, New York, New York

Coronet Instructional Films, 65 South Water Street, Chicago, Illinois 60601

Encyclopaedia Britannica Films, Inc., 1150 Wilmette Avenue, Wilmette, Illinois 60091

Greystone Corporation, Educational Activities Division, 100 Sixth Avenue, New York, New York 10013

The Jam Handy Organization, 2821 East Grand Boulevard, Detroit, Michigan 48211

Library Films, Inc., 79 Fifth Avenue, New York, New York

Official Films, Inc., Grand and Linden, Ridgefield, New Jersey

Society for Visual Education, Inc., 1345 Diversey Parkway, Chicago, Illinois 60614

Sterling Films, Inc., 6 East 39th Street, New York, New York 10016

Teaching Films Custodians, Inc., 25 West 43rd Street, New York, New York

Young America Films, McGraw-Hill Book Co., Text-Film Dept., 330 West 42nd Street, New York, New York 10018

MUSIC AND RECORD DISTRIBUTION SERVICES

American Educational Music, P.O. Box 126, Fort Worth, Texas 76101

Audio-Education, Inc., 55 Fifth Avenue, New York, New York

Belwin, Inc., Rockville Centre, Long Island, New York (books on music)

Children's Music Center, 5373 West Pico Boulevard, Los Angeles, California 90019

Educational Audio-Visual, Inc., 29 Marble Avenue, Pleasantville, New York (recordings)

Educational Music Bureau, 434 South Wabash Avenue, Chicago, Illinois 60605 (music)

Educational Record Sales, 157 Chambers Street, New York, New York 10007

Gamble Hinged Music Co., Inc., 312 South Wabash Avenue, Chicago, Illinois 60604 (records, books, teaching aids)

Ginn Library Service, Statler Building, Boston, Massachusetts 02117 (records)

Sam Goody, Inc., 235 West 49th Street, New York, New York 10019 (records)

Byron Hoyt's Sheet Music Service, 34 N.W. 8th Avenue, Portland, Oregon

Keynote Music Service, Inc., 833 South Olive Street, Los Angeles, California 90014 (sheet music)

J. W. Pepper, 231 North Third Street, Philadelphia, Pennsylvania 19102 (sheet music)

School Music Service, Inc., Champaign, Illinois 61824 (sheet music)

MUSIC THEATRE AGENTS

Century Library, Inc., 225 West 44th Street, New York, New York 10036

Chappell and Co., Inc., 609 Fifth Avenue, New York, New York 10017

The Dramatic Publishing Co., 86 East Randolph Street, Chicago, Illinois 60601

Samuel French, Inc., 25 West 45th Street, New York, New York 10036

Music Theatre International, 119 West 57th Street, New York, New York 10019

The Rodgers and Hammerstein Repertory, 120 East 56th Street, New York, New York 10022

G. Schirmer, Performance Dept. SD, 609 Fifth Avenue, New York, New York 10017

Tams-Witmark Music Library, Inc., 757 Third Avenue, New York, New York 10017

APPENDIX D

Music Publishers

Associated Music Publishers, Inc., 609 Fifth Avenue, New York, New York 10017

Augsburg Publishing House, 425 South 5th Street, Minneapolis, Minnesota 55415

Belwin, Inc., 250 Maple Avenue, Rockville Centre, Long Island, New York 11571

Big 3 Music Corporation (Robbins-Feist-Miller), 1350 Avenue of the Americas, New York, New York 10019

Boosey and Hawkes, Inc., Oceanside, New York 11572

Boston Music Co,. 116 Boylston Street, Boston, Massachusetts 02116

Bourne, Inc., 136 West 52nd Street, New York, New York 10019

Brodt Music Co., Box 1207, Charlotte, North Carolina 28201

Broude Bros., 56 West 45th Street, New York, New York 10036

Chappell and Co., Inc., 609 Fifth Avenue, New York, New York 10017

M. M. Cole, 823 South Wabash Avenue, Chicago, Illinois

Concordia Publishing House, 3558 South Jefferson Avenue, St. Louis, Missouri 63118

Consolidated Music Publishers, Inc., 240 West 55th Street, New York, New York 10019

Oliver Ditson (see Theodore Presser Co.)

Elkan-Vogel Co., Inc., 1712-16 Sansom Street, Philadelphia, Pennsylvania 19103

Fillmore Music Co. (see Carl Fischer, Inc.)

Carl Fischer, Inc., 56-62 Cooper Square, New York, New York 10003

J. Fischer and Bro., Harrison Road, Glen Rock, New Jersey 07452

H. T. FitzSimons Co., 615 LaSalle Street, Chicago, Illinois 60610

Harold Flammer, Inc., 251 West 19th Street, New York, New York 10011

Sam Fox Publishing Co., Inc., 1841 Broadway, New York, New York 10023

Frank Music Corporation, 119 West 57th Street, New York, New York 10019

Galaxy Music Corporation, 2121 Broadway, New York, New York 10023

185

H. W. Gray Co., Inc., 159 East 48th Street, New York, New York 10017

Handy-Folio Music Co., 5100 West 82nd Street, Minneapolis, Minnesota 55431

Hansen Publications, Inc., 119 West 57th Street, New York, New York 10019

Hargail Music Press, 157 West 57th Street, New York, New York 10019

Harms, Inc. (see Warner Bros.-Seven Arts Music)

Hope Publishing Co., 5793-TA6 West Lake Street, Chicago, Illinois 60644

Interlochen Press, National Music Camp, Interlochen, Michigan 49643

C. C. Jenkins Company, P.O. Box 149, Decatur, Illinois 62525

Jenkins Music Co., 1217 Walnut Street, Kansas City, Missouri 64100

Kalmus Music Co., 421 West 28th Street, New York, New York 10001

Kendor Music, Inc., Delevan, New York 14042

Neil A. Kjos Music Co., 525 Busse Highway, Park Ridge, Illinois 60068

Lawson-Gould Music Publishers, Inc., 609 Fifth Avenue, New York, New York 10017

Hal Leonard Music, Inc., 64 East Second Street, Winona, Minnesota 55987

Ludwig Music Publishing Co., 557-59 East 140th Street, Cleveland, Ohio 44110

Edward B. Marks Music Corporation, 136 West 52nd Street, New York, New York 10019

MCA Music, 543 West 43rd Street, New York, New York 10036

Mercury Music Corporation, 47 West 63rd Street, New York, New York 10023

Mills Music, Inc., 1619 Broadway, New York, New York 10019

Edwin H. Morris and Co., Inc., 31 West 54th Street, New York, New York 10019

New Jersey Educational Music Co., Box 748, Summit, New Jersey 07901

Novello (see H. W. Gray Co., Inc.)

Oak Publications, 701 Seventh Avenue, New York, New York 10036

Oxford University Press, Music Department, 200 Madison Avenue, New York, New York 10016

C. F. Peters Corporation, 373 Park Avenue South, New York, New York 10016

Plymouth Music Co., Inc., 1841 Broadway, New York, New York 10023

Morse M. Preeman, Inc., 733 South Spring Street, Los Angeles, California 90014

Theodore Presser Co., Presser Place, Bryn Mawr, Pennsylvania 19010

Pro-Art Publications, Inc., 469 Union Avenue, Westbury, Long Island, New York 11591

Remick Music Corporation (see Warner Bros.-Seven Arts Music)

G. Ricordi and Co., 16 West 61st Street, New York, New York 10028

Rubank, Inc., 5544 West Armstrong Avenue, Chicago, Illinois 60646

E. C. Schirmer Music Co., 600 Washington Street, Boston, Massachusetts

G. Schirmer, Inc., 609 Fifth Avenue, New York, New York 10017

Schmitt, Hall and McCreary Co., 527 Park Avenue, Minneapolis, Minnesota 55415

Shapiro-Bernstein and Co., Inc., 666 Fifth Avenue, New York, New York 10019

Shawnee Press, Inc., Delaware Water Gap, Pennsylvania 18327

Larry Shayne Music, Inc., 1619 Broadway, New York, New York 10019

Wm. J. Smith Music Co., Inc., 254 West 31st Street, New York, New York 10001

Southern Music Co., 1100 Broadway, San Antonio, Texas 78206

Staff Music Publishing Co., 374 Great Neck Road, Great Neck, Long Island, New York 11021

Summy-Birchard Co., 1834 Ridge Avenue, Evanston, Illinois 60204

Transcontinental Music Publishers, 1674 Broadway, New York, New York 10019

Warner Bros.-Seven Arts Music, 488 Madison Avenue, New York, New York 10022

Williamson Music Co. (see Chappell and Co., Inc.)

Willis Music Co., 440 Main Street, Cincinnati, Ohio 45201

M. Witmark and Sons (see Warner Bros.-Seven Arts Music)

B. F. Wood Music Co., Inc., 1619 Broadway, New York, New York 10019

APPENDIX E

Recommended Organization for Filing Music Materials

The supervisor cannot do much in music education unless he is knowledgeable about music in general. Yet, knowledge and information need not be entirely memorized; knowing how and where to locate information when it is needed is also of considerable importance. For this reason it is advisable that the supervisor maintain a file of information (articles, clippings, papers, pamphlets, personal research) on all facets of music.

For efficient use, the file must be highly organized. Therefore, it is recommended that something similar to the following plan be used for filing music materials. This will enable the music director to develop his own knowledge, as well as to meet the needs of his staff quickly and expertly, in organizing resource materials. Although the plan and most of the sub-divisions are my own, I am indebted to the thinking of sociologist Max Kaplan for the organization of the section on social foundations of music.

I. Systematic Musicology.
    A. Acoustics.
        1. The nature of vibration.
        2. General characteristics of sound (material on velocity, reflection, interference, resonance, etc.).
        3. Physical characteristics of sound (information on frequency, harmonic series, etc.).
        4. Acoustical properties of musical instruments.
    B. Psychophysiology of Music.
        1. Perception of sound (audition, hearing).
        2. Sensation and response (information on pitch, loudness, qualities of tone, dissonance, etc.).
        3. The creative process.
        4. Emotions and mood.
        5. Memorization and the learning process.
        6. Listening to music; music appreciation.
    C. Aesthetics of Music.
        1. The aesthetic experience.
        2. Materials of music (key, pitch, motives, themes, dynamics, etc.).
        3. Form and treatment.
        4. Meaning in music.
        5. Value, judgment, and taste (including criticism).
    D. Music Theory.
        1. Elementary theory (scales, notation, etc.).

   2. Rhythm.
   3. Melody (and counterpoint).
   4. Harmony.
   5. Arranging, instrumentation, and orchestration.
   6. Form and composition.
E. Social Foundations of Music.
   1. Social functions of music (material on collective, individual, moral, and incidental functions).
   2. Relationships of society to music (e.g., economic, political, educational, family, class, race, church, general environment, etc.).
   3. Relationships of music to society (information on the production of music, distribution of music, consumption of music, education for music).
   4. Roles in music: the social emphasis (creator-composer, creator-performer, distributor, audience, educator-teacher, educator-student).
   5. Roles in music: the aesthetic emphasis (social circle, the musician's function, status, and self-conception).
F. Music Education
   1. Philosophy of music education.
   2. Curriculum organization.
   3. Physical-plant organization.
   4. Administration and supervision.
   5. Elementary school instruction.
   6. Secondary school instruction.
   7. Music in higher education.
   8. Music in the community.
   9. The general music class.
  10. The music history-appreciation class.
  11. The music theory class.
  12. The comparative arts class.
  13. Choral organizations: general methods and materials (junior high school).
  14. Choral organizations: general methods and materials (senior high school).
  15. Instrumental organizations: general methods and materials (junior high school).
  16. Instrumental organizations: general methods and materials (senior high school).
  17. Individual and class voice instruction.
  18. Individual and class instrumental instruction.
  19. Extra-class music activities.
  20. Production of musical shows.
  21. Materials: instruction or method books, charts, pictures, exercises, music, etc.
G. Ethnomusicology.
   1. The study of ethnomusicology.
   2. Primitive music (materials arranged by region and society: e.g., American, North American Indian, etc.)
   3. Oriental and Eastern music.
      a. Far East, China, and Japan.

       b. Indo-China, Burma, and Polynesia.
       c. India.
       d. Persia, Arabia, and Arabic countries of the Eastern Mediterranean and Northern Africa.
    4. Folk music (materials filed alphabetically by countries).
II. Historical Musicology.
    A. Methods of Historical Research.
    B. Classical Music.
      1. Periods of music history.
        a. Music of antiquity and ancient civilizations.
        b. The medieval period.
        c. The Renaissance.
        d. The Baroque period.
        e. The Rococo period.
        f. The pre-Classical period.
        g. The Classical period.
        h. The Romantic period.
        i. Post-Romanticism.
        j. The twentieth century.
      2. Types of music, forms, elements, and miscellaneous topics. (Information here is filed alphabetically by subject. The list below is not intended to be complete, but indicates some of the major subjects which would be placed in this section.)
        a. Anecdotes, musical.
        b. Art song.
        c. Atonal music.
        d. Ballet music.
        e. Bibliographies, music.
        f. Cantata.
        g. Chamber music.
        h. Choral music.
        i. Church and religious music.
        j. Concerto.
        k. Copyright, musical.
        l. Dance, music and the.
        m. Discographies.
        n. Documents, musical.
        o. Electronic music.
        p. Expressionism.
        q. Festivals, music.
        r. Fiction, music.
        s. Film music.
        t. Forms, musical.
        u. Fugue.
        v. Gregorian chant.
        w. Gypsy music.
        x. Humor in music.
        y. Hymnody.
        z. Impressionism.
        aa. Improvisation.
        bb. Industry, music in.
        cc. Libraries, music.

      dd. Madrigals.
      ee. Mass, the.
      ff. Military music.
      gg. Minstrelsy (minnesingers, troubadours, etc.)
      hh. Motet.
      ii. Nationalism in music.
      jj. Notation.
      kk. Opera.
      ll. Oratorio.
    mm. Organizations and foundations, music.
      nn. Overture.
      oo. Polytonal music.
      pp. Publishers, music.
      qq. Recordings and recording techniques.
      rr. Serial music.
      ss. Sonata.
      tt. Symphony.
      uu. Theatre, music and the.
      vv. Therapy, music.
    ww. Tone-poems.
      xx. **Variation forms.**

3. Biography (information on composers, performers, patrons, etc., arranged alphabetically from Adolphe Adam and Isaac Albeniz to Vladimir Zakharov and Carl Zeller).
4. Instruments (historical information, arranged alphabetically from the accordion to the zither).
5. Performance.
    a. Techniques (material, arranged alphabetically, on technical facets of performance, such as accompanying, conducting, singing, etc.).
    b. Media (material, arranged alphabetically, on performance media such as bands, choral groups, string quartets, symphony orchestras, etc.).
6. Music of different countries. (Organized similar to the section on folk music, this section catalogues information on the composed music of countries, alphabetically from Africa to Yugoslavia.)

C. Popular Music, including Music Theatre.
1. History. (Information is arranged first by country and then, as much as possible, in chronological order.)
2. Types of popular music. (The following list suggests only a few of the topics to be filed here.)
    a. Barbershop singing.
    b. Calypso music.
    c. Dance music.
    d. Discographies.
    e. Extravaganzas.
    f. Hawaiian music.
    g. Latin-American style music.
    h. Minstrel shows.
    i. Musical comedies and plays.
    j. Operetta.
    k. Publishers, popular music.

   l. Recordings.
  m. Songs.
   n. Songwriting.
   o. Vaudeville.
  3. Biography (information on composers and performers, arranged alphabetically).
  4. Performance (information on dance bands, vocal styles, etc.).
 D. Jazz.
  1. History.
   a. Backgrounds (African music, Afro-American music and culture, Negro religious music, work songs, blues, minstrelsy, ragtime).
   b. Beginnings of jazz (Negro brass bands, archaic jazz).
   c. Traditional jazz era.
    1. New Orleans schools (classic jazz, Dixieland).
    2. Chicago schools (Chicago style, classic blues, boogie-woogie).
    3. New York schools (Harlem jazz, stride piano, New York Dixieland).
   d. Mainstream jazz era (Kansas City jazz and the Southwest circuit, early big bands, swing).
   e. Revival era (New Orleans and Dixieland jazz, San Francisco style).
   f. Modern jazz era (bebop, progressive jazz, cool jazz, West Coast jazz, hard bop, funky jazz, the new thing).
  2. Singers and singing.
   a. Jazz.
   b. Blues.
   c. Related areas.
  3. Instrumental developments (material arranged alphabetically by instruments).
  4. Topics. (The following list suggests only some of the subjects that would be filed here.)
   a. Arts, jazz and other.
   b. Broadcasting, jazz in.
   c. Classical music and jazz.
   d. Composition/improvisation.
   e. Concerts.
   f. Criticism.
   g. Discographies.
   h. Elements of jazz.
   i. Etymology of jazz.
   j. Europe, jazz in.
   k. Exportation, government.
   l. Festivals.
   m. Literature.
   n. Recordings.
   o. Sociology of jazz.
   p. Study of jazz.
  5. Biography (information on performers and promoters, filed alphabetically).

APPENDIX F

Selected Music Periodicals

MUSIC EDUCATION

In addition to the music education journals listed below, there are fifty magazines published by state associations. These vary in issue from three to eleven times a year. Since their editors change frequently, the addresses of state journals are not very stable and thus are not included here. A complete address list is published biennially in the directory issue of the *Music Educators Journal*, and current information on the state journals can be obtained from the MENC office during the interim.

American Music Teacher, 2209 Carew Tower, Cincinnati, Ohio 45202 (bi-monthly)

American String Teacher, Mankato State College, Mankato, Minnesota 56001 (quarterly)

Bandwagon, H. & A. Selmer, Inc., Box 310, Elkhart, Indiana (six times a year)

Conn Chord, Conn Corporation, Elkhart, Indiana (three times a year)

Council for Research in Music Education, Bulletin, College of Education, School of Music, University of Illinois, Urbana, Illinois 61803 (three times a year)

Guild Notes, National Guild of Community Music Schools, 244 East 52nd Street, New York, New York 10022 (quarterly)

The Instrumentalist, 1418 Lake Street, Evanston, Illinois (eleven times a year)

International Music Educator, International Society for Music Education, 1201 Sixteenth Street, N.W., Washington, D.C. 20036

Journal of Research in Music Education, Music Educators National Conference, 1201 Sixteenth Street, N.W., Washington, D.C. 20036 (quarterly)

Juilliard News Bulletin, 120 Claremont Avenue, New York, New York 10027 (monthly, November-April)

Keyboard and *Young Keyboard*, 1346 Chapel Street, New Haven, Connecticut (monthly, September-June)

Musart, National Catholic Music Educators Association, 620 Michigan Avenue, N.E., Washington, D.C. 20017 (bi-monthly)

Music Educators Journal, Music Educators National Conference, 1201 Sixteenth Street, N.W., Washington, D.C. 20036 (monthly, September-May)

National School Orchestra Association Bulletin, High School, Benton Harbor, Michigan (five times a year)

NATS Bulletin, National Association of Teachers of Singing, 2930 Sheridan Road, Chicago, Illinois 60657 (quarterly)

The School Musician, Director and Teacher, 4 East Clinton Street, Joliet, Illinois (ten times a year)

Youth Symphony News, 441 Washington Avenue, Palo Alto, California (six times a year)

VOCAL AND CHORAL MUSIC

American Choral Review, American Choral Foundation, 130 West 56th Street, New York, New York 10019 (quarterly)

Central Opera Service Bulletin, 147 West 39th Street, New York, New York 10018 (eight times a year)

Choral and Organ Guide, Music Enterprises, Box 714, Mount Vernon, New York 10551 (ten times a year)

The Choral Journal, American Choral Directors Association, Box 17736, Tampa, Florida 33612 (bi-monthly)

Harmonizer, SPEBQSA, 6315 Third Avenue, Kenosha, Wisconsin 53141 (bi-monthly)

Lyric Opera News, Lyric Opera of Chicago, 20 North Wacker Drive, Chicago, Illinois 60606 (three times a year)

Opera News, 1425 Broadway, New York, New York 10018 (weekly during opera season)

Research Memorandum Series, American Choral Foundation, 130 West 56th Street, New York, New York 10019 (nine times a year)

INSTRUMENTAL MUSIC

Accordion and Guitar World, Gerstner Publications, 11 Railroad Avenue, Bedford Hills, New York 10507 (ten times a year)

American Guild of Organists Quarterly, 630 Fifth Avenue, New York, New York 10020

American Organist, Organ Interests, Inc., 16 Park Avenue, Staten Island, New York 10302 (monthly)

The American Recorder, 141 West 20th Street, New York, New York 10011 (bi-monthly)

Brass and Woodwind Quarterly, Box 111, Durham, New Hampshire 03824

Brass World, Box 343, Waukesha, Wisconsin 53187 (three times a year)

Clavier, The Instrumentalist Co., 1418 Lake Street, Evanston, Illinois 60201 (nine times a year)

The Diapason, 343 South Dearborn Street, Chicago, Illinois 60604 (monthly)

Figa News, Fretted Instrument Guild of America, One East Fordham Road, New York, New York 10068 (bi-monthly)

Fretts, Randall Publishing Co., Inc., P.O. Box 928, Santa Ana, California 92702 (bi-monthly)

Journal of Band Research, McKeldin Library, University of Maryland (ABA Research Center), College Park, Maryland (quarterly)

Notes of NAOT, National Association of Organ Teachers, 7938 Bertram Avenue, Hammond, Indiana 46324

Orchestra News, Scherl and Roth, 1729 Superior Avenue, Cleveland, Ohio 44114

Organ Institute Quarterly, Organ Institute, Box 50, Andover, Massachusetts 01810

Percussionist, 111 East Grand, Carbondale, Illinois 62903 (quarterly)

Piano Quarterly, Piano Teachers Information Service, Box 3881, Grand Central Station, New York, New York 10017

Theatre Organ, Box 248, Alameda, California (quarterly)

Woodwind World, Gerstner Publications, 11 Railroad Avenue, Bedford Hills, New York 10507 (bi-monthly)

MUSICOLOGY AND THEORY

American Musicological Society Journal, 2901 Byrdhill Road, Richmond, Virginia (three times a year)

Current Musicology, Columbia University, Department of Music, New York, New York 10027 (semi-annual)

Electronic Music Review, Trumansburg, New York 14886 (quarterly)

Journal of Music Theory, Yale University, School of Music, New Haven, Connecticut 06520 (semi-annual)

The Musical Quarterly, 609 Fifth Avenue, New York, New York 10017

Musigram: Journal of Music History, National Sheet Music Society, Inc., 5010 Reeder Avenue, Covina, California 91723 (monthly, September-May)

Perspectives of New Music, Princeton University Press, Box 231, Princeton, New Jersey 08540 (semi-annual)

GENERAL MUSIC MAGAZINES

Bravo, 10 Columbus Circle, New York, New York 10028 (four times a year)

High Fidelity Magazine (incorporating *Musical America*), Great Barrington, Massachusetts (monthly)

Inter-American Music Bulletin, Pan-American Union, 18th and Constitution Avenue, N.W., Washington, D.C. 20006 (bi-monthly)

Music Journal, 1776 Broadway, New York, New York 10019 (ten times a year)

Musical Leader, McCormack Building, 332 South Michigan Avenue, Chicago, Illinois 60604 (monthly)

Stereo Review, One Park Avenue, New York, New York 10016 (monthly)

Variety, 154 West 46th Street, New York, New York 10036 (show business, including music; weekly)

A World of Music, 14011 Ventura Boulevard, Sherman Oaks, California (quarterly)

JAZZ

Blues Research, 65 Grand Avenue, Brooklyn, New York

Down Beat, 222 West Adams Street, Chicago, Illinois 60606 (bi-weekly)

Jazz & Pop, 1841 Broadway, New York, New York 10023 (monthly)

Jazz Report, 357 Leighton Drive, Ventura, California 93001 (monthly)

Music Memories—Jazz Report, 314 Windsor Drive, Birmingham, Alabama 35209 (quarterly)

Record Research, 65 Grand Avenue, Brooklyn, New York (bi-monthly)

The Second Line, New Orleans Jazz Club, 2417 Octavia Street, New Orleans, Louisiana 70115 (bi-monthly)

FOLK AND ETHNIC MUSIC

Archives of Traditional Music, Trimester Report, Archives of Traditional Music, Maxwell Hall, Indiana University, Bloomington, Indiana 47405 (three times a year)

The Broadside, 145 Columbia, Cambridge, Massachusetts 02139

Ethnomusicology, Wesleyan University, Middletown, Connecticut (three times a year)

Sing Out, 165 West 46th Street, New York, New York 10036 (bi-monthly)

ASSOCIATION JOURNALS

ACA Bulletin, American Composers Alliance, 170 West 74th Street, New York, New York 10023 (quarterly)

American Symphony Orchestra League Newsletter, Symphony Hill, Box 66, Vienna, Virginia 22180 (bi-monthly)

ASCAP News, 575 Madison Avenue, New York, New York 10022 (quarterly)

International Musician, American Federation of Musicians, 39 Division Street, Newark, New Jersey 07102 (monthly)

Journal of Music Therapy, National Association for Music Therapy, Inc., Box 610, Lawrence, Kansas 66044 (quarterly)

Junior Keynotes, National Federation of Music Clubs, 600 South Michigan Avenue, Chicago, Illinois 60605 (five times a year)

Keynote, Associated Male Choruses of America, 412-16 Lewis Street, Flint, Michigan 48506 (quarterly)

Music Clubs Magazine, National Federation of Music Clubs, 600 South Michigan Avenue, Chicago, Illinois 60605 (five times a year)

Musicana, Army, Air Force Bandsmen's Association, 54 Commerce Street, New Haven, Connecticut (bi-monthly)

National Band Association Newsletter and Journal of Proceedings, Band Department, Purdue University, Lafayette, Indiana (bi-monthly)

National Music Council Bulletin, 2109 Broadway, New York, New York 10023 (three times a year)

SESAC Music, 10 Columbus Circle, New York, New York 10019 (six times a year)

Notes, Music Library Association, c/o School of Music, University of Michigan, Ann Arbor, Michigan 48105 (quarterly)

RECORDINGS

American Record Guide, P.O. Box 319, Radio City Station, New York, New York 10019 (monthly)

Billboard Music Week, 165 West 46th Street, New York, New York 10016 (weekly)

New Records, H. Roger Smith Co., Tenth and Walnut Streets, Philadelphia, Pennsylvania 19107 (monthly)

CHURCH MUSIC

Children's Music Leader, 127 Ninth Avenue, N., Nashville, Tennessee 37203 (quarterly)

The Church Musician, 127 Ninth Avenue, N., Nashville, Tennessee 37203 (monthly)

Journal of Church Music, 2900 Queen Lane, Philadelphia, Pennsylvania 19129 (eleven times a year)

The Junior Musician, 127 Ninth Avenue, N., Nashville, Tennessee 37203 (quarterly)

Music Ministry, 201 Eighth Avenue, S., Nashville, Tennessee 37203 (monthly)

Music for Primaries, 127 Ninth Avenue, N., Nashville, Tennessee 37203 (quarterly)

MUSIC TRADE MAGAZINES

Music Tempo, King Enterprises, 4136 Peak Street, Toledo, Ohio 43612 (bi-monthly)

Music Trades Magazine, 111 West 57th Street, New York, New York 10019 (thirteen times a year)

Musical Merchandise Review, 114 East 32nd Street, New York, New York 10016 (monthly)

Piano Technician's Journal, Piano Technician's Guild, 512 First Avenue, N., Seattle, Washington 98109 (monthly)

PTM Magazine: The Business and Financial Journal of the Music Industry, Piano Trade Publishing Co., 434 South Wabash Avenue, Chicago, Illinois 60605 (monthly)

MISCELLANEOUS MAGAZINES

Guild-O-Gram Associate Notes, American Guild of Music, P.O. Box 2427, Zenesville, Ohio 43701 (monthly)

Hymn, Hymn Society of America, 475 Riverside Drive, New York, New York 10027 (quarterly)

Music Today Newsletter, American Music Center, 2109 Broadway, New York, New York 10023 (six times a year)

Music World, Box 1321, Music City Building, Nashville, Tennessee 37202 (monthly)

Musicians' Voice, Box 615, New York, New York 10019 (ten times a year)

The Songwriter's Review, 1697 Broadway, New York, New York 10019 (monthly)

APPENDIX G

Basic Music Book Series for the General Music Program

American Singer, Second edition (1954-55), by John W. Beattie, Josephine Wolverton, Grace V. Wilson, and Howard Hinga.
(American Book Co., 55 Fifth Avenue, New York, New York 10003)
Grades 1-6; teachers' guides, accompaniments, recordings.

Birchard Music Series (1958-62), by Karl D. Ernst, Wiley Housewright, Hartley D. Snyder, Alex H. Zimmerman, and Rose Marie Grentzer.
(Summy-Birchard Publishing Co., 1834 Ridge Avenue, Evanston, Illinois 60204)
Grades K-8; teachers' editions, charts, recordings.

Discovering Music Together (1966), by Charles Leonhard, Beatrice Perham Krone, Irving Wolfe, and Margaret Fullerton.
(Follett Publishing Co., 1010 West Washington Boulevard, Chicago, Illinois 60607)
Grades K-8; recordings.

Exploring Music (1966), by Eunice Boardman, Beth Landis, and Lara Hoggard.
(Holt, Rinehart and Winston, 383 Madison Avenue, New York, New York 10017)
Grades K-8; teachers' editions, instrumental supplements, recordings.

Growing with Music, Second edition (1966), by Harry R. Wilson, Walter Ehret, Alice M. Snyder, Edward J. Hermann, and Albert A. Renna.
(Prentice-Hall, Inc., Englewood Cliffs, New Jersey 07632)
Grades K-8; teachers' editions, charts, recordings.

The Magic of Music (1965-68), by Lorrain E. Watters, Louis G. Wersen, William C. Hartshorn, L. Eileen McMillan, Alice Gallup, and Frederick Beckman.
(Ginn and Co., Statler Building, Boston, Massachusetts 02117)
Grades K-6; teachers' editions, recordings.

Making Music Your Own (1964), by Beatrice Landeck, Elizabeth Crook, Harold Youngsberg, and Otto Luening.
(Silver Burdett Co., Box 362, Morristown, New Jersey 07960)
Grades K-6; teachers' editions, recordings.

Music for Living (1956), by James L. Mursell, Gladys Tipton, Beatrice Landeck, Harriet Nordholm, Roy E. Freeburg, and Jack M. Watson.

(Silver Burdett Co., Box 362, Morristown, New Jersey 07960)
Grades 1-6; teachers' editions, accompaniments, recordings.

Music for Young Americans, Second edition (1966), by Richard C. Berg, Lee Kjelson, Eugene W. Troth, Daniel S. Hooley, Josephine Wolverton, and Claudeane Burns.
(American Book Co., 55 Fifth Avenue, New York, New York 10003)
Grades K-8; teachers' editions, accompaniments and guides, recordings.

Music in Our Life, Enlarged edition (1967) and

Music in Our Times, Enlarged edition (1967), by Irvin Cooper, Roy E. Freeburg, Warner Imig, Harriet Nordholm, Raymond Rhea, and Emile H. Serposs.
(Silver Burdett Co., Box 362, Morristown, New Jersey 07960)
Grades 7-8; teachers' editions, recordings.

Our Singing World, Enlarged edition (1959-61), by Lilla Belle Pitts, Mabelle Glenn, Lorrain E. Watters, and Louis G. Wersen.
(Ginn and Co., Statler Building, Boston, Massachusetts 02117)
Grades K-8; teachers' editions, accompaniment books, recordings.

Singing School, Revised edition (1956), by Theresa Armitage, Peter W. Dykema, Gladys Pitcher, David Stevens, and J. Lilian Vandevere.
(Summy-Birchard Publishing Co., 1834 Ridge Avenue, Evanston, Illinois 60204)
Grades 1-8; teachers' manuals, accompaniments, recordings.

This Is Music, Second edition (1967-68), by William R. Sur, Adeline McCall, Mary R. Tolbert, Robert E. Nye, William R. Fisher, Charlotte DuBois, and Gladys Pitcher.
(Allyn and Bacon, Inc., 470 Atlantic Avenue, Boston, Massachusetts 02210)
Grades K-8; teachers' editions, accompaniment books, charts, recordings.

Together We Sing, Revised edition (1959), by Max T. Krone, Irving Wolfe, Beatrice Perham Krone, and Margaret Fullerton.
(Follett Publishing Co., 1010 West Washington Boulevard, Chicago, Illinois 60607)
Grades 1-8; teachers' editions, recordings.

APPENDIX H

Selected Literature on Music Education

GENERAL AND PHILOSOPHICAL WORKS

Andrews, Frances, and Clara Cockerille. *Your School Music Program.* Englewood Cliffs, N.J.: Prentice-Hall, Inc., 1958. 289 pp.

Dykema, Peter, and Hannah Cundiff. *School Music Handbook.* Revised edition. Boston: C. C. Birchard and Co., 1955. 609 pp.

Ernst, Karl D., and Charles L. Gary, eds. *Music in General Education.* Washington, D.C.: Music Educators National Conference, 1965. 224 pp.

Henry, Nelson, ed. *Basic Concepts in Music Education.* Fifty-seventh Yearbook of the National Society for the Study of Education. Chicago: University of Chicago Press, 1958. 362 pp.

Jones, Archie N., ed. *Music Education in Action.* Boston: Allyn and Bacon, Inc., 1960. 523 pp. (via William C. Brown Co., Dubuque, 1964; 571 pp.)

Kaplan, Max. *Frontiers and Foundations of Music Education.* New York: Holt, Rinehart and Winston, Inc., 1966. 261 pp.

Kowall, Bonnie C., ed. *Perspectives in Music Education.* Source Book III. Washington, D.C.: Music Educators National Conference, 1966. 576 pp.

Leonhard, Charles, and Robert W. House. *Foundations and Principles of Music Education.* New York: McGraw-Hill Book Co., 1959. 375 pp.

Murphy, Judith, and George Sullivan. *Music in American Society: An Interpretive Report of the Tanglewood Symposium.* Washington, D.C.: Music Educators National Conference, 1968. 72 pp.

Mursell, James L. *Music Education Principles and Programs.* Morristown, N.J.: Silver Burdett Co., 1956.

Schwadron, Abraham. *Aesthetics: Dimensions for Music Education.* Washington, D.C.: Music Educators National Conference, 1967. 112 pp.

Sprague, Carleton, and William C. Hartshorn. *The Study of Music: An Academic Discipline.* Washington, D.C.: Music Educators National Conference, 1963. 32 pp.

MUSIC SUPERVISION AND ADMINISTRATION

Dennis, Charles. *Music Supervision and Administration in the Schools.* Chicago: Music Educators National Conference, 1949. 32 pp.

Hermann, Edward J. *Supervising Music in the Elementary School.* Englewood Cliffs, N.J.: Prentice-Hall, Inc., 1965. 210 pp.

Marvel, Lorene. *The Music Consultant at Work.* New York: Bureau of Publications, Teachers College, Columbia University, 1960. 71 pp.

Phelps, Roger P. *National Conference to Improve the Effectiveness of State Supervision of Music.* Washington, D.C.: Educational Resources Information Center, U.S. Office of Education, 1966. 115 pp.

Schultz, G. Lloyd. *State Supervision of Music.* Washington, D.C.: Music Educators National Conference, 1959. 58 pp.

Snyder, Keith. *School Music Administration and Supervision.* Second edition. Boston: Allyn and Bacon, Inc., 1965. 332 pp.

Weyland, Rudolph H. *A Guide to Effective Music Supervision.* Second edition. Dubuque: William C. Brown Co., 1968.

ELEMENTARY SCHOOL MUSIC

Bergethon, Bjornar, and Eunice Boardman. *Musical Growth in the Elementary School.* New York: Holt, Rinehart and Winston, Inc., 1963. 320 pp.

Garretson, Robert L. *Music in Childhood Education.* New York: Appleton-Century-Crofts, Inc., 1966. 270 pp.

Gary, Charles L., ed. *The Study of Music in the Elementary School: A Conceptual Approach.* Washington, D.C.: Music Educators National Conference, 1967. 150 pp.

Ginglend, David R., and W. E. Stiles, comps. *Music Activities for Retarded Children.* Nashville: Abingdon Press, 1965. 140 pp.

Grant, Parks. *Music for Elementary Teachers.* Second edition. New York: Appleton-Century-Crofts, Inc., 1960. 422 pp.

Hartsell, O.M. *Teaching Music in the Elementary School: Opinion and Comment.* Washington, D.C.: Association for Supervision and Curriculum Development, 1963. 53 pp.

Hartshorn, William C. *Listening to Music in Elementary Schools.* Englewood Cliffs, N.J.: Prentice-Hall, Inc., 1968.

Heffernan, Charles W. *Teaching Children to Read Music.* New York: Appleton-Century-Crofts, Inc., 1968. 144 pp.

Hood, Marguerite. *Teaching of Rhythm and Classroom Instruments.* Englewood Cliffs, N.J.: Prentice-Hall, Inc., 1968.

Humphreys, Louise, and Jerrold Ross. *Interpreting Music Through Movement.* Englewood Cliffs, N.J.: Prentice-Hall, Inc., 1964. 149 pp.

Kaplan, Max, and Frances J. Steiner. *Musicianship for the Classroom Teacher.* Chicago: Rand McNally & Co., 1967.

Leach, John Robert. *Functional Piano for the Classroom Teacher.* Englewood Cliffs, N.J.: Prentice-Hall, Inc., 1968. 176 pp.

McMillan, L. Eileen. *Guiding Children's Growth Through Music.* Boston:

Ginn and Co., 1959. 246 pp. (via Blaisdell Publishing Co., Waltham, Mass.)

Myers, Louise Kifer. *Teaching Children Music in the Elementary School.* Third revised edition. Englewood Cliffs, N.J.: Prentice-Hall, Inc., 1961.

Nordholm, Harriet. *Singing in the Elementary Schools.* Englewood Cliffs, N.J.: Prentice-Hall, Inc., 1966. 94 pp.

Nye, Robert E., and Bjornar Bergethon. *Basic Music for Classroom Teachers.* Second edition. Englewood Cliffs, N.J.: Prentice-Hall, Inc., 1962.

Nye, Robert E., and Vernice T. Nye. *Music in the Elementary School.* Second edition. Englewood Cliffs, N.J.: Prentice-Hall, Inc., 1964. 405 pp.

Pierce, Anne E. *Teaching Music in the Elementary School.* New York: Henry Holt and Co., 1959. 239 pp.

Runkle, Aleta, and Mary LeBow Eriksen. *Music for Today's Boys and Girls.* Boston: Allyn and Bacon, Inc., 1966. 280 pp.

Swanson, Bessie R. *Music in the Education of Children.* Belmont, Calif.: Wadsworth Publishing Co., 1961. 304 pp.

SECONDARY SCHOOL MUSIC

Andrews, Frances M. *General Music Classes in the Junior High School.* Englewood Cliffs, N.J.: Prentice-Hall, Inc., 1968.

————, and Joseph Leeder. *Guiding Junior-High-School Pupils in Music Experiences.* Englewood Cliffs, N.J.: Prentice-Hall, Inc., 1957. 372 pp.

Cooper, Irvin, and Karl O. Kuersteiner. *Teaching Junior High School Music.* Boston: Allyn and Bacon, Inc., 1965. 440 pp.

Hartshorn, William C. *Music for the Academically Talented Student in the Secondary School.* Washington, D.C.: National Education Association, 1960. 127 pp.

Hoffer, Charles R. *Teaching Music in the Secondary Schools.* Belmont, Calif.: Wadsworth Publishing Co., 1964. 463 pp.

Leeder, Joseph A., and William S. Haynie. *Music Education in the High School.* Englewood Cliffs, N.J.: Prentice-Hall, Inc., 1958. 366 pp.

Music Educators National Conference. *Music Curriculum in the Secondary Schools.* Washington, D.C.: The Conference, 1959. 116 pp.

————. *Music in the Senior High School.* Washington, D.C.: The Conference, 1959. 112 pp.

Singleton, Ira, and Simon V. Anderson. *Music in Secondary Schools.* Second edition. Boston: Allyn and Bacon, Inc., 1969. 200 pp.

Sur, William R., and Charles F. Schuller. *Music Education for Teen-Agers.* Second edition. New York: Harper and Row, 1966. 603 pp.

VOCAL AND CHORAL INSTRUCTION

Appelman, D. Ralph. *The Science of Vocal Pedagogy.* Bloomington: Indiana University Press, 1967. 448 pp.

Garretson, Robert L. *Conducting Choral Music.* Second edition. Boston: Allyn and Bacon, Inc., 1965. 320 pp.

Ingram, Madeline D., and William C. Rice. *Vocal Technique for Children and Youth: Understanding and Training the Developing Voice.* Nashville: Abingdon Press, 1962. 175 pp.

McKenzie, Duncan. *Training the Boy's Changing Voice.* New Brunswick, N.J.: Rutgers Press, 1956. 146 pp.

Neidig, Kenneth L., and John W. Jennings, eds. *Choral Director's Guide.* West Nyack, N.Y.: Parker Publishing Co., Inc., 1967. 308 pp.

Wilson, Harry R. *Artistic Choral Singing.* New York: G. Schirmer, Inc., 1959. 374 pp.

INSTRUMENTAL INSTRUCTION

Bartlett, Harry R. *Guide to Teaching Percussion.* Dubuque: William C. Brown Co., 1964. 182 pp.

Berg, Richard, and Kenneth Hjelmervick. *Marching Bands: How to Organize and Develop Them.* New York: The Ronald Press Co., 1953.

Colwell, Richard J. *Teaching Instrumental Music.* New York: Appleton-Century-Crofts, Inc., 1968. 480 pp.

Dalby, John B. *School and Amateur Orchestras.* Long Island City, N.Y.: Pergamon Press, 1966. 225 pp.

Duvall, W. Clyde. *The High School Band Director's Handbook.* Englewood Cliffs, N.J.: Prentice-Hall, Inc., 1960. 209 pp.

Green, Elizabeth A. H. *Teaching Stringed Instruments in Classes.* Englewood Cliffs, N.J.: Prentice-Hall, Inc., 1966.

Holz, Emil A., and Roger F. Jacobi. *Teaching Band Instruments to Beginners.* Englewood Cliffs, N.J.: Prentice-Hall, Inc., 1966. 118 pp.

House, Robert. *Instrumental Music for Today's Schools.* Englewood Cliffs, N.J.: Prentice-Hall, Inc., 1965. 282 pp.

Hunt, Norman. *Guide to Teaching Brass.* Dubuque: William C. Brown Co., 1968.

Kuhn, Wolfgang E. *Instrumental Music: Principles and Methods of Instruction.* Second edition. Boston: Allyn and Bacon, Inc., 1969.

————. *The Strings: Performance and Instructional Techniques.* Boston: Allyn and Bacon, Inc., 1967. 168 pp.

Neidig, Kenneth L., ed. *The Band Director's Guide.* Englewood Cliffs, N.J.: Prentice-Hall, Inc., 1964. 308 pp.

Robinson, Helene, and Richard Jarvis, eds. *Teaching Piano in Classroom and Studio.* Washington, D.C.: Music Educators National Conference, 1967. 144 pp.

Spohn, Charles J. *The Percussion: Performance and Instructional Techniques.* Boston: Allyn and Bacon, Inc., 1967. 192 pp.

_____, and Richard W. Heine. *The Marching Band: Comparative Techniques in Movement and Music.* Boston: Allyn and Bacon, Inc., 1969.

Timm, Everett R. *The Woodwinds: Performance and Instructional Techniques.* Boston: Allyn and Bacon, Inc., 1964. 211 pp.

Westphal, Frederick W. *A Guide to Teaching Woodwinds.* Dubuque: William C. Brown Co., 1962. 328 pp.

Winter, James H. *The Brass Instruments: Performance and Instructional Techniques.* Second edition. Boston: Allyn and Bacon, Inc., 1969. 124 pp.

Wiskirchen, George, Rev. *Developmental Techniques for the School Dance Band Musician.* Boston: Berklee Press, 1961. 212 pp.

BIBLIOGRAPHIES AND GUIDES

Arberg, Harold W., and Sarah P. Wood. *Music Curriculum Guides.* Washington, D.C.: U.S. Department of Health, Education, and Welfare, 1964. 48 pp.

Berger, Kenneth, ed. *Band Music Guide.* Fourth edition. Evanston, Ill.: The Instrumentalist, Inc., 1964. 356 pp.

Collins, Thomas C., ed. *Music Education Materials: A Selected, Annotated Bibliography.* Washington, D.C.: Music Educators National Conference, 1968. 174 pp.

Music Educators National Conference. *Contemporary Music for Schools.* Washington, D.C.: The Conference, 1966. 88 pp.

_____. *Materials for Miscellaneous Instrumental Ensembles.* Washington, D.C.: The Conference, 1960. 90 pp.

National Interscholastic Music Activities Commission. *Selective Music Lists: Chorus, Orchestra, Band.* Washington, D.C.: Music Educators National Conference, 1964. 96 pp.

_____. *Selective Music Lists for Instrumental and Vocal Solos, Instrumental and Vocal Ensembles.* Washington, D.C.: Music Educators National Conference, 1965. 160 pp.

Orchestra Music Guide. Evanston, Ill.: The Instrumentalist, Inc., 1967. 47 pp.

Shetler, Donald J. *Film Guide for Music Educators.* Washington, D.C.: Music Educators National Conference, 1962. 128 pp.

MISCELLANEOUS TOPICS

American Association of School Administrators. *Creative Arts in Education.* Washington, D.C.: The Association, 1959. 256 pp.

Farnsworth, Paul R. *The Social Psychology of Music.* New York: Henry Holt and Co., 1958. 304 pp.

Gaines, Joan. *Approaches to Public Relations for the Music Educator.* Washington, D.C.: Music Educators National Conference, 1968. 44 pp.

Gary, Charles L., ed. *Music Buildings, Rooms and Equipment.* Fifth edition. Washington, D.C.: Music Educators National Conference, 1966. 119 pp.

Hermann, Edward J. *The Music Teacher and Public Relations.* Washington, D.C.: Music Educators National Conference, 1958. 48 pp.

Lehman, Paul. *Tests and Measurements in Music.* Englewood Cliffs, N.J.: Prentice-Hall, Inc., 1968. 99 pp.

Maltzman, Edward. *National Conference on the Uses of Educational Media in the Teaching of Music.* Washington, D.C.: Educational Resources Information Center, U.S. Office of Education, 1965. 295 pp.

Music Educators National Conference. *Comprehensive Musicianship.* Washington, D.C.: The Conference, 1965. 88 pp.

Music Industry Council. *Business Handbook of Music Education.* Washington, D.C.: Music Educators National Conference, 1962. 31 pp.

Schneider, Erwin H., and Henry L. Cady. *Evaluation and Synthesis of Research Studies Relating to Music Education.* Washington, D.C.: Educational Resources Information Center, U.S. Office of Education, 1965. 632 pp.

Index

A

Administration (personnel), relations with, 8-9, 54, 81-102, 164
Administration (process):
  definition of, 2
  duties in, 10, 11, 157-168
Adult education, 128-129
Aesthetic value of music, 16-20
  program based on, 20-21
  responsiveness to, 20
Aims of music education, 20-21, 23, 24-25
All-state performing groups, 76, 77
Alternating group rehearsals, 91
American Association of School Administrators, 3, 19, 117
American Federation of Musicians, 76, 117, 129
American School Band Directors Association, 3
American String Teachers Association, 3
Appreciation, music; course in, 55-58
Arts, combined; course in, 61-62, 64-65
Association for Supervision and Curriculum Development, 3
Associations, see Organizations and Associations
Audio-visual aids, 150-152
  manufacturers and distributors of, 179-183
Auditoriums, planning, 101-102

B

Balance in the music curriculum, 73-74
Band:
  concert, 46, 68, 69-70, 158
  marching, 68, 70
  stage, 68, 70-71
Basic content:
  in general music, 31-37, 48-51
  in general-special courses, 56-58, 59-61, 63, 64-65
  in performance classes, 67-68, 71-73

Basic music book series, 201-202
  selecting, 146-148
Board of education, relations with, 8-9, 83
Books, selecting, 146-148
Boosters clubs, 116
Broadcasts, school, 126-127; see also, Television, closed-circuit
Budgets, 157, 164-166; see also, Financial support
Bulletins, 138, 145-146
Business and industry, performances for, 118, 121; see also, Music Industry
Business transactions, 167-168

C

Cambiata, 52
Carnegie Foundation for the Advancement of Teaching, 75
Carnegie unit, 75
Cataloguing music and recordings, 159-162
Checklist, visitation, 133-136
Choruses:
  elementary, 41-42
  secondary, 65-67
  see also, Vocal music program
Chrisman, Lee, 43
Church musicians, relations with, 121
Civic and social organizations, 121, 127-128
Classroom teachers (elementary), 37-40, 132-139, 141-142; see also, Supervisory relationships
Clubs:
  parents, 116
  school music, 76
Community music council, 127-128
Community participation in the school program, 129
Community programs, 127-129
Community relations, 9, 113-129
Comparative arts course in high school, 61-62, 64-65

Competitions, musical, 76-77
Conant, James B., 87
Concert series, 128-129
Concerts, school:
  invitations to, 115
  programming, 72, 120-121
Conferences with teachers, 136-137
Consultancy in supervision, 7
Consultant, music, 6, 38-39, 132
Consumer, musical, 48, 50-51
Contemporary music, 149-150
Coordinator, music, 6
Copyright law, 118-119, 151
Correlation, 60-63, 64-65, 153-154
County supervision, 4, 5
Creativity, 20, 26-27, 59-60
  definition of, 26-27
Credit for music courses, 74-76
Cultural organizations and associations,
  169-170
Curriculum, definition of, 23
Curriculum development and imple-
  mentation, 9-10, 143-156
Curriculum guides, 122, 143-145
Curriculum organization:
  balance in, 73-74
  content, see Basic content
  duties in, 9-10
  in elementary school, 23-46
  in junior high school, 47-53, 65-67,
    68-70, 71-74
  in senior high school, 47, 54-65, 66,
    67-68, 69, 70-79
  objectives in, 20-21, 23-25
  procedures of, 23-25

D

Definitions:
  administration, 2
  creativity, 26-27
  curriculum, 23
  general education, 16
  general music, 47
  supervision, 2
Demonstrations, 137-138, 141-142
Department of Classroom Teachers, 3
Department of Health, Education, and
  Welfare, 2
Department of Superintendence, 19
Depreciation of instruments, 159
Director of music, 6; see also, Supervisor of music

District performing groups, 77
Duties of music supervisor, 9-12

E

Educational organizations and associations, 2-3, 169-170
Elementary school, music curriculum
  in, 25-46, 85-87, 152-153
Ensemble, wind-and-percussion, 46, 68,
  69
Ensembles, small, 67, 71, 76
Equipment, instructional:
  basic, 40-41, 43, 53, 58, 61, 158
  manufacturers, 175-177, 178, 179-
    180, 181-182
  purchasing, 116, 119, 151, 152, 157-
    159, 166, 167
  supervision over, 10, 157-164
Equipment, storage, 178-179
Evaluation, 12, 154-155
  of private instruction, 117
  of teachers and instruction, 108-109,
    133-137
Exhibits, public, 129
Extended-time scheduling, 91-93
Extra-class activities, 23, 76-79

F

Facilities, room and building:
  planning, 96, 100-102
  supervision over, 10
Festivals, music, 76-77
Filing:
  music and recordings, 159-162
  resource materials, 189-193
Financial support, 116
Five-fold music program, 26
Flexible schedules, 93, 96
Funds, music, 164-165

G

General education, 16, 19
  definition of, 16
General music class, definition of, 47
General music program:
  in elementary school, 25-41
  in junior high school, 47-53
  in senior high school, 54-65
General students, participation in special courses, 54-55, 58

Glee clubs, 65, 66-67
Guides, curriculum, 122, 143-145

H

Harmony, course in, 54, 58-61
High school, see Senior high school
History, music; course in, 54, 55-58
Human relations, 81-83, 107-108, 132, 133, 136; see also, Supervisory relationships
Humanities course, 61-65

I

In-service program, 11, 131-142
Instrument classes, 42-46, 68-69
Instrument method books, selecting, 148
Instrumental activities in general music, 30, 32, 33, 34, 35, 36, 37, 42, 52-53
Instrumental music program:
  band, 68, 69-70
  beginning program, 42-46
  classes, 45-46, 68-69
  in elementary school, 42-46
  in junior high school, 68-70, 71-73
  in senior high school, 68, 69, 70-73
  orchestra, 68, 69
  recruiting beginners, 44-45
  small ensembles, 71
  stage band, 68, 70-71
Instrumentation, 43, 46, 70, 158
Instruments:
  basic, school-owned, 40-41, 43, 158
  loans and rentals of, 43-45, 163
  maintenance of, 159, 166
  manufacturers of, 175-177
  pre-band, 30, 42
  purchasing, 158, 166, 167
Integration of learning experiences, 61-65, 153-154
Interpreting the music program, 12, 44-45; see also, Public relations
Interviewing teacher candidates, 104-105

J

Jazz, 56, 57, 70-71, 149, 193
Junior high school, music program in, 47-53, 65-67, 68-70, 71-74, 87

Justification of music curriculum, 15-21
Justification of special courses, 54-55, 58-59

L

Learning experience, setting for, 2, 10-11, 25-26
Library:
  music, 159-163
  professional, 139
Listening activities in general music, 30-31, 32, 33, 34, 35, 36, 37, 53
Literature, music; course in, 55, 66
Loan agreements, student, 163-164
Lunch periods, rehearsals during, 93, 94-95

M

Madrigal singers, 67
Magazines, see Periodicals
Marching band, 68, 70
Mass media, 122-127
Masserman, Jules, 18
Materials, teaching:
  basic, 40-41, 53, 58, 61, 157-158
  filing of, 159-162, 189-193
  manufacturers and distributors of, 179-181, 182-183
  purchasing, 116, 118-119, 157-158, 165-166, 167-168
  supervision over, 10, 157-164, 189
  types and selection of, 143-152
  use of, 143-154
Meaning of music, 17-19, 49
Meetings, teachers', 139-141
MENC, see Music Educators National Conference
Monotone, 29
Music (the art), purpose in curriculum, 15-21
Music (scores):
  library, 159-163
  ordering, 167-168
  selecting, 29-30, 149-150
Music and humanities course in high school, 61-63
Music dealers, relations with, 43-44, 118-119, 129, 167-168
Music Educators National Conference, 2, 3, 40, 101, 102, 117, 118

Music history-appreciation course in high school, 55-58
Music industry, 118-119, 167-168
Music Industry Council, 3
Music literature course in high school, 55, 66
Music nights, 115
Music organizations, national, 2-3, 171-174
Music Performance Trust Fund, 129
Music Teachers National Association, 3
Music theory course in high school, 54, 55, 58-61
Musicians, see Professional musicians

N

National agencies in supervision, 2-3, 169-170
National Association of Secondary School Principals, 3
National Association of Teachers of Singing, 3
National Catholic Music Educators Association, 3
National Education Association, 2, 3, 40, 75
National Elementary Principals Association, 3
National Interscholastic Music Activities Commission, 3
National Music Council, 3, 156
NEA, see National Education Association
News releases, 122-126
   preparation of, 123-125
   subjects for, 123
   submission of, 125-126
Newspapers, local, 122-126

O

Objectives of the music program, 9, 20-21, 23-25
Observations, 137-138
Orchestra, 46, 68, 69, 71-73, 89, 158
Ordering music and materials, 157-158, 167-168
Organizations and associations:
   affecting supervision, 2-3, 169-174
   community, 121, 128

Organizations and associations (*cont.*)
   national educational and cultural, 2-3, 169-170
   national music, 3, 171-174

P

Parent-Teachers Association, 115-116
Parents:
   organizations and clubs, 115-116
   relations with, 43, 44-45, 115-116, 117, 119
Performance classes:
   balance, 73-74
   content in, 71-73
   see also, Instrumental music program, Vocal music program
Performances, public, 42, 72-73, 118, 119-121, 126-127
Periodicals, music:
   in the United States, 195-200
   writing for, 126
Personnel:
   employment of, 10-11, 103-107
   evaluating, 108-109, 132-137
   full-time, 103-109
   orienting new, 106-107
   part-time, 109-112
   staff organization of, 5-7
   see also, Classroom teachers, Specialist (music), Student teachers, Supervisory relationships, Teachers
Plant, physical, 96, 100-102
Playing activities, see Instrumental activities, Instrumental music program
Popular music, 29-30, 56, 70-71, 77-79, 149, 193-194
President's Commission on National Goals, 17, 18
Press, see Newspapers, Periodicals
Principals, relations with, 8, 83, 84; see also, Administration
Private instruction, school credit for, 117
Private music teachers, relations with, 3, 117
Professional growth, 11, 156
Professional musicians, relations with, 109-111, 117-118, 119
Programming concerts, 72, 120-121
Psychological need for music, 18-19, 21

Public relations, 113-129
Publications:
  music, 195-200
  national, 126
  newspapers, 122-126
  school, 122, 143-146
Publishers, music, 185-187
  relations with, 118-119, 167-168
Purpose of music in the curriculum, 15-21

Q

Qualifications of music teachers, 103, 105-106
Qualities of music supervisor, 9, 12-13

R

Radio and television presentations, 39, 126-127, 152-153
Reading program, music, 26, 28, 29, 30, 32, 33, 34, 35, 36, 37, 52
Record companies, 119, 180-181
Recording equipment:
  manufacturers of, 181-182
  use and selection of, 151
Recording Industries Trusts Funds, 129
Records and reports, supervisory, 11, 84-85, 159-162, 163-164
Required subjects, 73, 74-75
Responsibilities of the music supervisor, 8-9
Rhythmic activities, 28, 32, 33, 34, 35, 36, 37
Rooms, music, 96, 100-102
Rotating schedules, 86-87

S

Scheduling the music program, 85-99
  alternate rehearsals, 91
  basic principles of, 88-89
  extended periods, 91-93, 94-95
  flexible schedules, 93, 96
  in elementary schools, 85-87
  in secondary schools, 87-99
  number of periods, 87-88
  use of lunch periods, 93, 94-95
  use of study periods, 89-91
  see also, Time allotment for music
Schoen, Max, 18
School committee, see Board of Education

Secondary schools, music curriculum in, 47-79, 87-96, 97-99
Seeger, Charles, 81-82
Senior high school, music program in, 47, 54-65, 66, 67-68, 69, 70-79, 87-96, 97-99
Shows, musical, 77-79, 166
  agents for, 183
Singing activities in general music, 28-30, 32, 33, 34, 35, 36, 37, 41-42, 51-52
Singing school, 1
Speaking engagements, 115, 116
Special activities in the high school, 76-79
Special music courses in senior high, 54-65
Special students, music classes for, 54-65
Specialist, music, 6, 38-40, 152; see also, Teachers, music
Staff, organization of, 5-6
Stage band, 68, 70-71
Stages, planning facilities, 101-102
State supervision, 4-5
Stearns, Marshall, 5
Storage equipment, manufacturers of, 178-179
Student needs, 20, 25-26, 29-30, 47, 48, 50-51
Student teachers, 111-112
Study periods, music classes during, 89-91
Superintendent, relations with, 8, 84-85; see also, Administration
Supervision:
  agencies of, 2-7
  autocratic, 7
  coordinate system of, 6
  county, 4, 5
  definition of, 2
  democratic, 8
  general, 6-7
  horizontal system of, 6
  invitational, 7
  local, 5-7
  national agencies affecting, 2-3, 169-170
  need for, 1-2
  representative, 7
  scientific, 7-8
  staff organization in, 5-6
  state, 4-5

Supervision (*cont.*)
  types of, 7-8
  vertical system of, 5-6
Supervisor, elementary music, 84, 132-138
Supervisor of music, role of, 1-2, 4, 5-7, 8-12
Supervisory relationships, 8-9, 81-129
  with administration, 8-9, 54-55, 81-102, 164
  with board of education, 4-5, 83
  with church musicians, 121
  with community, 9, 113-129
  with local press, 122-126
  with music dealers, 43-44, 118-119, 129, 167-168
  with music publishers, 118-119, 167-168
  with parents, 43, 44-45, 115-116, 117, 119
  with principals, 8, 83, 84
  with private music teachers, 3, 117
  with professional musicians, 109-111, 117-118, 119
  with superintendent, 8, 84-85
  with teachers, 8, 10-11, 103-112, 130-142
Supervisory responsibilities and duties, ties, 8-12
Supplying the schools, 10, 157-163

T

Tanglewood Symposium, 21
Tape recorders, use and selection of, 151
Taste and discrimination, musical, 20, 29-30, 50-51, 149
Teachers:
  classroom, 37-40, 85-86, 132-139, 141-142, 143
  evaluating, 108-109
  music, 37-40, 53, 58, 103-112, 131-138, 139-142
  orienting new, 106-107
  part-time music, 109-112
  professional musicians as, 109-111
  relations with, 8, 10-11, 103-112, 131-142
  selecting music personnel, 103-106
  student, 111-112
Team teaching, 61, 62, 64

Television:
  closed-circuit, 39, 152-153
  presentations on commercial stations, 126-127
Tests:
  achievement, 155
  aptitude, 42, 154-155
Textbooks, selecting, 146-148
Theory, music; course in, 54, 55, 58-61
Three-fold music program, 26-37
Time allotment for music:
  choral-vocal program, 42, 65, 66, 67
  general music program, 38-39, 40, 53
  general-special classes, 58, 61
  instrumental program, 46, 68, 69, 70, 71
  see also, Scheduling

U

Uncertain singer, 29, 52
Uniform and robe manufacturers, 177-178
Unit organization in teaching:
  in junior-high classes, 49-51
  in senior-high classes, 55-58, 60-61, 63
United States Office of Education, 2

V

Value of music, 15-20
Visitation, 7, 132-136
Vocal music program:
  elementary chorus, 41-42
  glee clubs, 65, 66-67
  in elementary school, 28-30, 32, 33, 34, 35, 36, 37, 41-42
  in junior high school, 51-52, 65-67, 71-73
  in senior high school, 65, 66, 67-68, 71-73
  mixed choruses, 65-66
  small ensembles, 67
  see also, Singing activities
Voice, changing, 52, 66, 67
Voice classes, 65, 67-68

W

Wagner, Richard, 18
Workshops, 141-142